PEDRO DE VALDIVIA

From Herrera's "Historia De Las Indias"

PEDRO DE VALDIVIA

CONQUEROR OF CHILE

BY

R. B. CUNNINGHAME GRAHAM

"El mas seguro don de la fortuna
Es no la haber tenido vez alguna."
            ERCILLA.

MILFORD HOUSE
BOSTON

Library of Congress Cataloging in Publication Data

Graham, Robert Bontine Cunninghame, 1852-1936.
    Pedro de Valdivia, conqueror of Chile.

    Reprint of the 1926 ed. published by W. Heinemann, London.
    1. Valdivia, Pedro de, 1500?--1554? 2. Chile--History--To 1565.
F3091.V15   1973   983'.02'0924 [B]   73-4895
ISBN 0-87821-134-9

This Milford House book is an unabridged
republication of the edition of 1926.
Published in 1973 by Milford House Inc.
85 Newbury Street, Boston, Massachusetts
Library of Congress Catalogue Card Number: 73-4895
International Standard Book Number: 0-87821-134-9
Printed in the United States of America

DEDICATORIA

Al Excelentísimo
Sr. DON EMILIANO FIGUEROA LARRAIN
Presidente de la República de Chile

HOMENAJE DE ADMIRACIÓN ENTUSIASTA
A LA NACIÓN CHILENA Y DE SINCERA
SIMPATÍA PARA SU PRIMER MANDATARIO,
GENUINO REPRESENTANTE DE LAS VIEJAS
Y GLORIOSAS TRADICIONES DE SU PATRIA

PREFACE

Commentators tell us that most men are savages at heart, and give more admiration to the qualities of courage, patience in hardships, and contempt of death, than they accord to the talents of the artist, man of science, or the statesman.

If this is true of men, they say it is doubly true of women, who rather would be roughly loved by a tall fellow of his hands, even though their physical and moral cuticle suffer some slight abrasion in the process, than inefficiently wooed by a philanthropist.

This may be so, and if it is, certainly Pedro de Valdivia was an archetype of all the elemental qualities nature implants in man.

Brave to a fault, patient and enduring to an incredible degree, of hardships under which the bravest might have quailed, loyal to King and country, and a stout man-at-arms, he had yet no inconsiderable talents of administration, talents not so conspicuous to-day amongst the Latin race.

Thus—and I take all the above for granted—the lives of men such as was Pedro de Valdivia must be of interest to us, not only on account of their historic value, but as human documents.

Born in Estremadura, the cradle of the Conquest, as were his greater countrymen the Pizarro brothers, Cortés, and Belalcazar, he naturally, as a good Estremenian, drifted to the Americas. Unlike the most of the conquistadores, he was brought up to arms. Cortés, Quesada, and Legaspi, the conqueror of the Philippines, all began life as lawyers; Pedro de Mendoza had passed most of his life about the Emperor's court.

Valdivia, on the contrary, had served in the Italian and German wars, and had been at Pavia, where Francis I. lost all, *fors l'honneur*. Probably his youth had been spent about his father's house at La Serena, and an hidalgo of the Estremadura of those days most probably was cousin german to the immortal gentleman of La Mancha, who Cervantes drew for the diversion and instruction of mankind.

Both in Estremadura and La Mancha, hidalgos had their "running greyhounds and their bold ferrets," though in the case of Pedro de Valdivia's father, probably Rocinante was replaced by a serviceable steed. The books of chivalry that turned Don Quixote's brain had their equivalent in the no less marvellous accounts that came in almost daily of the conquests in America.

Englishmen, often led astray by the aggressive Protestantism of Prescott, are apt to look upon the whole "Conquista" as a sordid, money-grubbing enterprise carried out by buccaneers. Spaniards, on the other hand, are to be pardoned if they regard Drake, Hawkins, Frobisher, and all the rest of Queen Elizabeth's sea-dogs, as pirates, who attacked and pillaged defenceless settlements in time of peace between their Kings.

The truth, as usual, lies between the extreme view in both cases. Most certainly the Spaniards carried fire and sword amongst almost defenceless Indians, as we ourselves have done, in the four quarters of the globe. Still, at the bottom of the minds of most of them there was a very real belief that they were introducing the true faith amongst the heathen. To Spaniards of those days their faith was more than it can ever have been to other nationalities, for, in addition to its religious aspect, it was the sign of national unity, in a land recently half dominated by the Moors.

The Elizabethan sea-rovers did not, as it appears, trouble themselves overmuch as to the particular kind of devil worship under which the heathen languished. No doubt they forced them to accept the Trinity, the Church of England as by law established, and to do homage to the charms of their royal mistress, Gloriana, to put on breeches at their own expense, for decency, and because in all their ships they carried stores of red cloth and hawksbells, those cowrie shells of the old navigators.

Still, Drake and all his bold compeers were no mere huckstering filibusters. They all seem to have had a confused idea that England had as good a right as Spain to a fair share of the Indies, and that the leopards and St. George's cross had as good right to fly in southern waters as had the castles of Castille.

Naturally, Spaniard and Englishman alike had no objection to gold gained easily, and when they saw it to be had for the picking up, stooped for it readily. Still, both of them had higher motives than mere greed of conquest and of pelf.

The English and the Spaniards of those days held loyalty as their chief duty, next to their faith in their religion, and Protestants and Catholics alike were possessed of faith, surmounting all the puny hills of common sense.

Each of them endeavoured stoutly, to extend their empires, not caring overmuch about the means. These faiths, or fetishes, together with the love of gain, formed types of men that have few parallels to-day.

Valdivia was imbued with patriotism, loyalty, and faith in the religion he professed, for from his letters to the Emperor Charles V. it is evident he really had the conversion of the Indians ever in his mind. His loyalty was above all proof, his faith in the future of his colony and its value as a field for Spanish enterprise, unbounded.

Though far from being one of the most interesting of the conquistadores, he was without doubt, one of the most typical of all of them, embodying in himself most of their failings and their virtues.

Without the genius of Cortés, the military talents of Pizarro, the broad humanitarian views of Alvar Nuñez or the administrative powers of Domingo de Irala, Pedro de Alvarado's gallant bearing and romantic life, Quesada's magnanimity or his literary vein, Valdivia had in him that fierce tenacity of purpose and shrewd common sense that nearly all the others shared.

His conquest, compared to those of Mexico, of New Granada, and Peru, had not the element of romance about it that makes the others read like fairy tales.

Difficult of access and further off from Spain than were the other conquests, it had the attraction of great wealth to be won easily. There was no settled kingdom, with its emperor and hierarchy, as in Peru and Mexico, no stone-built temples, and the inhabitants were not so far advanced in any of the arts as were the Peruvians or the Mexicans. It had one countervailing interest, for it possessed the stoutest warriors in the Americas.

No other Indians warred for three hundred years against their conquerors, adopting all the tactics of their enemies, their horses, and their arms. None of the races that the Spaniards ever encountered in America had such highly disciplined and well-drilled forces. None were so chivalrous, and none gained the respect and admiration of their enemies, as did the Araucanians.

All the authorities, Ercilla, Gongora Marmolejo, Bascuñan, and Figueroa, speak of them in terms of admiration, although the two first fought against them and Bascuñan suffered captivity at their hands for a considerable time.

They were the only Indians who never went to war with the invaders of their country without first sending heralds to let them know that they were going to attack.[1] Cruel, no doubt, they were, but then the example that the Christians showed them was little edifying.

Lastly, no other Indians have preserved their speech, dress, customs, and their polity, down to quite recent days.

Valdivia himself, in his third letter to the Emperor Charles V., although he never mentions them by name, draws a sympathetic picture of their life, their love of family, their patriotism, and their drinking bouts.

Except Quesada and Cortés, most of the chief conquis-

[1] "Nunca jamás han peleado con españoles, que han sido infinitas veces, que primero no lo hagan saber y envien a decir."—*Gongora Marmolejo*.

tadores met violent deaths, but at the hands of their own countrymen. Nuflo de Chaves and Valdivia alone suffered poetic justice, slain by the Indians.

Both met their fate through over-confidence, and both of them perished with their work unfinished, and with the prospect of long years of life before them. Just as the swimmer's fate is to be taken by the sea, as say the Arabs, so did the sword at last claim him who lived by it. After a thousand perils, bravely confronted, Valdivia died as he had lived. He perished miserably, but still well in the picture, conquered alone by numbers and by death.

Firmly he set his seal upon the Chile of his day. So well the impress has endured, that in the length and breadth of that long, narrow, sword-shaped land, cities he founded and provinces[1] he won, still bear his name and keep his memory green.

R. B. CUNNINGHAME GRAHAM.
ARDOCH,
May, 1926.

[1] "Es el reino de Chile y la Tierra, de la manera de una vaina despada, angosta y larga."—*Gongora Marmolejo.*

PEDRO DE VALDIVIA
CONQUEROR OF CHILE
BEING A SHORT ACCOUNT OF HIS LIFE, TOGETHER WITH HIS FIVE LETTERS TO CHARLES V.

PEDRO DE VALDIVIA

CHAPTER I

PEDRO DE VALDIVIA was born either at Villa Nueva de la Serena or at Castuera,[1] both of them little towns in the ancient province of Estremadura, the cradle of so many of the conquistadores, in the year 1500.

He came of a family of gentlefolk. His father's name was Pedro Oncas de Melo, and his mother's Isabel Gutierrez de Valdivia. His wife was Doña Maria Ortiz de Gacte, a lady of good family from Salamanca.

His mother seems to have been of better family than his father, for he took his mother's name. The Spanish proverb says, " He who has a worthless father takes his mother's name."[2] This may have been Valdivia's case.

In 1520 he became a soldier,[3] and appears to have seen service at once, under the Emperor Charles V. in Italy, being present at the siege and taking of Milan and at the battle of Pavia. This was a good preparation for a conqueror, for at that time discipline was strict in the Spanish forces, and the Castilian infantry was the best in Europe. How long he remained in the armies of the Emperor is uncertain, or in what capacity he went to America. Probably as a captain, for in 1530 he distinguished himself in the conquest of Venezuela.

In 1532 he accompanied Pizarro in his second expedition to Peru, and from that time onward served him faithfully

---

[1] Neither place is very notable, although Castuera boasts its seven castles, Los Siete Castillos de Castuera. As he himself called the first town he founded La Serena, it is probable that it was his place of birth.

[2] El que tiene ruin padre, toma el nombre de la madre.

[3] Abrazó la carrera de las armas.

and was much esteemed by the veteran conqueror, whose side he took against Almagro at the conference of Mara, helping him greatly by his counsel, his talents for diplomacy, and by his knowledge of mankind.

The conference of Mara, a little town not far from Cuzco, was called to prevent a civil war between Pizarro and Almagro as to the boundaries of their respective territories.

Few partnerships have been more far-reaching in their results than that entered into between Pizarro and Almagro, at Panama, in the year 1524 or 1525. Both were men already past fifty years of age, and both had seen much service in the New World. They both were natives of Estremadura, cradle of the conquistadores of America.

Neither, it is said, could read or write,[1] arts not absolutely indispensable to conquerors.

Pizarro was born in Trujillo, an old-world town in Estremadura.

His father was a gentleman, Captain Gonzalo Pizarro, and his mother, according to Gómara, was an Old Christian[2] —that is, a woman without Jewish or Moorish blood. His parents were not married, and at his birth tradition says he was exposed at the church door, and was suckled by a sow. It is said he was a swineherd when a boy, as was Sebastian de Belalcazar, conqueror of Pasto and of Popayán, in what is now Colombia.

[1] Presbyter Juan Tena in his life of Pizarro (Trujillo, 1925) denies this hotly as far as Pizarro is concerned. He brings no proof, however, and only tells us (p. 28), in a letter written at Cuzco in the year 1535, preserved at Seville in the Archives of the Indies, that Pizarro placed his rubric and his antirubric to it, but that his secretary, one Picado, signed. This is not much as regards proof. "In spite of this" (so says the Presbyter), "I cannot believe Pizarro could not write."

One likes his simple faith in his great countryman. What he does not see is that he makes him less, not more to be admired by his belief. It also wounds him that Gómara and others have said Pizarro was a swineherd in his youth. He fails to see that to surmount such difficulties as want of education and humble occupation, but serve to make Pizarro more remarkable.

[2] "Era Christiana Vieja": "Historia de las Indias," Francisco Lopez de Gómara.

His father married off his mother to a farmer,[1] one Fulano[2] de Alcantara. Captain Pizarro afterwards recognized his son,[3] and presumably found better employment for him.

In a great waste of blocks of limestone, that rise out of the plain, as a shoal rises from the sea, sun-scorched in summer, and in winter scourged by the winds that sweep down from the Sierras, the strange old town of Trujillo stands up as starkly from the Castilian plain as St. Paul's rock stands up from the sea. But for the shoal on which it lies, no object breaks the surface of the plain after the wheat is cut. It basks in the shimmering heat, brown, arid, and adust. Great clouds of stour[4] rise in the distance from a train of carts drawn by mules harnessed in Indian file, and led invariably by a little donkey, who looks preternaturally wise, as he zig-zags across the road when it is broken into holes.

The great collegiate church, built of a warm, brown stone that seems at eventide to give forth the heat it has imbibed at noon, is the first feature as you approach the town. It dominates the low-roofed houses, all painted dazzlingly white. Just as it must have looked in the Pizarros' time, it looks to-day. Possibly far fewer worshippers fill its aisles than they did on the fateful day when the child Francisco[5] was exposed before its doors.

[1] Un honrado labrador.
[2] Fulano = "So and so," for Gómara did not know Alcantara's Christian name.
Fulano is from the Arabic "Filán-Filán" = "So and so." The Spaniards have continued the phrase, and speak of "Fulano, Zutano y Mengano."
[3] The Marquis (Francisco) Pizarro had four brothers, Gonzalo, Hernando, Juan Francisco, and Martin de Alcantara. The last was a half-brother, being the son of his mother's husband. He died bravely defending the Marquis when he was assassinated. Hernando was the only one of the five born in wedlock.
[4] There is no word in English to express dust in motion; "stour" is, of course, a Scotticism.
[5] The legend of the porcine foster-mother chiefly rests on a passage in the work on the conquest of Peru by Francisco Lopez de Gómara: " He was Francisco Pizarro, the bastard son of Gonzalo Pizarro, who was a captain in Navarre; he was born in Trujillo and was exposed

Sometimes a motor-car stands where the Pizarros tied their horses to the great iron rings, placed at a proper height for tying horses, before the door of almost every house. Slop suits and store clothes, surmounted by straw hats, have replaced doublets and trunk hose. The people strike a note that is in accord with the mediæval aspect of the town. Still, when a group of swarthy peasants passes, dressed in knee-breeches and short jackets, their vitals wrapped round with the countless folds of thick, black sashes, the clock seems to have been put back three hundred years. Their ancestors marched with Pizarro, sweltered on the coast, and froze upon the icy Parameras of Peru. They can have been but little different from their descendants of to-day, as they sit sideways on their asses, wrapped in striped blankets, with their black, wide-brimmed hats worn over handkerchiefs tied like a turban on their heads. The Spanish saying used to run, this place " smells of the saints "[1] when speaking of a town like Avila.

It might be said, Trujillo smells of the Pizarros. The little house where lived the father of the five brothers, Captain Gonzalo Pizarro, with its horseshoe door, still stands and is inhabited. His tomb is in the church of the Conception, upon the Gospel side,[2] and also that of the most noble lady, Doña Isabel de Vargas, his wife.

---

at the church door; he sucked a sow for several days, not finding anyone willing to give him milk."

The Inca Garcilaso is indignant with Gómara and produces many quite reasonable arguments against him. So does a modern writer, a priest of Trujillo.[*] Neither seem to see that if there never was a sow, and if Pizarro was swaddled and nurtured as an hidalgo's child, much of the picturesqueness of his career is taken from him.

Who would have thought so much of Romulus without the legend of the wolf ?

[1] Este lugar huele a santo.
[2] " En la banda del Evangelio ": " Francisco Pizarro," por Juan de Tera, Trujillo, p. 7.

---

[*] " Francisco Pizarro," por Juan de Tena, Presbitero, Trujillo. Tip. Solerimo de B. Peña, 1925.

In the great plaza paved with cobble-stones, at the west corner, stands the palace known as La Casa de la Conquista. The arms of the Pizarros[1] are sculptured over the great door. Upon the angle of the house that fronts the square they are again emblazoned, with Indians in chains beneath them, above the wrought iron balcony. Figures and urns adorn the roof, and a long stretch of high arcading keeps off the sun from the interior court.

It is a noble building of the sixteenth century, fit for the conqueror to take the ease in, that fate denied him all his life. It was not so decreed, and perhaps his end, bloody and violent by the assassin's hand, with but time to call on Jesus, and with his finger dipped in his own blood to make a cross upon the stones, was the most fitting for him.

He died as he had lived, and the old city with its great church, its winding streets, and granite castle dominating it upon the highest rock of the great reef on which the town is built, might have been too restful for him, and he would have regretted Cuzco and the City of the Kings.[2]

Francisco Pizarro went first to the island of Santo Domingo, from thence to Urabá, on the gulf of the same name.[3] He served there for several years with the celebrated Alonso de Ojeda, and was with Vasco Nuñez de Balboa when he discovered the Pacific Ocean. Afterwards he served long and faithfully with Pedrarias Davila,[4] the celebrated governor of Panama.

[1] There seems some doubt about who built the palace. It may have been built by Hernando Pizarro, who lived nineteen years in Trujillo, after his release from confinement in El Castillo de la Mota. El Presbitero Juan Tena, in his "Francisco Pizarro" (Trujillo, 1925), has a note (p. 17) in which he says: "Francisco Pizarro no tuvo casa levantada por el en Trujillo."

[2] Lima. La Ciudad de los Reyes.
In the church of Santa Maria de la Concepcion his effigy in armour kneels, though his body is in Lima. The helmet is said to have been his own.

[3] It is situated in Colombia almost opposite the once celebrated and unlucky Scottish colony at Darien.

[4] Pedrarias Davila, known as El Justador (the Tilter), who so unjustly put Vasco Nuñez de Balboa to death.

Diego de Almagro, according to Agustin de Zarate,[1] was born in Malagon, a little town that the rhyme says " has a rogue at the corner of each street."[2]

Gómara says, with more apparent reason, that he was born in Almagro, and that it was never known with certainty who was his father, although some said he was a priest.

He, too, had seen much service in the Indies, and had settled down at Panama. In neither of the two captains had their advancing years blunted the zeal for conquest and adventure.

The Inca Garcilaso de la Vega says they were both rich, and famous for their exploits.[3]

Not daunted by the perils that they had undergone, upon the mere rumours of the existence of the rich empire of Peru, they determined to stake their all upon a cast of fortune. Into their fellowship they took one Hernando de Luque, a schoolmaster of Panama.[4]

They executed a deed, and swore publicly not to break up their fellowship, either on account of the expense or the misfortunes it might entail, and that they would share equally all the gains that might accrue. This[5] they did, not knowing if the land they were to conquer was rich or poor, or, in fact, exactly where it was.

" The good fortune " (says the Inca) " of those who now enjoy it, called them, and even forced them to undertake the enterprise, as it were, in the dark.

---

[1] " Historia del Peru."

[2] " En Malagon, a cada esquina, un ladron." This may be observed in almost every town in both hemispheres; but luckily for them most of them have not names that rhyme so easily with " thief " (ladron).

[3] Eran hombres ricos y famosos por las Haçanas, que en otras conquistas ava in hecho: " Comentarios Reales," Book I.

[4] A schoolmaster in the Spanish America of those days seems to have been better paid than his modern brethren in Spain, where " to be as hungry as a schoolmaster " (tener hambre de maestre-escuela) has become proverbial.

Hernando de Luque in addition to his profession was Señor de la Taboga and presumably, therefore, rich.

[5] " . . . Tan a ciegas que ni sabian adonde ni a que tierra iban, ni si era rica, ni pobre, ni lo que era menester para la ganar ": " Comentarios Reales."

"But the chief thing was that God had mercy on those heathens,[1] and wished by that road to send them His Gospel."[2]

Who shall dive into motives, especially the motives of a power quite uncontrolled by human reason?

Still mere historians may be allowed to wonder without comment on the peculiar way that the great Power adopted to make His wishes clear.

Latin, we know, goes in with blood, and it may well be that the Gospel, at least in these days, wanted blood to make it manifest.

Luque, the schoolmaster and lord of La Taboga,[3] remained in Panama to collect arms and provisions, and take charge of the finances. From that time he almost disappears.

Pizarro and Almagro set out in 1525 with the small following of but one hundred and twenty men, to found an empire and to leave their names, after that of Cortés himself, the most renowned of all the conquerors of the New World.

What chiefly differentiates the tasks most of the conquistadores undertook, from all the adventures of the kind that men have undertaken, is that the greater part of them were plunges into the unknown. Cortés had heard of Montezuma and his empire, but by the vaguest rumours. Quesada had not even rumour to spur him on, but fell upon the Chibcha Empire on the plains of Bogotá, just as a miner working in a mine by a chance blow lights on a vein of gold.

Pizarro and Almagro knew not even where they were going to, and yet they risked all that they had amassed in danger and in toil, at an age when the majority of men are thinking of repose.

Chance favoured them, and they hit upon Peru, that put

---

[1] The Peruvians.

[2] Pero lo principal era, que Dios avia misericordia de aquellos Gentiles, y queria por este camino enbiarlos su Evangelio.

[3] Taboga is an island in the Gulf of Panama, celebrated for its pearl fisheries.

the spoils of Mexico into the shade, and for three hundred years became proverbial for its wealth.[1]

Rarely have men embarked on a more desperate enterprise.

At the first place they landed, three hundred miles southward from Panama, probably somewhere near Buenaventura, for it was very rainy,[2] the Indians attacked them as they tried to disembark. Pizarro received seven arrow wounds and Almagro lost an eye.

Their bad success left them undaunted, and Almagro, leaving Pizarro and the remnants of his force encamped further down the coast, returned to Panama to beat up reinforcements. It speaks well for the spirit of the Spaniards of those days that he could have found anyone to accompany him on what must have seemed a fruitless quest. Nevertheless, he managed to persuade some eighty soldiers, who probably were either desperate in their fortunes or inspired by the love of adventure that was their common heritage.

So great, however, were the hardships and the losses, that even the hardy adventurers were daunted and wished to return to Panama.

Almagro and Pizarro were unmoved, and when Almagro once again was forced to return to Panama for fresh supplies of men, he would not take a single man back with him, or carry letters to their friends.

However, a certain man from Trujillo,[3] called Faravia, sent the following rhyme wrapped up in a cotton cloth:

> " Pues Señor Governador
> Mirelo bien por entero
> Que alla va el Recogedor
> Y aca queda el Carnicero."[4]

---

[1] " Vale un Peru " occurs again and again in Spanish books, as a comparison of wealth.

[2] Casi nunca escampa: " Comentarios Reales," p. 10.

[3] Fulano de Faravia—*i.e.*, one Faravia, or " ane they ca' Faravia," as we say in Scotland.

[4] This may be paraphrased:
> Lord Governor, Lord Governor,
> The case is very clear,
> The gleaner has gone back to Panama
> But the butcher still is here.

This little bit of doggerel, quoted both by the Inca Garcilaso and by Gómara in his " History of the Indies,"[1] upset all the plans of the two would-be conquerors.

When Almagro returned to Panama, he found a new governor in power, called Pedro de los Rios. When the doggerel rhyme came to his notice, he at once dispatched a judge, one Tafur,[2] to the island where Pizarro was encamped,[3] to inform any of the soldiers that they were at liberty to return to Panama. The journey and the recruiting of new men had taken Almagro a whole year. When the new men heard about the mission of the judge, they refused to accompany Almagro, and when the news came to Pizarro in his camp, his followers all wished to leave him and return. Then he showed that he was a conquistador on all four sides,[4] as goes the Spanish saying, for he unsheathed his sword, and with the point of it he drew a line upon the sand.

" Gentlemen," he said, turning his face towards his men, " this line means toil, thirst, hunger, weariness, wounds, illnesses, and all the other dangers and the difficulties that in this conquest we shall have to pass, until life finishes. Those who are brave enough to risk and conquer them, let them pass across the line, in sign and proof of the stoutness of their souls and in testimony that they will be my faithful followers, and those who feel themselves not worthy of so great a hazard, let them return to Panama, for I force nobody; but with those who remain, no matter if they are but few, I trust in God for His greater honour and His glory, and the perpetual renown of those who follow me, His eternal Majesty may so assist me, that I shall never miss those who elect to go."

Even Cortés when he set fire to his fleet upon the shores of an unknown and powerful empire did not show more heroism than did Pizarro on that fateful day. Cortés was in the flower of his age, had not endured long, arduous

---

[1] " Historia General de las Indias."
[2] Fulano Tafur.
[3] La Isla del Gallo.
[4] Los cuatro costados. A man is said to be " un hidalgo por los cuatro costados," if his parents are all nobles.

campaigns in the enervating climates of the New World, had not been badly wounded many times, as had Pizarro, and, above all, he had behind him all his army, that, though not very large, was yet devoted to him. Moreover, he was in a country where food was plentiful.

Not Xenophon or any of the commanders of old days showed more heroism and force of character than did Pizarro on that day, when, even had not fortune smiled upon him, he entered definitely into the fellowship of conquerors.

The milk that he had imbibed, when cast out at the church door, from the sow that fostered him, had proved as potent as the she-wolf's that suckled Romulus.

Gómara, Zárate, the Inca Garcilaso, Jérez, and Pedro de Cieza de Leon, all have preserved some of the names of the thirteen who passed the Rubicon that Pizarro traced with his sword upon the sand. He himself, in the Capitulation that he entered into with the Emperor Charles V. after Peru was won, gives all of them.

As Bernal Diaz del Castillo sets down the names and gives the qualities of all the horses and the mares that, as he puts it, " passed to the conquest of New Spain," so did Pizarro faithfully set down the names of his staunch followers.[1]

None rose to fame during the conquest. After it, Pedro de Candia and Juan de la Torre turned out traitors, deserting frequently to one side or another, until they met their fate during the civil wars. The one great moment of the lives of all of them was on the beach of the lost, little island of Gorgona, where they exhausted all the heroism that nature gave them, but then cut off the stream.

The Greek, Pedro de Candia, who was in command of the artillery at the battle of the Chapas, was slain for treachery

---

[1] Unluckily he set down nothing but their names: Bartolomé Ruiz (Pilot), Cristoval de Peralta, Nicolas de Ribera, Alonzo de Molina, Garcia de Jérez, Alonzo Briceño, Juan de la Torre, Pedro de Candia, Domingo de Soria Luce, Francisco de Cuellar, Pedro Alcon, Anton de Carrion, Martin de Paz.

by his commander, the young Almagro, who had observed he pointed all the cannons over the enemy.

Juan de la Torre made a great fortune, joined first one side and then the other in the civil wars, and met a traitor's fate.

After the initial hardships the conquest of Peru presented far less dangers than that of Mexico. Never once were the two partners in such imminent, deadly peril of their lives as was Cortés during the retreat known as "La Noche Triste," nor did they have to storm a city well fortified and manned by savage warriors as was Tenochtitlán.[1] They did not, at any rate, during the progress of the conquest, have to endure the almost superhuman hardships that Quesada passed in his advance on Bogotá. There does not seem to have been one pitched battle in the field between the Spaniards and the Inca's armies.

The effects of the conquest of Peru were, on the whole, much more far-reaching than were those of Mexico, not to speak of Bogotá. To the astonished Spanish world was opened up a country richer far in the precious metals than was Mexico, and that almost without a blow.

The hardships that Pizarro had to undergo were before he ever landed in Peru, and afterwards, during the civil wars and in the various revolts.

Uneducated as he was, his mind was naturally formed both to command and to inspire the utmost confidence in his followers. Above all things he was ambitious, not of mere wealth, but honour, that all his life he put before mere wealth.

After three years of hardships, and having only seen the outside fringe of the great empire fate was about to put into his hands, so certain was he of his power to conquer it, that he went back to Panama, to lay before his partners all that he had done and to return to Spain to see the Emperor. In Panama he found Diego de Almagro and the rich schoolmaster Luque anxiously waiting for him. When they heard of the riches of Peru, although the conquest still was in the

[1] Mexico.

air, they resolved Pizarro should return at once to Spain, to legalize their position, and to petition Charles V. to make them governors.

Fortune had not smiled upon them during the three years Pizarro had been absent, and he had brought but little of the riches of Peru, though he had had a sight of some of them in the great temple in the Vale of Tumbez where he had stayed so long.

In this place Pedro de Candia had an astonishing adventure, one that would seem incredible had it not occurred during the conquest of the Indies.

Becoming tired of staying in the camp one day, being a goodly man of a fine presence, he dressed himself in his best coat of mail and bravest helmet, taking a buckler of polished steel upon his arm and in his hand a sword with a cross handle, on which he relied more than on the strength of all his armament. He walked along with a grave air as dignified as if he had been lord of the province, and as he walked, the natives fled before him, seeing he was one of the Children of the Sun.

When he got to the town, the trembling Indians dare not attack him, though they were numerous and armed. To try his valour they let a tiger and a lion out upon him; these animals did not attack him, frightened perhaps by his steel buckler, in which they saw themselves as in a looking-glass, or by his grave and knightly air (semblante grave y señoril).[1] They fawned about his feet and he patted their heads, holding the cross handle of his sword before their eyes, which of course pacified them.

All lingering doubts that he was really one of the Children of the Sun were dissipated by this ordeal of battle. The Indians led him into the temple, where everything down to the very kitchen pots and pans was wrought of finest gold. He walked in fairyland through a great, golden garden where all the plants, the trees on which sat birds, the flowers growing in the beds, were of the purest gold. Much did he marvel, and much the simple Indians must have marvelled

[1] "Comentarios Reales," Garcilaso de la Vega.

at his stature, his shining armour, and his grave, knightly air.

Both must have been contented, for it is given to few to see a god walking and talking in their midst, and to few conquerors has been vouchsafed so much of fairyland.

Pedro de Cieza de Leon, the most authoritative of all the chroniclers of the conquest of Peru, touches but gingerly upon the story, though all the rest accept it faithfully. Such as it was, it was the basis of Pizarro's confidence in the great riches of Peru, for at the time when he first returned to Spain he had seen none of them.

Between the three partners they managed to collect a thousand dollars, the greater part of which they had to borrow. With this exiguous treasure, but with his dauntless spirit still unquenched, Pizarro set out on his voyage.

CHAPTER II

AFTER a prosperous journey Pizarro arrived in Spain and at once went to court to see the Emperor. Most likely he at that time made his pilgrimage to Guadalupe, the great Estremenian shrine, not far from where he himself was born.

At a session of the Council of the Indies[1] he related all that he had done, and begged the Emperor Charles V. to make him governor of the country he had discovered, on account both of his past and present services, offering to conquer it at his own cost, and by the exertions of himself and of his friends. No monarch was ever better served than Charles V. Cortés, Pizarro, Ojeda, Valdivia, Mendoza, and the rest of the conquistadores undertook their conquests at their own expense.

It was a rare thing that they received assistance from the Crown. Charles almost invariably treated them with neglect, and the same policy was followed by his son. The House of Hapsburg always seems to have considered all efforts of its subjects as their due, and that their great position placed them above the need of gratitude.

The Inca Garcilaso[2] says that those who listened to Pizarro thought he exaggerated the riches of Peru and promised more than he could perform. The reverend, wise dullards, seated securely in their chairs at home, their feet on the brasero[3] in the winter, and in the summer with a cool tumbler of Agraz beside them, naturally knew more about

---

[1] El Concejo de Indias. It sat in Seville.
[2] "Comentarios Reales," Book I., p. 16.
[3] A brasero is a pan for charcoal. Agraz is a beverage made of unripe grapes.

Peru than the scarred soldier who stood before them[1] proffering the richest country in the world. Garcilaso well says, in a few years they saw he had performed far more than he promised them.

Charles V. gave him the title of Adelantado Mayor of Peru and Captain-General and Governor of the empire that he might subdue. He also gave him the right to use the title " Don " before his name. Pizarro lost no time in embarking at Seville for the Indies, taking his four brothers with him. Unfortunately Pizarro, either by the ill-advice of those about him or through forgetfulness—for all his life he was a man devoid of envy or of jealousy of any kind—omitted to secure any title or recognition for the services of Almagro, his partner and old friend.

When Pizarro arrived in Paranas loaded with honours, and Almagro found nothing had been secured for him, he was furious, and from that moment began the misunderstanding that in the long run caused the death both of Pizarro and himself and, incidentally, gave Pedro de Valdivia the first chance to make his name. Almagro's first action was to cut off supplies, an action that left Pizarro without means to move. Hernando Pizarro, the only one of the five brothers born in wedlock, a brave but proud and haughty soldier, fanned the flames, insulting Almagro personally, and railing at his brother for not proceeding to extremes. Pizarro, who was a prudent man, who moreover always loved his old companion in perils and in arms, refused to be pushed on, and strove to reconcile his outraged partner and friend by the renunciation in his favour of the title of Adelantado, promising to write to Charles V. for confirmation of it. This for the moment bridged the difficulty, and on Almagro giving him a thousand ducats and all the horses and the arms he could collect, Pizarro once more set out for Peru.

---

[1] History repeats itself. The dullards, apostolically descended from those who doubted Pizarro, but fifty years ago called Du Chaillu a liar, when he spoke of the gorillas he had seen in Africa. He, like a llama, took a salivary revenge, and promptly spat in the face of the honourable chief dullard.

Throughout the conquest, that was mainly carried out by the Pizarro brothers, the ill-feeling still grew and increased between the ancient partners.

When the Peruvians were finally subdued, Pizarro sent his brother Hernando back to Spain to see the Emperor, and get him confirmed in his government. As there were now rich spoils to offer, the Council of the Indies took another view of his position. The Emperor promptly confirmed him in the government, and in addition made him a marquis, an honour which he well deserved, and one which already had been bestowed upon Cortés.[1]

Marquis has always been the title that the Kings of Spain seem to have conferred upon the conquistadores. So common has it become to-day, few can escape it if they chance to commit an action out of the ordinary, not actually a crime.

In the days of Pizarro, it conferred a real distinction, and he esteemed it greatly, having been all his life a man to whom honours ranked higher than mere pelf. In addition, twenty thousand Indians were adjudged to him and his descendants " in service," a state which though not actually one of slavery, yet made them subject to " corvée," though they could not be bought or sold.[2] Almagro was made Marshal of Peru, and given a hundred leagues of territory, which was called New Toledo to distinguish it from that Pizarro held under the name of New Castile.

Once again he was furious, and hastening to Cuzco, which was outside his jurisdiction before the Emperor's confirmation had arrived, he had himself proclaimed its governor.

[1] He was made Marqués del Valle (of Mexico). Pizarro was not given a territorial designation as was Cortés, but merely styled Marqués Pizarro.
The title of Marqués de la Conquista was given to Pizarro's great-grandson.
Pizarro had a daughter by an Inca princess, the daughter of the Inca Huayna Capac. She was sent to Spain to be educated, and married her uncle Hernando Pizarro (the brother of the Marquis), who had been long in prison in El Castillo de la Mota, in Medina del Campo, on account of his having ordered the execution of the elder Almagro.
Cesare Borgia was also confined in the Castillo de la Mota.
[2] De servicio.

Some of the Spanish captains who had a grudge against Pizarro gave their adhesion to him. Juan and Gonzalo Pizarro and other Estremenian cavaliers,[1] as Gabriel de Rojas, Garcilaso de la Vega,[2] the father of the historian, and others, protested indignantly.

Pizarro posted up from Trujillo, the town that he had founded, two hundred leagues from Cuzco, carried by Indians,[3] to arrange matters before things went as far as civil war. Almagro, angry as he was, could not resist his old companion in arms, and they were reconciled. They had had many quarrels, but in all of them Pizarro always had held out the olive branch.

Their meeting this time was at the little town of Mara,[4] not far from Cuzco, and at this conference Pedro de Valdivia played the part of mediator between the rival chiefs. After much wrangling, so fierce at one time that they had nearly drawn their swords, it was arranged that Almagro should set out to conquer Chile and leave Pizarro free to consolidate the conquest of Peru.

Almagro recruited five hundred and fifty men, according to Garcilaso.[5] Molina, in his "History of Chile,"[6] says five hundred and seventy, and fifteen thousand Indians. Amongst his followers were many men of fortune who had been attracted by the accounts of the great wealth of Chile to join the enterprise, leaving their estates in Cuzco to the care of friends. In those days, says Garcilaso, every Spanish soldier, no matter how poor he was, held all Peru[7] a small possession for himself alone.

[1] Y otros cavalleros, estremeños.
[2] His mother was the Inca princess La Palla Isabel, daughter of the Inca Huayna Capac.   [3] En ombros de Indios.
[4] Some of the historians of the conquest write it "Mala."
[5] "Comentarios Reales," Book II., Cap. XIX.
[6] "History of Chile," from the Italian of P. Ignatius Molina, London, 1889. Figueroa, in his "History of Chile," says he had only one hundred and fifty men. This seems incredible, as Almagro's losses were severe, both of his Spanish troops and of his Indians.
[7] "Que en aquellos principios, qualquiera Español por pobre soldado que fuera, le parecia poco todo el Peru, para el solo": "Comentarios Reales," p. 87.

Almagro set out under the best of auspices, and lent the friends that joined him, who were unable to equip themselves, thirty thousand dollars to buy arms and horses, and all things necessary for such a journey as they were about to undertake.

He sent on Juan de Saavedra, a Sevillian, with one hundred and fifty men to explore the road for him.

In the beginning of the year 1535 he set out from Cuzco, taking with him an Inca called Paullu, the brother of the Inca Manco Capac, and the high priest of the Temple of the Sun in Cuzco.

Manco, who had hopes of being reinstated on the throne that he had lost by the conquest of his country by Pizarro, did all he could to aid Almagro in his preparations, bringing up both provisions and Indians to act as baggage carriers.

Juan de Saavedra marched to Charcas,[1] two hundred leagues from Cuzco, without a skirmish by the way, for all the Indians seem to have been entirely cowed by the death of their Inca Atalhualpa, and by the impossibility of resisting the well-armed Spanish troops. Almagro followed him, after an interval.

There were two roads to Chile, in those days—one by the mountains and the other by the coast.

The mountain road was the shorter of the two, but far more dangerous, and though the Inca Paullu strongly advised him to take the coast road, Almagro plunged into the hills, although the paths were only practicable at certain seasons of the year. From the first league his difficulties began. The snow lay deep, for it was in the month of June,[2] midwinter in the Southern Hemisphere.

The cold was terrible, because, as Garcilaso says,[3] "according to the Astrologers and the Cosmographers that great Cordillera is so high that it reaches to the middle region of the air."

In this high altitude the miserable Indians, clad in the

---

[1] It is now known as Chuquisaca.   [2] El mes de San Juan.
[3] "Segun los Astrologos y Cosmografos aquella gran Cordillera llega con su altura a la Media Region del Aire."

unsubstantial clothes that they wore in Peru, perished like flies. Even the hardier Spaniards suffered terribly. Garcilaso puts the Indians' loss at ten thousand, and that of the Spaniards at one hundred and fifty, who sank and died amongst the snows. All baggage had to be abandoned, and the miserable remnant of the army pushed on for life, taking no notice of those who fell behind.

The Sierras once surmounted, they descended into a better climate, and luckily for them the Indians that they met received them hospitably, for they were in no fit condition for a fight. As they were still within the jurisdiction of what had been, so short a time ago, the Inca Empire, the natives flocked to see the Inca Paullu and to make obeisance to him.

He and the High Priest induced them to collect two hundred thousand ducats' worth of gold, telling the Indians that the Spaniards were great friends of the Incas, and were Children of the Sun.

They also brought provisions in great quantities, for even Children of the Sun must eat.

In a few days they brought a further sum of three hundred thousand ducats, and all this gold Paullu presented to Almagro, who at once divided it amongst his followers.

Then, having called them all together, he destroyed the receipts for the money that he had advanced them in Peru. Certainly neither Almagro nor Pizarro, with all their failings, had any meanness in their composition, and both of them poured out the money that they wrung from the Indians, to their own followers with an unsparing hand.

Gómara says: " This was the liberality of a prince[1] rather than of a soldier, but when he died there was found no one willing to put a cloth upon the scaffold." When the remainder of his forces had recovered and rested from their arduous passage of the Andes, Almagro marched into the interior of Chile. From the first he met with a stiff

---

[1] " Historia de las Indias," Francisco Lopez de Gómara.
"Era liberalidad de Principe, mas que de soldado, pero cuando murió no tuvo quien pusiese un paño en su degolladero."

resistance from the Indians, who were of quite a different stamp from the peaceable Peruvians, and, moreover, never had been conquered by the Incas. After a few days' march, the influence of the Inca Paullu and the High Priest of Cuzco disappeared. The further he went the greater opposition he encountered on the way. Almagro, who had never had much stomach for the expedition, for his heart was still in Cuzco, the Inca capital, soon began to be discouraged. His followers, who had expected to overcome the country without difficulty, were even more discouraged than their general. No one had counted with the Araucanians, the fiercest and most warlike Indians the Spaniards ever faced in the New World, more to be dreaded even than were the Mexicans, for they fought with the courage of despair, but the Araucanians out of reasoned patriotism.

Their military organization was as good as that of the Spaniards, and had their arms been equal, perhaps they never would have been subdued.[1] After five months of incessant warfare, in a climate rigorous compared to that to which they had been accustomed in Peru, Almagro's depleted forces were joined by Captains Ruy Diaz and Juan de Herrera, with a hundred fresh recruits. They, too, had passed great hardships in the Andes before emerging in the fertile valley of Copiapó. Reduced almost to the last gasp by hunger and by cold, they had been forced to eat the flesh of the horses that had been frozen and left stiff, standing upon their feet, during Almagro's passage through the hills. Although five months had passed, the intense cold of those high altitudes had preserved their flesh as fresh as on the day they died.

Juan de Herrera brought with him the Emperor's confirmation of Almagro's governorship of one hundred leagues of territory to the south of that to which Pizarro had been nominated governor.

Cuzco was included in Almagro's governorship. Almagro, who loved honour, and especially position, far above riches —for in this respect he and Pizarro were identical—at once

[1] They remained independent well into the nineteenth century.

resolved to abandon his attempt to conquer Chile, and to return to take possession of the Inca capital that he had coveted so long.

It was to cost him dearly, as it proved. Many of his captains urged him to remain and settle in the rich territory of Charcas, for they were sick of turmoil, and they foresaw that civil war would follow on his return to Cuzco, a prize that the Pizarro brothers were not likely to give up.

Pizarro himself protested strongly against Almagro's resolution, as did the town council of Cuzco, but they all pled in vain.

Many of Almagro's captains, although they had acquired great landed properties in the northern parts of Chile, where the Indians were not so warlike as in the south, pressed on Almagro to return.

With their encouragement he set out northward, abandoning the conquest of the country that he had overrun but not subdued. Thus, for the present, Chile was left unconquered, and remained so until Valdivia undertook the task.

The lure of Cuzco, and the hope of finding still more riches in Peru, enticed Almagro to his doom.

He set out northwards by the route along the coast, not caring once again to face the Andes and their snows.

His road lay for full a hundred leagues[1] through Atacama, a trackless desert in those days. This time the sufferings of his men through thirst were terrible, for wells were few and far between, and water not too plentiful, even when the water-holes were reached.

Almagro, who had had long experience of the hottest countries of the New World, and was perhaps a better leader than an actual general in the field, passed through the desert by an ingenious plan.

[1] Valdivia calls it one hundred and twenty leagues, in his first letter to Charles V. It is at least one hundred leagues—that is, three hundred miles. In those days the want of water was the difficulty, as wells were few and far between, and only known to the Indians. To-day great condensing works and pumping stations have obviated much of the difficulty, but it will always remain difficult to cross.

He formed his forces into small groups of ten or at the most a dozen men, so that when they arrived at any of the wells they should not exhaust the water, for his Indian guides had told him of its scarcity. Thus strung out in a string, like wild geese migrating, the various groups followed each other's tracks and then passed on, leaving the wells time to fill up for those who followed them. The infantry went first, and when Almagro judged that the last group had passed the thirsty eighty leagues, he followed with the horse. Although they suffered terribly from thirst their loss was small and bore no ratio to that they suffered in the snows upon their southern march.

Nothing could daunt either Almagro or Pizarro, or, in fact, any of the conquistadores, who affronted all the extremes of cold, thirst, hunger, perils and the unknown, taking them all as but the daily incidents of life.

How terrible Almagro's sufferings had been upon his southern march is curiously confirmed by an " Unknown Conqueror,"[1] who left a marginal note upon a copy of Gómara's history of the conquest of Peru, as Garcilaso tells .

Geronimo de Alderete, wishing to see the remains of Almagro's expedition, five or six years after the event, followed the mountain route from Chile to Peru, and found upon the road " a negro[2] standing propped up against the rocks without having fallen, and his horse also still standing (frozen) as if cut out of wood, and the decaying reins still in the negro's hand." The poignant episode recalls the sentinel at Pompeii, dead at his post, preserved to show what Roman discipline was, after a thousand years.

No doubt the " Unknown Conqueror " had been with Alderete on the mountain trail and seen the moving sight,

[1] " Conquistador desconcido." It and the Unknown Warrior are the two finest titles history has bestowed on any man. They are finer even than that of Liberator, that was the chief pride and glory of Bolivar, the greatest man that either North or South America has as yet produced.

[2] " Un negro arrimado a las peñas en pié sin averse caido, y un caballo tambien en pié, como fuese de palo, y las riendas en las manos del negro, ya podridas ": " Comentarios Reales," Book II., p. 91.

and, like a true and veritable conqueror, recorded it, for his own satisfaction, without his signature.

After Almagro had returned to Cuzco, civil war soon broke out between Pizarro and himself, for neither would relinquish Cuzco. The war, Almagro's fate and miserable death upon the scaffold, when an old, gouty man, broken with hardships and with toil, fall into the history of Peru. The Inca Garcilaso, Gómara, Zárate and Jérez all give accounts of his sad fate. That of the Inca Garcilaso is the most copious and sympathetic to him. It appears that the Marquis Pizarro, his old companion in the first conquest, might have stayed the execution had he had the opportunity, but his stern brother Don Hernando, who was in Cuzco at the time, hurried it on, as he had quarrelled bitterly with Almagro from the first day that they had met. He paid for his vindictive conduct with twenty years' imprisonment in Spain. So perished Diego de Almagro, whom the Indians called "Armero," not being able to pronounce his name.

Pizarro for some reason or another they styled "Lapomocho." He, too, met his doom, assassinated by the partisans of the young Almagro,[1] fighting to the last like an old lion,[2] at seventy years of age.

[1] Diego de Almagro's illegitimate son, by an Indian woman of Panama.
[2] He killed three of the assassins with his own hand, and had he had time to put on his armour, would probably have escaped.

CHAPTER III

CHILE was left abandoned by the Spaniards through the failure of Almagro's expedition, until in 1538 Pizarro entrusted the subjugation of the country to his friend and lieutenant, Pedro de Valdivia.

Since his first landing in America, Valdivia had served the Pizarros faithfully, both in the council chamber and in the field. He fought for the Pizarros in the bloody battle of Las Salinas, against Almagro's faction, and did good service at it.

The battle left Pizarro absolute master of Peru. Had he but used his triumph with more clemency, and not brought his old companion to the scaffold, he might have died honoured and loved by all, instead of perishing by the assassin's steel. Pizarro named Valdivia Captain General and Governor of Chile in the year 1538.

One Pedro Sanchez de la Hoz opposed him, alleging certain rights he had to the position, under a letter from the Emperor; but Pizarro was not a man to look at mere technicalities, and confirmed Valdivia in his command. In 1540 he set out from Cuzco with Captains Pedro Gomez, Pedro de Moncada, and Alonso de Monroy, the latter destined to play a great part in the conquest.

Almagro's veterans had brought such bad accounts of Chile, spreading abroad there was no gold there, and that there was nothing to be gained except hard knocks, that there were few who cared to join Valdivia in his enterprise. His utmost efforts only resulted in enlisting one hundred and fifty men, and these their comrades looked upon as mad to leave Peru on such a barren quest. One thousand Indians were pressed as porters,[1] and with this poor following he set out.

[1] Indios de carga.

In spite of his small forces, Valdivia, though he speaks of hardships and of dangers that he encountered on his journey in his letter to the Emperor Charles V., had not the additional difficulty of embarking into the unknown, for Almagro had already, so to speak, blazed the trail.

He followed the coast route, and arrived in the fertile valley of Coquimbo, known to the Spaniards as El Valle de la Posesion, probably because it was the only part of Chile that Almagro really subjugated. The Indians called the valley Coquimbo, and by that name it is so called to-day. There Valdivia founded the first city of the many that he was destined to found in Chile in the valley, and called it La Serena, after his birthplace in the Estremenian wilds.

He then passed on, subduing all the country without great trouble, although the Indians resisted his advance as far as possible.

On the 12th of February, 1541, he founded Santiago, that has remained the capital of Chile, and named it Santiago del Nuevo Extremo. El Nuevo Extremo was the name that Valdivia and the other conquerors applied to Chile; but it soon fell into disuse.

He founded Santiago[1] in the name of God and of His Blessed Mother and of the Apostle St. James (Santiago). The adjoining province he called Nueva Estremadura, after the province where he was born.

His first act[2] was to get himself elected Captain General

[1] "Fundó esta ciudad en nombre de Dios, y de su bendita madre y del Apostol Santiago, el muy magnifico señor Pedro de Valdivia teniente del Gobernador y Capitan General por el muy ilustre señor Don Francisco Pizarro, Gobernador y Capitan General en las provincias del Peru por S.M. y pusole nombre la ciudad de Santiago del Nuevo Extremo, y a esta provincia y sus comarcas, y aquella tierra de que S.M. fuese servido que sea su Gobernador la provincia de Nueva Extremadura": "Historia de Chile desde su Descubrimiento Hasta el Año de 1575," compuesta por el Capitan Alonso de Gongora Marmolejo (publicada el año de 1850 en el tomo 42 del Memorial Historico Español, por Don Pascual de Gayangos).

[2] ". . . Electo Gobernador y Capitan General en nombre de S.M. por el cabildo, justicia y regimento y por todo el pueblo . . .": Marmolejo.

and Governor in the name of His Majesty (Charles V.) by the town council, by the magistrates and all the citizens.

For this portion of Valdivia's life and conquests there is no better authority than that of his own letters, five in number, to the Emperor.

Figueroa in his " General Biographical Dictionary of Chile " writes that " the letters that he (Valdivia) wrote from Chile to the Emperor Charles V. constitute[1] the first spring of exact historical information of this country in the first period of the conquest. . . ."

They are written in a soldier-like but cultured style, and are, as Figueroa says, our only first-hand authority for the first period of the conquest. Marmolejo, although he served with Valdivia, did not write whilst the actual conquest was in progress, as did his general.

One of Valdivia's first acts was to set about to build a church, for he was careful of the public welfare[2] both in the spiritual and the material spheres.

He himself fixed the length and breadth of the cathedral. He drew up plans for the porch and for the sacristy, taking

---

Marmolejo was born in Carmona, near Seville, and served long under Valdivia. Valdivia's own account of his election to the Emperor is in the best " Nolo episcopari " style: ". . . Therefore the Procurador of the city resolved to request the cabildo to choose me as governor in Your Majesty's name, owing to the news of the said Marquis's (Pizarro) death, whose lieutenant I was. . . . And so they and the people all with one opinion met together and gave their approval, giving reasons why I should accept, and I giving mine why I should be excused; in the end they overcame me, though not by arguments, but through showing me the advantage to Your Majesty, and since it seemed to me that it were best for that state of things, I accepted": Valdivia's first letter to Charles V.

[1] " Las cartas que escribió de Chile al emperador Carlos V., constituyen la primera fuente de noticias historicas de este pais en el primer periodo de la conquista . . . ": " Diccionario Biografico General de Chile," Santiago de Chile, 1808.

[2] " . . . Para el beneficio comun, tanto en lo espritual como en lo temporal ": " Cordoba y Figueroa," Cap. X., p. 79.

good care the architect should put a fireplace[1] in it, for even this did not escape his far-reaching eye.

He showed he knew the labour question thoroughly, for in the contract he put down that the master builder should bind himself to execute the work within three years, and to encourage him to keep his bargain, ordered him a gratuity of ten thousand dollars above his estimate. All this he did with the sole object that divine service should not be held in a straw hut, a thing he held unseemly and intolerable.[2]

His piety was such that the Apostle Santiago came from the celestial sphere to drill his soldiers.[3]

How few poor mortals, Figueroa says, have merited so great a blessing! That is so, though Santiago had had great practice of guerilla warfare, and must have passed much of his time out of the celestial sphere, to judge by all the paintings of him and his horse trampling the infidel.

Valdivia, like the rest of the conquistadores, set his hand lightly to build cathedrals; but there was something far more difficult to do in his new founded town. That was the question of the tithes, a matter thorny and beset with difficulties ever since the days of Hofni and of Phineas. It must have been a still more arduous task when the tithes had to be gathered with the sword.

The city naturally grouped itself around the hill of Santa Lucia, that rises in the middle of the modern capital.

As far as Santiago, all had been relatively easy work, for Valdivia had not encountered any very serious opposition from the Indians. His difficulties lay ahead, and from the year 1541, in which he founded Santiago, he was to know no rest from fighting, either in Chile or Peru. To the southward lay the independent territory of the Araucanians, whom the Incas never had subdued.

[1] " . . . Ordenó que se construyese la catedral y expresó su longitud y latitud ": " Cordoba y Figueroa."
" . . . Con la chimenea, que aun esto no desacordó su providencia."
[2] " Solo tuvo por objeto que se celebrase el divino culto con toda decencia, y no en una choza pajiza ": " Cordoba y Figueroa."
[3] " Cordoba y Figueroa."

This country, only twenty leagues in extent, as Ercilla says in his celebrated "Araucana,"[1] lay sheltered by the Andes, across which several passes gave access to the great Pampas of the south. As time went on, and the great plains became the home of countless herds of cattle, no doubt the Araucanians got supplies of food from the Pampa Indians, who Father Falkner, in his most interesting book,[2] says spoke the same language as themselves. This, no doubt, helped them to continue their long wars against the Spanish settlers.

Ercilla goes on to say,[3] "certainly it is a thing to wonder at that with the scant territory they possessed that they were able to resist so long." However, they were the people with whom Valdivia was fated to contend for the next ten years, and amongst whom he lost his life.

However, before he attempted the conquest of Arauco he had plenty on his hands. As he says himself, in his first letter to the Emperor Charles V., he did his best on arriving in the valley of Mopocho—that is, the valley in which Santiago stood—to attempt to conciliate the chiefs. By a judicious disposition of his men he made the Indians think his forces were far stronger than they actually were. He says the Indians were so friendly at the first, that they built the town of Santiago, erecting houses of wood, thatched with the grasses of the country, from plans he furnished them.

When the Indians saw Valdivia was actually settling in the country, they very naturally took alarm. Valdivia, who had had long experience of Indian warfare under such skilled commanders as Pizarro and Almagro, was not the least deceived by the pacific attitude the Indians adopted at the first. He collected a great stock of provisions of all kinds, sufficient for two years. The Inca, Manco Capac,[4] had sent beforehand to warn the Indians of the Spaniards' coming and to prepare them to resist.

---

[1] "La Araucana," Alonso de Ercilla, Madrid, Año de MDCCLXXVI., por Antonio de Sancha, con las licencias necesarias.

[2] "A Description of Patagonia," Thomas Falkner (Jesuit), Hereford, 1774.   [3] "La Araucana," Canto XXX., p. 17.

[4] Valdivia calls him Mango Ynga.

He advised them to hide all gold, and sweep the country bare both of corn and cattle, so that the invaders should not find a livelihood. Valdivia, in his first letter to the Emperor, says they did this thoroughly, so thoroughly that they themselves were left half starving, until the harvest could be gathered in.

News reached Valdivia of a plot amongst the Indians to kill him and cut off his garrison, and so expel the Spaniards from the land. Some of the Indians were taken prisoner and under torture confessed their chief, lord of the Canconcagua valley, had had news of Pizarro's death by the chiefs of Copiapó, news that had come to them from the chiefs of Atacama, the nearest territory to Peru.

As there was no direct communication with Peru by sea, and Valdivia was still uncertain as to Pizarro's death,[1] and feared if it were true Peru would be in revolt, he determined, with the disregard of difficulties that characterized all the conquistadores, to build a vessel in which he hoped to get news from Peru, for the land journey was a desperate enterprise. He went down to the coast himself to superintend the building of the brigantine.[2] "God knows the trouble that it cost," he says pathetically. He left twelve men to build his vessel, with a guard of eight horse soldiers[3] to protect them at their labours. While he was at the coast, encouraging and urging on the work, a letter reached him from Captain Alonso de Monroy, his second in command, informing him that there was a plot to murder him, afoot, contrived by some of the partisans of the Almagro faction who were serving in his ranks.

These men, no doubt stimulated by the murder of Pizarro, thought the time ripe to kill Valdivia, and hand over Chile to Almagro's half-caste son, who for the moment held the first place in Peru.

The letter came at midnight, but Valdivia at once saddled

[1] " . . . I did not believe what the Indians said of the Marquis's death (for they lie) ": First letter to Charles V.
[2] Un bergantin y el trabajo que costó, Dios lo sabe.
[3] Ocho de a caballo.

up, and took the road to Santiago on the spur. Before he started he enjoined upon the workmen and the few horse soldiers that he left, to be upon their guard, and promised to return within a day or two.

They, after the fashion of all those unused to frontier warfare, seeing no signs of danger, thought none existed, and, as Valdivia told the Emperor, went about carelessly, not even carrying arms. One night they were suddenly attacked, and all but two of them paid for their folly with their lives. Then the whole country at once rose in revolt.

Valdivia was undaunted, and before dealing with the revolted Indians, took a swift vengeance on the traitors in his camp. Well did he understand the pith and substance of the saying, there is no worse thief than the one in your own house.[1]

Five of the rogues he hung incontinently, not daring to hang more on account of "the straits in which I was," he wrote regretfully. He turned a blind eye[2] on the others who had been guilty of participation in the plot, and with the sight of the five corpses dangling in the air, instilled such terror into all his men that he had no more mutinies to quell throughout his whole career.

The worst blow that Valdivia suffered was the loss of his new vessel, that had cost him so much difficulty to build, burned by the Indians. Thus, for the present, he was obliged to give up any hope of communicating with Peru, and to remain uncertain as to how matters stood with the Pizarros, to whom he was most loyally attached.

The Indians gave him little time to think about such matters, for they attacked the newly founded town of Santiago in overwhelming force. Being built of wooden houses thatched with grass, it was not easily defensible. The Indians divided their forces into two great companies.

Valdivia, with ninety men, all he could muster, anxious to get in the first blow, sallied out and attacked the larger body of the enemy, leaving his lieutenant, Captain Alonso de

---

[1] No hay peor ladron, que el de casa.
[2] Hizo la vista gorda.

Monroy, to defend Santiago with fifty men, thirty of whom were mounted, and therefore equal in those days to a whole regiment.

Whilst he was dealing with the greater army of the Indians, the rest of them fell on Monroy and his small forces in the town. All day they fought, dealing death and destruction on the Indians, both with their lances and their swords. Slowly the Indians pushed the Spaniards back into the town, which they set fire to and consumed utterly.

As night came on, seeing the desperate straits that they were in, Captain Monroy resolved to stake his future on a charge. Most of his men were wounded, but luckily his horses all had escaped, so with the men on foot clinging to the riders' stirrups, they sallied out and charged.

"So by the favour of 'our Santiago'[1] we fell upon them," and the Indians, seeing the wounds made by the lances and the swords, and terrified by the fierce aspect of the charging horses, first weakened, and then fled. A priest,[2] one Father Lobo from San Lucar, fought in the front, dealing such blows he seemed a wolf amongst sheep, and helping greatly towards the victory. Lobo was evidently a true priest of the church militant, and understood the full force of the saying " praying to God and battering with the mace."[3] Monroy sent to advise Valdivia next day that he had put the Indians to flight, but that the town was burned down and all provisions lost. He sent a list of the small stock of property left unconsumed.

It included the precious horses, their arms, the clothes they had upon their backs, mostly in rags, two small pigs, a sucking-pig, a cock and hen, and about two handfuls of wheat. Valdivia was in an almost desperate position, but, like the rest of the conquistadores, never despaired. He

[1] Nuestro Santiago: First letter to Charles V.
[2] " . . . Y viendo los golpes de lanzas y cuchilladas que los el daban tan bravos, en especial un clerigo natural de San Lucar, llamado Lobo, que andaba entre ellos como lobo en las pobres ovejas y con este temor alzaron (los Indios) el campo": "Historia de Chile," por el Capitan Alonso de Gongora Marmolejo.
[3] A Dios rogando, y con la maza dando.

writes to Charles V.: " It seemed to me that if we were to cling to the land and make it Your Majesty's for ever, we must eat of the fruits of our own hands, as in the beginning of the world, and I set about to sow. I divided my men into two bands, and we all dug, ploughed, and sowed in due order, being always armed and with our horses saddled all the day. One night the one half kept watch in its quarters, and so for the other half; when the seed had been sown, some kept guard over it and the town in the said way, while I, with the other half, moved all the time eight or ten leagues around it, breaking up the bands of Indians, for they surrounded us on every side. And with the Christians and the people we brought from Peru, I built up the town again, and we made our houses and sowed to feed ourselves. It was no easy thing to find maize for seed, and it was got with great risk. I also had the two handfuls of wheat sown, and from them twelve fanegas[1] were harvested."[2]

The Indians, on their side, were no less heroic and determined in the defence of their own land. They sowed no crops, hoping to starve the Spaniards out, feeding themselves with roots and herbs, and a scanty crop of maize that they sowed in the mountains in places unknown to the Spaniards.

It is difficult which most to admire, the patriotic Indians or the band of adventurers, few in number, cut off from all supplies, and with but the advantage of their horses and their arms.

Theirs was no conquest such as those of Africa in modern times, when with arms of precision, countless resources, and well provisioned, " Christians " mow down the " natives " like ripe corn.

The Indians tried their best to destroy the crops Valdivia cherished like the apple of his eye. However, so strict was the watch he kept upon the growing corn, that all their efforts were in vain.

Still, situated as he was, it was imperative to have communication with Peru, for from there and there alone could

---

[1] The fanega contains about one bushel and three-quarters.
[2] First letter to Charles V.

he expect to get provisions and more men. He therefore determined to send Captain Alonso de Monroy with men and the best horses that he had, to tempt his fortune over the trackless desert that lay between them and Peru. Hitherto no small body had crossed Atacama, and now it was more dangerous than before, for all the wells and waterholes were occupied, or known, but to the Indians alone.

In order that Monroy should be in a position to recruit more soldiers, Valdivia gave him seven thousand dollars, and that the horses should not be distressed, for he well knew nothing fatigues a horse more than being ridden without stirrups, he had six pairs made, scabbards for the riders' swords, and two iron cups for the men to drink from on the way.

The stirrups, probably, he had made of wood, for he says: " Out of the iron stirrups, harness, and some few things I found, I had horseshoes made by a smith whom I had brought with his forge, with which the horses were well shod; and each man carried four spare shoes and a bag of a hundred nails, and with my blessing I entrusted them to God and sent them off upon their way. . . ."[1]

[1] First letter to Charles V.

CHAPTER IV

CAPTAIN MONROY and his five soldiers set out upon their adventurous ride with but scant chance of getting through the hostile Indians, who now had risen in great force. Few rides in all the history of the conquest of the Indies were more desperate, with the exception of that undertaken by Captain Gonzalo de Sylvestre, so movingly related by the Inca Garcilaso in his " Florida."

Monroy started from Santiago in the month of January, 1542.

Riding continuously by day and night, he reached the valley of Copiapó. There, in spite of the warning he had received from Valdivia, to be upon his guard, he fell into an ambush, four of his companions were killed, and he himself with the remaining horseman of his little band were taken prisoners.

Nothing more curious or dramatic can be imagined than his subsequent escape.

The Indians took possession of the seven thousand dollars' worth of gold that they were carrying with them to buy arms and horses in Peru. Two of the horses had survived. The Indians spared the lives of the two Spaniards on condition they would teach them how to ride.

Weeks passed, and it was the delight of the cacique to ride out with one or other of his prisoners. It happened that, living amongst the Indians, was a Spanish soldier[1] who had been taken prisoner or deserted from Almagro's forces, on his return towards Peru. This man had settled down and married, and become almost an Indian.

He spoke their language, and enjoyed some reputation in the tribe. Valdivia blames him, and says he was the cause

[1] First letter to Charles V.

of the death of Monroy's followers; but this was most probably on account of his having become a renegade.

At any rate, he was the means, perhaps involuntarily, of Monroy's wonderful escape. Three months had passed, and it appeared Monroy and his companions were destined to pass their lives amongst the Indians. All their arms had been taken from them. Their clothes hung on their backs in rags. One thing was in their favour and one only—the horses had got into first-class condition, and were fit for a man to ride for life upon them.

Each morning the two Spaniards gave the chief his riding lesson. Monroy rode one of the horses, and the other Spaniard trotted beside the chief to help him if the need occurred. It was the fashion of the times to have a running footman[1] who trotted dutifully behind the horses of the great. Perhaps Monroy, who must have had his mind fixed on escape, had told the chief all Spaniards of rank were so accompanied. Probably the chief was but an inapt pupil, for the Indians at the first conquest stood in great dread of horses, animals quite unknown to them, and that had spread death and destruction in their ranks.

The renegade, who perhaps had a lurking, not unnatural sympathy with his own countrymen, furnished Monroy with a knife, possibly with a knowledge of how it was to be employed. One morning, as the chief went out to take his morning lesson, with Monroy riding by his side as usual and the soldier jogging after them, their minds made up to escape or die in the attempt, Monroy, drawing his knife, stabbed the unsuspecting Indian to the heart.

The soldier jumped upon his horse, and urging both the horses to full speed, broke through the Indians and rode for liberty.

How they fared on their journey through the desert of Atacama, without provisions and unarmed, only they could have told. Such journeys were so usual at the time, and strange adventures were such commonplace occurrences to the conquistadores, that no one seems to have recorded what

[1] He was called " un espolique."

happened to Alonso de Monroy and his companion upon their desperate ride.

Valdivia says they took the renegade Christian with them, but he does not say how they managed it, for Monroy had but two horses, and it seems strange on such a ride that he should have made one of them carry the burden of two men.

He says the country that they traversed was a desert, and that they got over it by the will of God and the great care they took.[1]

Courage and diligence were of the first necessity, and the will of God was proved to demonstration, seeing that they got through their difficulties.

Monroy at once went to the Viceroy, Vaca de Castro, who had just won a victory over Diego de Almagro,[2] Almagro's half-caste son.

The royal treasury was empty, and the Viceroy was heavily in debt.

Hearing of Valdivia's almost desperate situation, and the great need he stood in, both of provisions and of arms, the Viceroy, having no money in his treasury, set about at once to raise as much as possible amongst the colonists. Meanwhile, in Santiago, Valdivia was in the direst straits imaginable. The town had been rebuilt, not very substantially, but sufficiently for the immediate shelter of the citizens and troops. Valdivia had it surrounded with a fence, one and a half " estados "[3] high. It was sixteen hundred feet square, and took two hundred thousand bricks of a yard long[4] and a palm in height to construct. Valdivia himself laboured at brick-making, beside the rest of " His Majesty's vassals," with their arms at their sides, and sentinels posted ready to warn them of an Indian attack.

[1] " Mediante la voluntad de Dios y su buena diligencia."
[2] After the victory he was executed, and went to the scaffold bravely.
[3] The estado was 1·85 yards long. Thus the fence would be about five feet or a little more in height.
[4] These bricks were most probably sun-dried and of the kind known as adobes.

When the warning came, the people with their few possessions took refuge in the square, in which the little food they had was carefully disposed. For three long years this state of siege continued, with ploughing, sowing, and the harvest all taking place in constant fear of an attack upon the colonists.

Their arms were never taken off, even for an hour, Valdivia informs the Emperor, in his most interesting account of the long struggle to maintain themselves in their newly founded capital. Throughout these three eventful years Valdivia and the mounted men patrolled the country ceaselessly, breaking up the Indian forces when they sought to concentrate for an advance against the town.

Writing to the Emperor he says: " The toils of war, ever-victorious Cæsar, men can bear, since it is the soldier's boast to die upon the field; but if the pangs of hunger are added to them, it is more than men can stand."

They certainly were called upon to bear a good deal, both from hunger and their enemies. Still, there were no revolts, as Valdivia's short method with the sceptics who had planned to murder him had showed that he recoiled before no measure to preserve discipline amongst his men.

No people in the world have ever suffered hardships better than the Spaniards. Even to-day, hunger is the national disease.

To read Valdivia's letters is to wonder how ever the conquistadores endured the miseries of which he writes: " And many of the Christians had to go sometimes to dig up roots for food . . . for there was no meat, and the Christian who got fifty grains of maize a day thought himself well off; and he who had a handful of wheat did not winnow it to take away the husks."

" Christians " seemed to have deserved their name in those days, for faith and faith alone could have enabled them to endure such misery, and yet be always ready at the sentinel's alarm to buckle on their swords.

Valdivia says nothing as to how he kept his horses in condition; but one may suppose that as one horse was at least as valuable in those days as three Christians, they got more than fifty grains of maize. " And so we went about like ghosts, and the Indians called us Capais, which is the name they give their devils."

It is strange how many of the conquistadores, as Pedro de Cieza de Leon, Bernal Diaz del Castillo, Cortés, Quesada, and Valdivia had a gift as chroniclers. No practised writer, with an eye upon his style, and a heart trembling beneath the critic's lash, could have produced a phrase more telling than " we went about like ghosts."

Yet phrases such as this—happy descriptions of men, of horses, and of battles; apt musings upon life; ponderings upon the customs of the Indians; simple and touching instances of faith fit to remove that highest of all mountains, reason, from her foundations—abound in all the writings of these men, whose hands must have been made so callous by the sword one wonders that they could have ever wielded so small a weapon as the pen.

Although Vaca de Castro was without money, yet there were wealthy citizens of Peru ready to come to Valdivia's aid. A certain Portuguese, whose name unluckily is not preserved in Valdivia's letters, set about to find out men willing to come forward in the hour of need. The Portuguese does not appear to have been a moneyed man himself. He found, however, one Cristobal de Escobar, who advanced five thousand castellanos.[1] With this sum Captain Alonso de Monroy fitted out seventy horsemen. A priest called Gonzalianez lent another sum of five thousand castellanos in gold. Not content with this, both Escobar and Father Gonzalianez joined Valdivia in Chile and served him faithfully.

The spirit of adventure inspired all classes of society in those days in the Americas; and as to loyalty, Spaniards in all ages have been only too loyal to their Kings.

Vaca de Castro, who had his hands full enough of public

---

[1] The castellano varied a good deal in value, according to where it was coined. It was the fiftieth part of a gold mark, and may have been worth a little less than a dollar.

business, yet bestirred himself nobly to send Valdivia help.

He dispatched Monroy to Chile, with all the arms and men he could collect, promising to send another ship loaded with everything required as soon as possible.

Monroy set out from Lima, and went to Arequipa to await the coming of the ship that Vaca de Castro had promised him. Owing to some reason unexplained, perhaps on account of the bad savour Chile had in everybody's estimation, the master of the vessel refused to leave the port. Instantly one Lucas Martinez Vegazo stepped into the breach and gave a vessel of his own. This ship he loaded up with arms, ironware, and all sorts of necessaries, putting aboard some casks of wine. This wine Valdivia was specially in need of, for for four months there had been no celebration of divine service in his newly built capital, for lack of the chief element.

Vaca de Castro also kept him informed of what was going on in Europe, and how the most Christian King of France had made an alliance with the Turk to the great scandal of all Christendom.

Castro also reminded Valdivia that the royal fifths would prove most acceptable to the Emperor to help him in his wars against the French. Money was scarce in Chile at that time, and Valdivia writes cautiously, for all his loyalty, saying that he " would look on it as salvation "[1] if he could find two or three hundred thousand castellanos in the country.

In September, 1543, Lucas Martinez Vegazo's ship reached Valparaiso, to Valdivia's great joy. Alonso de Monroy and his recruits came overland, travelling by the coast route.

The Indians who had retired into the province of the Promocaes, on the arrival of Monroy and his fresh men, now sent Valdivia a challenge to come and fight them, promising to submit if they found the Spaniards braver than themselves.

Valdivia, who was not the kind of man to miss an opportunity of fighting on such terms, sent them a message to expect him.

When Monroy's men and horses had recovered from their

[1] Valdivia's first letter to Charles V.

long march and constant fighting by the way, Valdivia set out. He found the Indians had left their stronghold, wasted and burned the country, and retired into the hills.

In April, 1544, a ship arrived upon the coast laden with provisions and with stores, but before she could be unloaded, the Indians attacked and burned her, after having killed the crew. The loss was most severe, for provisions were beginning to run short.

In the month of June (1544) Vaca de Castro's long-promised second ship arrived. Her master was a Genoese, one Juan Bautista de Pastene, a man who had already showed himself an able navigator.

Valdivia with that ever-present desire for knowledge that characterizes men of nations in the ascendant, as were the Spaniards of those days, instantly made him his Lieutenant General by sea, and sent him off on an expedition to explore the Magellan Strait. He gave him another vessel to accompany him, charging him to take possession of the land, in the name of the Emperor.

He also sent his Maestre de Campo, Francisco de Villagra, to drive back the Indians from the neighbourhood of Santiago, and to explore the provinces towards the south. Captain Francisco de Aguirre he stationed on the river Maulé[1] to guard the frontier. Valdivia's schemes were wise and far-reaching, and he seems to have seen that above all things it was necessary to settle his people on the land.

With pardonable pride, in a fine and manly passage, he tells the Emperor the scope and tenor of his aims. Aims widely differing from those that swayed Pizarro and Cortés with their thirst for gold.

". . . Since I came into the land and the Indians rose against me, what I have aimed at, to carry out my intention to make it Your Majesty's power, is to have been governor in your royal name with authority over your vassals and over it, and a captain to encourage them in war and to be the first in danger, for so it was best; a father to help them as I could, and grieve for their toils, aiding them like sons to bear up;

[1] Valdivia always calls the river Mauli. It is now the Maulé.

a friend to speak with them; a geometrician to trace out and people; an overseer to make channels and share out water; a tiller and worker at the sowings; a head shepherd for the breeding of flocks; and, in short, peopler, breeder, defender, conqueror and discoverer."

A noble and unselfish letter, and one that Charles V., who was no ordinary man, should have appreciated.

In return he asked the Emperor to confirm him in his government, setting forth that he had never had more than two hundred men-at-arms.

With a noble confidence he writes the Emperor, telling him all the hardships that the soldiers had to undergo, and how after all they had undergone they were still loyal to him.

" Withal they do not hate, but love me, for they begin to see all was needful. . . ."

His men were raging, as he says, to push farther into the country, but he restrained them, thinking it best to conquer by degrees.

" For though I have few men, if I had the same intention as other governors have had, which is not to stop till I find gold enough to enrich myself, I could have gone searching with them, but since this is at best for Your Majesty's service and the holding of the land, I go with a leaden foot."[1]

The fruit of his wise policy was manifest by the fact that from the two small pigs that he had saved when the Indians burned down Santiago, he had now a herd of many thousand swine, and chickens " were as the blades of grass," all bred from the solitary cock and hen that had escaped the flames. He also expected to harvest ten thousand fanegas of wheat. One of his chief preoccupations was to keep open the main road to Peru, for from that country alone could he expect supplies. Experience had taught the settlers, both in Chile and Peru, that the road by the Andes was impossible. Thus it had become of the first importance to develop traffic by the coast.

[1] " Con pie de plomo "—*i.e.*, slowly.

Vaca de Castro, by his wise government, had made all safe upon the road as far as Atacama, in Peru.

Between that town and the valley of Copiapó, where Valdivia had founded his first town, La Serena, lay the great difficulty. Nature had done all that she could to make the district hostile to mankind. Few wells, and those far distant from each other; but little pasturage, and that sparse and salitrose; fogs that swept down from the Andes, in which the traveller was as helpless as a ship at sea, befogged, rendered the passage of the hundred leagues of sand a perfect Calvary. In addition to all these natural difficulties, the Indians often held the wells, or filled them up with sand.

Nothing could shake Valdivia's confidence in his conquest.

He never tires of dwelling on the climate, so mild in winter that there is no need to draw near the fire. In summer, so temperate that a man may be all day in the sun without annoyance.

If a man will but work, he says, he will find plenty, and all those gentlemen who in Castile go short of food should emigrate to Chile, where there is land and food for everybody.

Had many of the other conquistadores held the same views Valdivia expressed, the history of the New World would have been different.

Valdivia was greatly intent on getting a good breed of horses, for on them in those days, especially in such a land as Chile, where there was much flat, open ground, so much depended, for by horsemen alone could the marauding bands of Indians be broken up.

Cavalry in those days played the part now played by aeroplanes. His policy was by degrees to detach the natives from their tribal chiefs, and to induce them to settle amongst the Spaniards. This policy, that was followed in a way unconsciously in all the Spanish colonies, had the result of breaking down the colour line, that has been such a curse in British colonies, and that seems destined to provide problems of the greatest difficulty to solve.

The result of Valdivia's policy has been to breed up a race in Chile, active, athletic, and eminently fitted for the conditions of their life. Moreover, as the European stock has proved far more persistent than the Indian, even those families who are known to have had a strong admixture of the native blood have now become quite white.

Above all things Valdivia wished to be left alone, to pursue the policy that he had laid down. Repeatedly he begged the Emperor not to send any other captain out, whether from Spain or from Peru. The Council of the Indies, from its snug armchairs in Seville, delighted to have a finger in all pies in the New World. Cortés was bothered all his life with foolish appointments of men ill suited to command, sent by the governor of Cuba, and so of almost every one of the conquistadores of America. Court influence, and the too ready ear the Council of the Indies gave to the discontented, hampered Quesada all his life, and at one moment very nearly wrecked his colony of New Grenada, that he had won with so great hardships and such toil.

Valdivia was quite determined that this should not take place in Chile under his command. He writes to Charles V. in that independent, democratic style that Spaniards may have received from their long contact with the Moors. Like them, whilst understanding thoroughly the difference that exists between a Sultan and a camel driver, the camel driver never forgets he is a man, and in his manhood equal to any other of the sons of Adam.[1] Thus, though Valdivia kisses, in all his letters, "Your Catholic Majesty's sacred feet and hands," that does not in the least prevent him from standing stoutly for what he considers are his rights.

At times he even pretty plainly advises His Catholic Majesty as to the course he ought to take. Such frankness could not have been repugnant to Charles V. himself, a Fleming reared in camps. His own description of the friars at Yuste as " yellow sons of whores "[2] shows pretty plainly that, though an Emperor and pleased to be known as Brother Charles,[3] amongst the aforesaid yellow bastards, he was at heart a Prince of Light Horsemen, as he was dubbed when still the darling of the camp.

[1] Beni-Adam. [2] Hideputas bermejos. [3] Fray Carlos.

After having prayed the Emperor to send out no raw captain[1] to bother him, a demand he also made upon the Viceroy of Peru, he gives his reasons just as one captain speaking to another at a war council would speak. Indeed, just as a gentleman includes a nobleman, for though the gentleman is not of necessity of noble birth, no rank avails unless the holder of it is a gentleman, so captain includes general, for no general is more than a mere wearer of a gaudy uniform unless he be a captain, tried and experienced in war.

So he says, " I tell Your Majesty the exact truth. If men are not accustomed to the food here, before they turn their bellies into skin bags to profit by it, they die the half of them, and the Indians soon finish off the rest." He then tells Charles V., quite frankly, if he sends out a governor to supersede him, and sees opposite orders given, he will retire and become a private soldier, but will continue to serve with the zeal and the will that he has always shown. By this time (September, 1545) Valdivia had got the Indians pretty well subdued around the capital. The conquest of Arauco still lay before him, though he was never fated to achieve it thoroughly. Before he even could attempt it, events occurred that called him to Peru, where he once more did yeoman service for the Emperor.

[1] Bisoño.

CHAPTER V

VALDIVIA, who in some things resembled the great Cortés, was always anxious to explore as well as conquer.

Just as Cortés sent several expeditions to the Gulf of California, so did Valdivia occupy himself with the exploration of the Magellan Straits, and all the extreme southern portion of his government.

His energy was boundless. Few of the conquistadores wasted less time in searching after mines.

In the year 1544 he sent off the Genoese, Juan Bautista de Pastene, to examine the southern portion of his territory.

He reached the Straits, but did not venture to sail through them. Valdivia, in his second letter to the Emperor, says, "If it is Your Highness' wish that the Strait be sailed through, send me your orders to do so, for the navigation is nothing (under God's will) if Your Highness is served thereby. . . . I will bring it about that from the day when Your Highness' orders shall come, in a very short time there shall be a ship in Seville, which has come through it."

No thought of profit seems to have occurred to him in this respect. He was chiefly interested, as it appears from what he says to the Emperor, to enlarge the dominions of the Crown.

Captain Pastene gave a favourable account of the lands in the south of Chile, and Valdivia immediately resolved to conquer them. He did not know that, between Santiago and the country Captain Pastene had reported on so favourably, the Araucanians barred the way.

For the first time, in his third letter to the Emperor, he mentions that he has been occupied in working certain mines, somewhere about Coquimbo in the extreme northern portion of his territory.

When he had extracted from the mines, after nine months' labour, sixty thousand castellanos' worth of gold, he sent off Captain Alonso de Monroy, in Juan Bautista de Pastene's ship, to Lima, to buy arms and horses, and to recruit more men.

He says he hopes that Monroy will return in six or seven months—in those days a voyage from Chile to Peru was a most formidable task. After appointing a Cabildo[1] in his newly founded town of La Serena, he returned to the capital. In 1546, for the first time for two years, things were so quiet in his government that he determined to head an expedition to explore fifty leagues towards the south.

After the harvest, that was the best that he had had in Chile, he picked out sixty of his best mounted men and set out to see, as he says, where he could plant another town.

On the 10th of February, 1546, he left Santiago, and for the first thirty leagues no one molested him. The country through which he passed had been half conquered, and the Indians had felt the full force of the Spanish weapons, and most of all that of the mounted men, for above all things the horses terrified them. After ten leagues' journey on, he came upon a country that was well populated, to which the Spaniards had not penetrated. The Indians did not at once attack him, but six leagues farther on he encountered warriors[2] who came out to defend the road. He attacked them,[3] charging upon them with his cavalry. The Indians could not resist the mounted men, and fled, leaving fifty dead upon the field. Valdivia found that the farther he advanced towards the south, the fiercer and more warlike the Indians became. Not the least daunted by their ill success in the first skirmish, that very night during the first watch they attacked again more fiercely than before, to the number of seven or eight thousand warriors. The conflict raged two hours, the Indians fighting desperately in serried

---

[1] Town council.   [2] Gente de guerra.
[3] Dimos en ellos y matamos hasta 50 y los demas huyeron: Third letter to Charles V.

squadrons, like the Germans,[1] as Valdivia says, who had had experience of every kind of troops in the Italian wars. " At last they weakened and we slew many, including the captain who was leading them. They killed two of our horses and wounded five or six more, and as many Christians."

Christians and horses were not upon a par, for a good horse was worth at least three Christians, no matter how strongly the Christians held their faith.

" When the Indians fled, we passed what remained of the night in curing our horses and ourselves.[2] Next day we marched four leagues and came to a great river, just where it flows into the sea, called Biubiu " (El Biobio).

He chose a good site for a town, but as he had suffered a good deal in the skirmish, and had but a few men with him, and the Indians were gathering in large number to oppose his crossing, he judged it prudent to return. His expedition lasted forty days. On his return to Santiago, all were rejoiced at the report he gave of the fertile country to the south.

The settlers were glad to hear that there were so many Indians there, for they looked forward to enslave them, after an easy conquest, as had happened in Peru, for they had no idea of what stern stuff the Araucanians were made.

Eleven months had now elapsed without communication with Peru, and Valdivia was quite in the dark as to what was going on.

In September, 1546, he dispatched a vessel under the

[1] Aquella misma noche al cuarto de la prima dieron sobre nosotros siete ó ocho mil Indios, y peleamos con ellos mas de dos horas, y se nos defendieron barbaramente, cerrados en un esquadron como Tudescos; al fin dieron lado y matamos muchos dellos y al capitan que los guiaba; mataron dos caballos y hirieron cinco o seis, y otros tantos Cristianos. Huidos los Indios entendimos lo que quedaba de la noche en curar a nuestros caballos y a nosotros, y otro dia anduve cuatro leguas y di en un rio muy grande donde entra en la mar, se llama el Biubiu (Biobio).

[2] What they used for dressing wounds, Valdivia does not specify. Perhaps, as Bernal Diaz del Castillo writes, their chief specific was "grasa de Indios," a loathsome remedy, and not even rendered less so by the fact that the Indians had never been baptized.

command of one Juan Davalos, with eighty thousand dollars destined to purchase arms and horses, " these being," as he says, " what is most needed here." The eighty thousand dollars, he says, would have been a great sum had it been destined for any other country than Peru. There it would be looked upon as nothing, he tells the Emperor, although " each dollar cost a hundred drops of blood, and more than two hundred drops of sweat." Thirteen months more he waited. Luckily time was what he had the most to spare, and then one morning Captain Juan Bautista de Pastene sailed into the bay. Twenty-seven months had passed since Valdivia had dispatched him to Peru, and he had given up all hope of ever seeing him. All this time Valdivia was sowing, ploughing, reaping, and keeping off the Indians by ceaseless vigilance, with men who were becoming discontented, and without communication from the outside world.

The conquistadores, besides having bodies made of iron, were endued with souls of steel. Even Valdivia shows a little human weakness in the following affecting words, that he writes to the stony-hearted Charles V. Pastene had returned with his ship empty, without goods, arms, or horses, and almost starving, so that it is not wonderful that Valdivia was moved.

" When I saw him I was so overcome with joy that tears came up from my heart when I bade him welcome. I embraced him as I asked him the reason for so long a delay and how and where the friends were he had taken with him. He answered telling me he would give me an account, and he had much indeed to tell me, and I should be filled with wonder (at what had happened in Peru) and that God had allowed the devil to have those provinces in his hand. And so they sat down to eat, he and his fellows, whereof they had the utmost need."

An affecting narrative and rendered more affecting by the simple words Valdivia uses, words in all respects fitting a conquistador. Valdivia was a man of education, but nearly all the conquistadores seem to have had the gift of a straightforward, simple style, no matter from what rank of society they sprang. Captain Pastene indeed had a strange tale to tell.

Of all the Viceroys of Peru up to that time, Vaca de Castro was easily the best.[1] Peru for some time past had been in a state bordering on civil war.

Fray Bartolome de las Casas, the Apostle of the Indians, had induced the Emperor Charles V. to have drawn up a set of laws, known as the Laws of the Indies, in order to protect the Indians against the exactions of the Spanish conquerors. These naturally were most unpopular with the conquistadores, who were in a fair way of becoming great feudal chiefs.

Far the most prominent of the old conquistadores of that time was Gonzalo, the brother of the murdered marquis, the first conqueror. He not unnaturally hoped the Emperor would continue him as governor in his murdered brother's place.

His talents and position fully justified his hopes.

Known and beloved by all, he had added to his military fame by his well-known exploring expedition to the Montaña.[2]

On his return, after having suffered dreadful hardships, he learned for the first time of his brother's murder, and that the Emperor, who had never forgiven the Pizarros for the death of Almagro, had appointed Vaca de Castro as his governor. Passed over once, his fury knew no bounds when at the end of Vaca de Castro's term of office he was once more left in the cold. The Emperor appointed one Blasco Nuñez Vela as Governor-General. Pedro de Cieza de Leon, the most authoritative of all the writers of the conquest of Peru, thus describes Vela, who he knew well, having served under him:

" Blasco Nuñez Vela had occupied important posts in

[1] " . . . Que sin lisonja, y sin agravio ageno, en voz de todo el Peru fué el mejor Governador, que alla ha pasado, como se podrá ver por todos los tres Historiadores, que del hablan, que ninguno de ellos, dice cosa mal hecha que huviese hecho."

The three historians of whom the Inca speaks are Gómara, Xeres, and Zárate.

[2] The Montaña is the eastern province of Peru on the other side of the Andes.

Spain, where he had been chief magistrate of Malaga and Inspector General of Navarre.

"He had also once made a voyage to this country (Peru) as Captain General of the fleet to fetch the treasure that was here.

"He was tall, of good bearing and gentle mien, he had clear light blue eyes, aquiline features, a broad forehead, a thick and very imposing beard, was an excellent horseman on both saddles,[1] and quick of apprehension, though it was not very sure. . . . He was a passionate man and quick to anger. After reaching this country (Peru) he placed full confidence in no person, and thus, impulsive as he was in his wrath, he was equally so in killing those who had angered him."[2]

It fell to his lot to enforce the Ordinances—that is, the new code of laws drawn up by Charles V. and his Council of the Indies, greatly owing to the influence of the great Fray Bartolome de las Casas, and directed chiefly to the protection of the Indians. In addition to this difficult duty, it fell to him to "take the residence"[3] of Vaca de Castro. This meant to enquire into and report upon all that he had done during his governorship, and, if necessary, arrest and send him home a prisoner to Spain.

No worse system could have been devised, when, as was Blasco Nuñez Vela's case, he himself had been already named governor in the place of him he was to judge.

Vaca de Castro, a much more judicious man[4] than Blasco

---

[1] That is, in the Moorish saddle, riding with short stirrups "à la gineta," and in the style called "à la brida"—that is, in the European saddle, with long stirrups. With the "gineta" saddle the strong Mameluke bit with the solid curb, and a single rein, were used, with a high hand. In the saddle "à la brida," double reins and a low hand.

[2] "The War of Chupas," Pedro de Cieza de Leon, taken from his "Civil Wars of Peru," and translated by Sir Clements R. Markham, K.C.B., for the Hakluyt Society, London, MCMXVIII.

[3] Tomar la residencia.

[4] Cieza de Leon says that Vaca de Castro was avaricious and vainglorious and fond of amassing money; yet although Vaca de Castro had the vices of meaningless presumption, vainglory, and avarice,

Nuñez Vela, had already incurred much odium in the attempt to enforce the Ordinances.[1]

As these Ordinances were specially aimed against the enslavement of the Indians by the means of what were called " Encomiendas "—that is, grants of a district with fixed boundaries to a colonist with power to appropriate the land tax (tributo) of the Indians or to exact personal service from them, or both—it is easy to understand what opposition they evoked.

Both in Mexico and in Peru these Encomiendas were the sources from which the original conquistadores drew a great portion of their wealth.

The Marquis Pizarro[2] granted Encomiendas after his first settlement at San Miguel de Piura, soon after landing in 1532.

The poorer Spaniards and the new colonists, who held no " Encomiendas," were not so much opposed to the introduction of the Ordinances, for men who do not suffer by them are always eager for reforms.

The conquistadores, and in especial the Pizarros, naturally prepared to defend what they considered were their rights by conquest and by the use and custom of the land.

Vela's first action on arriving in Peru was to imprison the man who he had come to supersede, without proceeding to a trial. He seems to have designed to send him back to Spain, for he imprisoned him on board a caravel. Castro, who evidently thought he was in danger of his life, eventually escaped, and made his way to Spain, but was arrested on his arrival at the court. For five long years he was confined in the fortress of Arrevalo. Then, when his trial came on, he was absolved of all the charges Blasco Nuñez Vela had made against him, and all his acts during his viceroyalty were solemnly approved.

---

apart from them he was a good governor and did useful things for the kingdom: " War of Chupas," Sir Clements Markham's translation, Chapter LXXXIII., p. 296.

[1] Las Ordenanzas.

[2] Note on p. xlvi of Sir Clements Markham's Introduction to his " War of Chupas."

Justice proceeded with deliberation in the Spain of those days, and Vaca de Castro's case was not unsimilar to that of Alvar Nuñez Cabeca de Vaca, the good governor of Paraguay.

As a solatium, Castro was made a member of the Royal Council of Castille. It was a case of what is called in Spanish " tarde piache "—that is, grace comes too late.

Blasco Nuñez Vela soon made himself detested by his pride and arrogance. He applied the new laws with severity, executing those who failed to comply with them, doubling the taxes, and doing all within his power to make himself detested in Peru. Each day the faction of Gonzalo Pizarro grew more powerful, and city after city declared upon his side. Vela, though cruel, was a brave man, and far from bowing to the storm, set about levying forces, and in a short time had a great army under arms. After a long series of skirmishes in which now one side, sometimes the other, had the advantage, the armies met near Quito. At a fierce battle in which the Viceroy fought most desperately, killing and wounding several of Pizarro's captains with his own hand, one Hernando de Torres brought him to the ground with a blow on the head with a mace or battleaxe.

Seeing his fall, his followers gave way, and a negro slave cut off the dying Viceroy's head and stuck it on a pole.

The victory made Gonzalo Pizarro master of the whole country for the time being. The Inca Garcilaso says that he made wise laws[1] and governed temperately. For a considerable time all things went well with him. News took months to arrive in Spain, and there was no one in the country able to dispute his will. His Lieutenant-General, Francisco de Carvajal, who was over eighty years of age, but still as fit to carry arms and pass long days and nights on horseback as he had been when he fought in the Italian wars, full fifty years before, urged him to marry one of the Inca princesses and make himself King of Peru. It was the first time and the last in all the history of the conquest that such a thought had ever entered into the mind of any of the conquistadores.

---

[1] "Las buenas leyes, que hiço para el buen govierno de aquel imperio": " Comentarios Reales," Libro Quarto de la Segunda Parte, p. 250.

Carvajal then advised him to set up a titular Inca, choosing the best of the royal family, so as to gain the suffrages of the Indians, who loved even the simulacrum of an Inca government. Many of Gonzalo's captains gave him the same advice, counselling him to institute Peruvian orders of nobility and make his captains marquises and dukes.

Carvajal, who must have been as good a statesman as a warrior, put the case to him most ingeniously. "No King can be a traitor,"[1] he exclaimed, quoting the Spanish adage. "This country was the Incas'. You and your brothers conquered it at your own cost and peril of your lives. Therefore you have a better right to it than the King of Castille, who neither helped with treasure nor with men."

To Gonzalo's answer that he preferred to send ambassadors to Spain to ask to be confirmed perpetual governor, Carvajal answered, "Cannons and arquebusses, swords and warhorses, are the best ambassadors in cases of this kind. They will speak for you with their deeds."

"Take," he advised him, "the royal revenues, that the Secretary for the Indies takes, without having done anything to deserve them, and use them in Peru."

However, Gonzalo Pizarro, who was a man more fitted for the field than for the council chamber, could not make up his mind.

On the one hand, he had the innate and almost superstitious loyalty of the Spaniards of those days, and on the other he had never lost the hope that Charles V. would confirm him in his government, in recompense for all that he had done.

He counted without the congenital ingratitude of Charles and all the sovereigns of his race, who took all sacrifices as being their just due.

Had he made up his mind in time, it is probable that all Peru would have acclaimed him, and Spain most certainly could have done little to unseat him, once established on the throne.

The destinies of Peru might have been altered, and as far

[1] No hay Rey, traidor.

as the Indians were concerned they would have gained immensely, for a King situated as Gonzalo would have been, and almost certainly married to an Inca princess, must have done all within his power to win their suffrages.

The Inca Garcilaso knew Gonzalo in his youth, and has left an interesting description of him.

"Everyone honoured him,"[1] the Inca says, "as a superior, accompanying him wherever he went, either on horseback or on foot, and he was courteous to everyone, both to the citizens and to the soldiers, treating them all so like a brother, that no one murmured at him. I never saw him give his hand for anyone to kiss, even although they begged him out of courtesy. He took off his cap to everyone (who saluted him), and called everyone 'your grace.'"

Old Carvajal he always called his father, and showed him great respect, both as a soldier and a counsellor. For all his courtesy and his good manners, when people saw his vacillation they began to lose respect for his authority.

His captains treated the Indians badly, commerce was at a standstill, and everyone did best in his own eyes. The Inca Garcilaso says sententiously, "In troubled rivers, fishers find their gains."[2]

Like many another general, Gonzalo Pizarro, brave as a lion in war, yet lacked the mental fibre to solve the far more intricate problems that peace presented to him.

By this time the ambassador that Gonzalo had dispatched to Spain had arrived at the court, that in those days was held in Valladolid. There he met the envoy that Blasco Nuñez Vela had sent out before he met his fate in the great battle with the Pizarros.

Each envoy laid his case before the Emperor.

Charles V. was not unnaturally disposed against Gonzalo Pizarro, on account of the execution of his Viceroy; but there were other reasons that may have moved him. Himself a great commander, he always manifested great jealousy of any other captain's military fame. This he showed

[1] "Comentarios Reales," Libro Quarto, p. 204.
[2] Rio revuelto, ganancia de pescadores.

plainly in the rout before Algiers. When things looked blackest, one of his officers came to him saying, " Hernando de Cortés, the conqueror of Mexico, is in the camp. If any man can save us, he is the man."

The Emperor made no answer, and the greatest Spanish captain of those days had not the chance to exercise his skill. This jealous temperament Charles perhaps inherited from his father, Ferdinand V., who, in the midst of his career, recalled Gonzalo de Cordoba, known as " El Gran Capitan," through jealousy of his success.

At the time that the envoys arrived, Charles had a thousand cares upon him. The German wars absorbed his full military strength. Luther and his reformation kept his diplomatic energies always on the stretch. Money was always wanting, in spite of all the treasures of Peru and Mexico, on account of the bad financial system that prevailed.

The plate fleets went to Antwerp, not to Seville, as a rule, and often all their cargoes were hypothecated months before they arrived.

To send a fleet to carry a sufficient force to conquer such a foe as was Pizarro by the force of arms was a most formidable affair.

Moreover, to equip a fleet and raise a force fit to attack Pizarro in a country that he knew intimately, and where he was beloved, required much time. The Emperor temporized, a line of conduct that he was well acquainted with, and had pursued with great success in many a desperate strait.

Therefore, as Garcilaso says, having no lion ready to his hand, he sent a sheep. His choice was most remarkable indeed, for it fell on an ecclesiastic, a member of the Council of Inquisition, the licentiate Pedro de la Gasca, who had done well in the negotiations with the revolted Moriscos of Valencia.

He was, says Gómara,[1] a man of better understanding than disposition, and renowned for prudence, which renown

[1] " Historia de las Indias," Fray Francisco Lopez de Gómara, Cap. CLXXIV., p. 163.

he certainly showed was justified by all his actions in Peru.

Gómara says he had a very little body on long and stilty legs. On horseback he looked still smaller than he really was, for as he was all legs, his body seemed to disappear. His countenance[1] was very ugly, but nature had endowed him with great powers of mind. His exploits, as the Inca says, were not those either of lance or sword, but of prudence and of counsel, of patience in all the actions that he undertook, for he had much to suffer from the rough conduct and the lawlessness of his soldiery. In the year 1546, in the month of February, he arrived with the title of President, and furnished with letters from the Emperor giving him plenary powers.

Of followers he had but few, and for his officers and suite, a chaplain and two licentiates. He went in a small fleet, with little luxury or show, so as to save the Emperor expense, and to show the colonists that he came, not as a warrior, but a man of peace.

His first act on his arrival at Panama was to repeal the Ordinances provisionally.

Though he had written to Gonzalo Pizarro from the Emperor's court in Germany, he sent an ambassador from Panama to Gonzalo Pizarro, telling him of his appointment by the Emperor as President of the Audiencia to judge between the various parties in Peru.

The ambassador took with him a letter from the Emperor.

In it Charles displayed all his unrivalled forms of diplomacy. After a long preamble, conducted most skilfully so as to give no cause to take offence, he said he understood Gonzalo Pizarro never intended to rebel against the Crown, but took up arms against the Viceroy Blasco Nuñez Vela, moved by the unyielding disposition that he showed. Then having, as no doubt he hoped, quieted Pizarro's fears, he finishes by calling on him to comply with all the licentiate

---

[1] De rostro era muy feo: "Comentarios Reales," por el Inca Garcilaso de la Vega, Book V., Cap. II., p. 269.

La Gasca orders, just as if it were " we ourselves who ordered you."[1]

He signs the letter, " I the King."[2] La Gasca also wrote himself from Panama. His letter was of inordinate length, dealing in the main with generalities, such as it is the duty of a good subject to obey his King, and matters of the kind.

In it he recounts all the campaigns and victories of Charles V., as if he wished to show that it was vain to strive against a King at once so powerful and so fortunate.

Most likely it was written to gain time, and to feel his adversary's blade before engaging with him.

From the first La Gasca showed himself a skilful negotiator. He kept no state, treated all men with affability, and, above all, displayed that courtesy of manner that Spaniards of all nations upon earth most value and appreciate.

His first success was to detach Pizarro's fleet from him.

Pizarro had seized both Panama and Nombre de Dios, thinking thereby that he could stop all egress from Peru or ingress from the mother country. It must have been a severe blow to him when his fleet deserted him, offering its services to La Gasca, almost without persuasion being used. Letters[3] passed between the two high contending parties, in which they addressed one another as most magnificent lord,[4] and illustrious envoy of the Cæsar, but said but little in them, as both La Gasca and Pizarro were anxious to gain time. This did not prevent them from levying men and getting ready for the worst, as both of them knew well the matter could alone be decided by an appeal to arms. After La Gasca's initial successes with the fleet, and the adhesion to his side of several celebrated captains, in especial Diego Centeno, who for a long time had been discontented

---

[1] " Por ende yo os encargo y mando que todo lo que de nuestra parte el dicho Licenciado os mandáre, lo pagais y cumplais como si por nos os fuere mandado ": "Comentarios Reales," Book V., Cap. XVII., p. 274.   [2] Yo el Rey.
[3] Both letters are to be found *in extenso* in the fifth book of the " Comentarios Reales." Garcilaso seems to have copied them from " La Historia del Descubrimiento y Conquista del Peru," by Agustin de Zarate.   [4] Muy magnifico señor.

with the Pizarro government, fortune veered round again to the Pizarros' side. La Gasca made Centeno general of his forces. After much skirmishing the rival armies met at Huarina, and Gonzalo Pizarro completely routed La Gasca's forces, and for the time again became absolute master of Peru. During the battle, Gonzalo Pizarro was in great danger of his life, escaping only by his cool courage and fine horsemanship. Having drawn up his infantry in line of battle, Pizarro placed himself on the right wing with a troop of cavalry. Diego de Centeno, seeing him, charged with great fury. He came upon Pizarro's men with all the impetus of a long charge, and catching him before he had the time to get his squadron under weigh, he overthrew them like a flock of sheep. Only Pizarro and ten horsemen were not dismounted, and they were forced to fly to the protection of their infantry. Three horsemen darted forward to make him prisoner, one of whom was Gonzalo Silvestre, who told the tale to Garcilaso in after years, in Spain. They pressed upon Pizarro, striking repeatedly both at his head and sides, but doing him no damage, for he wore armour of the best Milan steel. Silvestre's horse had his head on the quarters of the horse Pizarro rode, hindering his galloping.

Pizarro turned in his saddle, and with a battleaxe struck the pursuer's horse three rapid blows, so starkly given that one of them cut through its nostrils to the teeth; another broke the bony orbit of its eye, but left the eye itself uninjured.

All this was done, as Silvestre told the Inca, with as much coolness and dexterity as if he had been playing at "The Canes."[1] This gave Pizarro time to reach his infantry, who raised their pikes and let him ride into the square.

[1] El Juego de Cañas was a military sport the Spaniards had inherited from the Moors. In it, two parties of men, mounted à la gineta—that is, on the Moorish saddle, with short stirrups that forced them to stand upright and lean back against the high cantle when they galloped—charged and threw canes at one another. It was a rough sport, and if the cane was not parried or caught in the hands, it gave a severe blow.

The sport was called El Jerid by the Moors, and simulated a skirmish with javelins.

It was in this battle also that the Inca Garcilaso's father gave Gonzalo Pizarro his good horse Salinillas, when Pizarro's horse was wounded.

Just at this juncture of events, and when La Gasca's party had suffered so severe a check, news reached Valdivia in Chile, who at once determined to set out to help the President.

CHAPTER VI

AMONGST the other items of bad news Captain Pastene had brought with him from Peru, perhaps that which must have touched Valdivia the most was the death of Captain Alonso de Monroy.

From his first coming to the south, Monroy had been his right-hand man.

When others murmured, Monroy had always remained staunch. His desperate escape and adventurous ride over the wilds of Atacama must have endeared him to Valdivia's heart.

In his letter to the Emperor, Valdivia gives no details of Monroy's death, but merely says, "Captain Alonso de Monroy died when landing," and then adds grimly, "He had the most of my money with him."

Men of the stamp of Alonso de Monroy were common in the annals of the conquest, but he was certainly an archetype of them. Patient in hardships, active in the fight, a splendid horseman; of undaunted courage, intolerant, religious after the lights that the education of his time had given him, bloodthirsty, although not of a nature naturally cruel, honourable, that is to say, honourable towards those of the same faith he held himself, Monroy was a finished product of the eight hundred years of warfare between the Spaniards and the Moors. Without him and without Alonzo de Ojeda, Gonzalo de Silvestre, Soto, who found his burial-place in a hollow log sunk in the waters of the great river he discovered, Heredia, Belalcazar, with Bernal Diaz del Castillo and a hundred more hard-riding captains, who knew no scruples and were never torn by any doubts as to the righteousness of their leader's motives, the conquest never would have been achieved. They were the steel that tipped the spear that the Pizarros, Quesada, and Cortés wielded so skilfully. In the main, take them for all in all, their virtues were their own, their faults those of the times in which they lived.

Valdivia had entrusted his dispatches to the Emperor, to the care of one Captain Antonio de Ulloa, who had sailed, seven and twenty months ago, for Lima, in Captain Juan Bautista de Pastene's brigantine. This man proved quite unworthy of his confidence, and must have been a scoundrel of the lowest kind. When he arrived in Lima, upon the death of Captain Alonso de Monroy, he opened Valdivia's dispatches to the Emperor, read them, and tore them up. He then took all the money that Valdivia had given to Monroy, although no one knew better than himself what straits Valdivia was in, both for reinforcements and for arms. By means of one Lorenzo de Aldana, who Gonzalo Pizarro had made Chief Justice, probably not knowing his character, for Gonzalo was a man of honourable character, he got an embargo laid upon Pastene, forbidding him to leave the port, under the pain of death.

Luckily for Pastene, for the two rogues would probably have had him killed, the fierce old warrior Francisco de Carvajal, Gonzalo's right-hand man, happened to arrive in Lima.

Captain Pastene instantly went to him and complained, recalling to his memory that Valdivia and Carvajal had been old friends in Italy, and had served together. Nothing he could have said would have weighed more with Carvajal, who had been all his life a soldier, and though not, as the Inca Garcilaso says, too good a Christian, adored all that related to the career of arms.[1]

Carvajal instantly sized up the situation. He told Pastene that Aldana and Ulloa had represented to Gonzalo Pizarro that they wished to employ the money they had taken after the death of Alonso de Monroy entirely in Valdivia's interest, and would lay it out in arms, in horses, and in men.

Their real intent, said Carvajal, was to go back to Chile with the men they had enlisted, assassinate Valdivia, and make themselves the masters of the land.

[1] " Tuvo la milicia por idolo, que adorava en ella."

He told Pastene that Pizarro was ignorant of their designs, for he was a well-wisher to Valdivia, and believed the reinforcements were to be used solely to aid Valdivia in his conquest, for only on that plea would he allow a single man to leave Peru.

"It is no use," said Carvajal, "to reveal what I have told you, for you will never be believed, and Aldana and Ulloa will contrive to kill you, so as to carry out their aims.

"Save yourself, therefore, and take the news to Valdivia, for I know him to be one who can make head against men with teeth in their mouths,[1] and much more against skinned rabbits[2] such as these rogues."

Carvajal raised the embargo that Aldana had placed upon Pastene, and advised him to go at once to Quito to see Pizarro, pretending to believe Aldana's story and to offer to command one of the ships when it should be ready to set sail.

Captain Pastene set out at once for Quito, no slight journey in those days, but one that all the conquistadores performed repeatedly without twice thinking on it, although they suffered[3] just as much as men do to-day when they leave sea-level and suddenly journey to the high altitudes of the Paramos.

As Valdivia up to that time had been a staunch adherent of the Pizarros, he received licence from Gonzalo Pizarro to recruit men for service in the south, and purchase horses, arms, and merchandise.

This licence Pizarro said he would have given to no one but to a friend of Valdivia's, for he had need of every man that he could lay his hands on, for the troubles that he foresaw he was certain to encounter after the Viceroy's death.

Captain Pastene then hastened back to the coast. There he at once bought a vessel, paying a thousand dollars for her, and engaging that Valdivia should pay seven thousand more

---

[1] Hombres que tienen dientes.

[2] Conejos desollados: Valdivia's third letter to Charles V.

[3] "Es ordinario a los Espanoles, qe de nuevo, o recien, salidos de los calurosos llanos, suben a las nevadas, marearse": "Historia de las Indias," Gómara, Cap. CXL., p. 128.

on her arrival in the south. Ulloa had bought two ships and freighted them with men and merchandise, intending, "as a man who risked his life by night upon a raft," to kill Pastene, to sink his ship, sail down to Chile, and, after having killed Valdivia, share out the Indians and the land.

Ulloa then embarked fifty picked musketeers on board the swiftest of his ships and sallied out to attack Pastene, thinking to catch him unawares.

However, the skilful Genoese was able to outmanœuvre him, and, getting the weathergage, outsailed and left him in the rear. Ulloa, seeing that it would be impossible for him to take Valdivia by surprise, owing to the start of him Pastene had secured, gave up his enterprise.

Pastene kept on with his empty ship, without provisions and almost without arms, till he made Valparaiso harbour, half starving and in rags, as Valdivia says.

As soon as Pedro de Valdivia heard the news of the rebellion of Gonzalo Pizarro, and his determination to appeal to arms against all comers to make good his title to the governorship, all his old friendship for him vanished, for above all things Valdivia put loyalty to the Emperor, although he had received such scant consideration from him.

Long-suffering loyalty, that endureth all things, such as was so frequently wasted upon Charles V. and his son Philip by the conquistadores, must be born with a man. It is no more to be acquired than are a sense of colour, good hands on a horse, humour, or faith—faith, that is, that can remove the Cordillera of the Andes, as distinct from mere belief.

Immediately, Valdivia made all arrangements to leave Chile well protected whilst he was absent in Peru.

He appointed Captain Francisco de Villagra, a man who was to figure greatly in the conquest of Chile, to be his "Maestre de Campo," as he held him, as he says, "for a true servant and vassal of Your Majesty."

On the 1st of December, 1547, Valdivia embarked, accompanied by "ten noblemen," but did not sail from Valparaiso till the thirteenth of the month.

He raised all the available money that he found in Chile,

that amounted to one hundred thousand castellanos, for which he and his friends all pledged themselves.

In two days' sailing he reached the town of La Serena,[1] and stayed two days there, to tell everyone that he was going to join the President La Gasca, and the army of the King.

On Christmas Eve, 1547, he reached Tarapaca, and sent on shore to learn the news. His messenger came back to tell him that Gonzalo Pizarro's fleet had joined the President, but that he had defeated Captain Diego de Centeno, the only leader who had ventured to oppose him hitherto.

The messenger had heard that within twenty days Pizarro would be in Lima, and that La Gasca had no followers.

It took Valdivia eighteen days to reach Callao, and by that time the position of affairs had altered mightily. There he learned that La Gasca had landed, and in a few days had been joined by powerful forces, and was upon the march towards Cuzco to meet Pizarro in the field. Valdivia landed without delay, and marched to Lima, taking with him all the gentlemen who had accompanied him.

He sent word to the President of his arrival, asking him to await him eight or ten days, till he had bought arms and accoutrements for his followers. In ten days' time he laid out sixty thousand castellanos, in arms and horses and all things necessary for a campaign.

Then he set out, and overtook La Gasca in the valley of Andaguailas, fifty leagues from Cuzco, having marched in three days the distance that La Gasca had taken ten days to perform.

When he arrived in La Gasca's camp he was received with great rejoicing. A holiday was proclaimed, and they played at the " Game of Canes "[2] and tilted at the ring.

Valdivia says that Gasca made him general of his forces.[3]

[1] Near Coquimbo.

[2] El Juego de Cañas (see Chapter V.). " Se holgó Gasca, y todo el campo, y corrieron Cañas y Sortija de placer ": " Historia de las Indias," Gómara, Cap. CLXXXIV., p. 171.

[3] " He at once gave me all the authority that he held from Your Majesty for warlike matters, and handed me over the whole army and put it in my hands ": Third letter to the Emperor.

PEDRO DE VALDIVIA

Gómara, however, says that Gasca made Valdivia the colonel of his infantry. This seems more likely, for certainly, according to the Inca Garcilaso and all the other historians of the conquest of Peru, Diego de Centeno was in command at the time Valdivia arrived, and continued in command till the battle of Sacsahuana, in which Gonzalo de Pizarro was routed and made prisoner. It is not to be doubted that Valdivia was a skilled and an experienced commander. Still, it seems hardly likely that so cautious and so prudent a diplomatist as the licentiate La Gasca would have promoted an officer, however skilful or however brave, over the heads of all the other leaders, especially amongst men so prompt to take offence as Spaniards always have been, as a race.

Moreover, Valdivia's own lengthy and interesting account of all he did before the battle seems more to be the work of an infantry commander than of a man in the supreme command.

On the 12th of March, 1548, he writes to " His Cæsarean Majesty " a long account of what he did, and of the difficulties that he encountered till he came to a great river called Aporima, twelve leagues from Cuzco.

He tells the Emperor how he caused bridges to be made of oziers.[1] The oziers, he says, were plaited into cables ten or twelve paces longer than the breadth of the river to be passed, and two palms thick. These ropes of ozier were fastened either to trees or stakes, or made fast round great rocks.

When made, a flooring was placed upon them of light boards, and though they oscillated fearfully above the torrent, the men and baggage all passed safely.

The horses had to swim farther down the river, under the protection of bands of musketeers.

In fact, they were the bridges that the Incas used, and which the Spaniards found in use throughout Peru. They still are used in the High Andes, and the country people

[1] These " oziers " were most likely lianas, brought up from the hot countries by the coast, and called " bejucos " in South America.

cross them upon their mules, although they swing about just like a sailing ship at sea.

When some of his men had crossed to test the bridge, he waited for the President and the main army, in terror all the time that either Pizarro or his enterprising second in command, old Carvajal, would appear and attack them, when they were swinging in the air.

On Easter Day, 1548, the President arrived, and Valdivia, who must have counted every minute till he came, took him at once to see the bridge. Then, pointing out some rising ground upon the other side, he said, " Sir, it is my wish to cross and take the heights, for if the enemy take them before us, we shall be in difficulties."

La Gasca, who had no military skill, but had the sense to take advice from those who had it, a thing not always to be observed with the civilians who direct campaigns, said, " Cross, for the love of God, for the King's honour lies between your hands."

" And so," he says, " I crossed the bridge in God's name, and to Your Imperial Majesty's good fortune."

This was no gasconade, for when he had crossed and marched a league or two, he fell in with one Juan Nuñez Prado, a deserter from Pizarro's army.

This man informed him that Captain Juan de Acosta was on his way with a band of two hundred arquebussiers[1] to defend the passage of the bridge.

Valdivia hurried strong reinforcements across, and the whole night lay under arms. Next day, the whole army crossed, and after resting for two days, advanced two leagues towards the enemy's position at Sacsahuana.[2] The so-called battle took place next day.

Valdivia gives but a meagre account of it, merely saying that he drew up the forces of the President in line of battle,

[1] Arcabuceros.
[2] Valdivia writes it " Jaquijaguana," and some of the other writers on the conquest of Peru, " Xaquixaguana." It is a moot point amongst grammarians whether the letters x and j were pronounced gutturally then as they are now. Some incline to think that " Quixote " was pronounced with a soft x.

that only thirty of his men were killed, and that the ringleaders of the enemy were taken prisoner and then executed.

The strange incidents that took place before the battle, and the executions of Gonzalo Pizarro and Francisco Carvajal by the vindictive licentiate La Gasca, are to be found in the "Comentarios" of the Inca Garcilaso.[1]

At this famous battle the forces of the two parties were about equal, with perhaps a slight advantage, especially in cavalry, on the side of Gonzalo Pizarro.

It is probable, however, that some of those who had adhered to him had done so through fear. Moreover, the intense spirit of Spanish loyalty was a factor that Gonzalo Pizarro, and even Carvajal, who had a much more far-seeing mind than his commander, do not seem to have appreciated at its full value.

Before the battle, the President La Gasca had put out offers of free pardon to all who would rally to the royal cause. All through the day before the battle desertions were taking place. Garcilaso, who in his youth knew many of the chief actors, describes some of them with an inimitable touch, compounded of the simplicity, mingled with realism, that makes his chronicle, although less authentic than that of Pedro de Cieza de Leon, a complete compendium of the history of the times. Without it we should have known but little of a whole series of most interesting men, whose lives, but for him, we should have seen only through the writings of their enemies.

[1] Sir Clements Markham, speaking of the executions after the battle of Sacsahuana, says: "The executions and barbarities of that cunning and cruel priest, Pedro de la Gasca, were, it is true, unjustifiable, after Sacsahuana; but Mr. Prescott did not condemn them." This passage is on p. xliii of the Introduction to his translation of Pedro de Cieza de Leon's "Civil Wars of Peru" for the Hakluyt Society, London, MCMXVIII.

Sir Clements Markham is right as to the cunning and cruelty of La Gasca. These qualities marred his considerable powers of mind, his talents of diplomacy, and his great energy. Churchmen and non-combatants are often more bloodthirsty in the hour of victory than are those whose own lives have been in peril. Prescott, of course, was always on the side of authority.

The charm of Garcilaso is that, descended as he was from a Spanish father of high rank and a Peruvian princess, he had a foot in either camp. Moreover, having known the chief participants in the great struggle as a youth, too young to carry arms, he writes of them as it were from the outside, dwelling more on their personal attributes than on the justice or injustice of their cause.

His father being one of the first to leave Pizarro for the royal army, he naturally has much to say about it. There had been a coolness for some time, as it appears from the Inca, between his father and Gonzalo Pizarro, about the good horse Salinillas, who Garcilaso had mounted Gonzalo upon at the battle of Huarinas, when his own was killed.

Pizarro always delayed returning him to Garcilaso de la Vega, in spite of his requests.

At last, a day or two before Sacsahuana, he returned Salinillas to his owner, who was overjoyed to get him back. The Inca says: "He sent Salinillas, and when he (the Inca's father) saw him in his house, he thought an angel from heaven must have brought him."[1]

It is not to be forgotten that in those days a good horse was very valuable in Peru. Gonzalo Pizarro gave five thousand crowns in gold for one.

The Inca says his father had been constrained to take the side of the Pizarros, and that he deserted openly, in the full sight of both armies. That is as it may be; but naturally his son had to present his father in a favourable light. However, every historian of the conquest of Peru speaks of the elder Garcilaso's chivalrous and high character.

The next to go was the licentiate Cepeda, who had been Gonzalo Pizarro's chief councillor. He almost lost his life in the attempt.

Riding out from Pizarro's camp under the pretence of looking for a good position, he suddenly clapped spurs to his horse, a fine dark chestnut, and galloped towards La Gasca's

[1] "Le embió el caballo Salinillas, y quando lo vio en su casa, le pareció que lo avia traido un angel del cielo": "Comentarios Reales," Book V., Cap. XXXV., p. 333.

camp. His horse was covered with armour made of cowskin, which was varnished black.

It seemed, says Garcilaso, very handsome, both by its rarity and its singularity. For all that it was so heavy that the licentiate's horse could not gallop properly.

One Pedro Martin de Don Benito, who is described as an old, dried-up, hard, nut-coloured man,[1] galloped out after him.

His horse was fitting to him, for he was " long and dry as a stick." The Inca says: " I knew him; he was of a dark brown colour, and in one stride covered more ground than any horse in two or three."

This nut-coloured rider on his apocalyptic horse came up with the licentiate just as he was entering a marsh that lay between the two contending armies. In despite of his cowskin accoutrement, the dour old man drove his spear through the armour and wounded the licentiate's horse. Then, with a second thrust that pierced the licentiate's thigh, he laid him in the mud. He was shortening his lance to give the *coup de grâce*, when four cavaliers, seeing the danger of the fallen man, spurred out to help him. On seeing them, the tough old spearman wheeled his long horse as a hawk turns in the air when it has missed its quarry, and in a bound or two was back in safety.

La Gasca received the licentiate Cepeda joyfully, embracing him " though his face was all daubed with mud " after his tumble in the marsh.

Before the battle began Gonzalo Pizarro had lost at least the half of his followers. Of all his officers, only Francisco de Carvajal was left, for he knew he was fighting with a halter round his neck. His cruelties and ruthlessness, and above all his cynicism, had marked him out for certain death if he should chance to fall a prisoner.

In reality there was no real battle, for from the first it was a foregone conclusion that the licentiate La Gasca must gain the day, after the numerous desertions from the enemy.

When all was lost, Carvajal exhorted Gonzalo Pizarro to

[1] Un Vejaco, seco, duro y avellanado: Garcilaso de la Vega.

charge with him into the thickest of the foe and die like ancient Roman warriors.

Gonzalo, though he had proved his courage on a hundred fields, refused, saying, " Rather let us die like Christians." He gave his sword to Captain Diego de Centeno, Gasca's commander of the cavalry, scorning to fly, and perhaps thinking, as did the vast majority, that the licentiate La Gasca would keep him prisoner, whilst he spared his life.

Nothing was further from the mind of the bloodthirsty priest, who in the hour of triumph stood revealed in his true colours, arrogant and hard. Old Carvajal, though he was eighty-four years of age, fought to the last, and finally cutting his way alone through all the enemy, he took to flight.

He rode a horse called Boscanillo[1] that, though it had been once a first-rate charger, was now long past his prime. Passing a muddy stream, it fell upon him and he was taken by his enemies.

Despite his age, he was treated shamefully, struck, beaten and abused. To all of which he made no answer, but maintained a stoical silence, like an Indian at the stake. A cowardly bishop, whose brother Carvajal had executed, struck the old man, whose hands were bound behind his back, three or four blows across the face. Luckily for him, Diego de Centeno, a soldier and a gentleman, came and rescued the defenceless man from the long-robed miscreant, and took him to his tent, after presenting him to La Gasca. To all the questions that La Gasca asked, he refused to answer, looking as if he did not see him, and never opening his mouth. During the days before his execution he laughed and jested all the time with all the captains who came to talk with him.

To Diego de Centeno, whom he had once chased half across Peru, and would most certainly have hanged had he come up with him—for he was one of those who never pardoned—he said, " I am glad to see your face, for hitherto I have only

---

[1] " En un caballo mediano, castaño algo vejecido, que yo conoci, le llamavan Boscanillo avia sido muy buen caballo de obra ": Garcilaso, " Comentarios."

seen your back." Centeno, who was an honourable man, took no offence at him, knowing that what he said was true. Carvajal died as he had lived, game to the last, saying no word upon the scaffold, except to thank Centeno for his kindness to him.

He had had a most remarkable career.

Born in a village near Arrevalo, called Magama, no one knew anything about his lineage. He first appears as an alferez (ensign) at the battle of Ravenna, where he fought bravely. He was at Pavia, and saw Francis I. give up his sword. Then, as a captain, he was at the sack of Rome, where he had a strange experience. The Inca says, being a good soldier, he got nothing by the sack, as he was on duty all the time. Happening to find some papers left in the house of a notary, that had been sacked, he took them to his tent. After the sack, the notary, hearing a Spanish captain had found a mass of papers and that they were all that he had got by the sack of Rome, came to redeem them from him. He gave Carvajal two thousand ducats for the papers. With this money he went to Mexico, fought with Cortés, and ultimately drifted to Peru. He was a better soldier than a Christian, having passed all his life in arms.

So, at least, says Agustin de Zarate,[1] from whom the Inca copies.

His wife was Doña Catalina Leyton,[2] a lady of a well-known family in Portugal.

Over his cuirass he always wore a Moorish albornoz, of a brown colour. His arms, his accoutrements, and the horses that he rode, were only fitting for the poorest soldier, except a plume of feathers that he wore in his helmet.

In spite of his great age, his natural strength was unabated, and he passed days and even nights on horseback, and endured hardships under which the youngest soldiers sank.

His faults were cruelty and disregard of suffering, blood-

[1] "Historia del Descubrimiento y Conquista del Peru."
[2] Her name in Portuguese must have been Leitão, which the Spaniards had changed to Leyton.

thirstiness and inhumanity. His virtues, fidelity to the cause that he had once espoused, courage, patience, and a contempt of death that in a way gave him a savage kind of nobility and lifted him above the herd. He merited his death, and few regretted him, and had the battle gone the other way La Gasca would have had but a short shrift at the old warrior's hands.

Gonzalo Pizarro was a nobler victim, and him La Gasca might have spared had there been any generosity in his character.

To have pardoned him would have been an act of grace that would have rendered La Gasca popular in Peru during his lifetime, and would have kept his memory sweet. National sympathy has gone out to the unfortunate but gallant cavalier, who was done to death by the harsh minion of a cruel tyrant from afar. All the historians of the conquest of Peru concur in the opinion that Gonzalo Pizarro was unusually beloved. Moreover, under the greatest of temptation, he remained loyal to an Emperor who had done nothing, either for him or for Peru.

Had he assumed the crown at the advice of Carvajal and almost all his captains, and married an Indian princess, it is difficult to see how he could have been dispossessed of it.

Garcilaso says: "For his virtues and his military exploits he was loved by all, and though it was proper that he should lose his life (leaving apart the service of His Majesty), yet all were sorry at his death on account of his many and good parts,[1] and afterwards I never heard any one speak ill of him, but all with great respect."

His countrymen loved him, not unnaturally, for his easy manners, his accessibility, and because he was one of the first pioneers. Moreover, except in his expedition to the Montaña, he had not been cruel. The Indians also looked

[1] "Por sus virtudes morales y Haçañas militares, fué muy amado de todos y aunque convino quitarle la Vida (dejando a parte el Servicio de su Majestad) a todos en general les pesó de su muerte por sus muchas y buenas partes y asi despues, jamas oi que nadie hablase mal del sino todos con mucho respeto": "Comentarios Reales," Book V., p. 351.

up to him as a demi-god. He had all the personal qualities fitted to endear him to both races, as he was handsome,[1] very enduring of all kinds of hardships, and a dexterous shot both with the crossbow[2] and the arquebuse. So dexterous, indeed, that with a pellet bow he could draw anything he liked upon a wall.

A splendid horseman in " both saddles," the Inca says he was the best lance who passed to the Indies. He was very fond of horses, and always had the best. At the beginning of the conquest he owned two brown chargers, one called El Villano, on account of his small size, but very good for work.

The other's name was El Çainillo, so good a horse that when Gonzalo Pizarro[3] (may he be in glory) found himself on his back, he cared no more for squadrons of Indians than if they had been squadrons of flies.

He was an honourable and noble-minded man, and after the fashion of the times deeply religious. A most fervent Christian and a most devout adorer of Our Lady, so much so that he could never deny any request put forward in her name. Old Carvajal knew this weakness (or strength) of Gonzalo's character, and always executed all his prisoners before their friends were able to ask for their release in Our Blessed Lady's name.[4]

A stranger to any form of falsehood or underhanded dealing, he was no match for the astute and crafty licentiate La Gasca, who, by his execution of Gonzalo Pizarro and the other unnecessary and cruel hangings and beheadings of the prisoners after the rout of Sacsahuana, brought odium on the name of Spain.

Valdivia deals rather summarily with the whole affair, saying the rebel leaders were taken and duly dealt with,

[1] Gentil hombre de cuerpo.
[2] "Diestro Arcabucero y Ballestero, con un arco de bodoques pintava lo que queria en la Pared ": " Comentarios Reales."
[3] " Quando Gonzalo Pizarro (que avra gloria) se veia en su Çainillo no hacia mas caso de Esquadrones de Indios, que si fueran de moscas.'
[4] " Era muy devoto de Nuestra Señora la Virgen Maria Madre de Dios."

and that La Gasca thanked him, saying, " Ah, Sir Governor, how much His Majesty owes to you."

For the first time La Gasca addressed Valdivia as Governor, having only called him Captain till the victory was won. Then both Valdivia and La Gasca returned to Cuzco, and Valdivia was to learn that his reward for all that he had done, was but the barren phrase.

When he asked La Gasca, then master of Peru, for some reward for having left his government, perilled his life, and pledged his credit, he was told to apply to the Royal Council of the Indies. He got permission, as a great favour, to buy a galleon and a galley, and receive credit for the purchase money. With these scant favours, and his parsnips just smeared a little with the butter of fair words, Valdivia set about making preparations to return to his government.

CHAPTER VII

ONE thing, in addition to the permission to buy a ship on credit, Valdivia received.

The President, La Gasca, confirmed him in his government of Chile, in the name of the Emperor.

Well did he deserve the somewhat barren honour. By his own efforts, without the slightest aid from the home government, he had conquered, or at least begun the conquest of, a territory that before his time had baffled the efforts of the Spaniards to obtain a footing.

He then bade goodbye to La Gasca, and prepared to set off on his return to Chile.

La Gasca certainly had justified the confidence reposed in him by the Council of the Indies and the Emperor. Landing alone in Panama, accompanied but by a secretary and a priest or two, through his adroit use of the powers invested in him by the Crown, almost without military advisers at the first, he had put down a formidable rebellion headed by the most beloved of the original conquistadores of Peru.

Courage La Gasca had most certainly, and the gift of handling men. What he lacked was the power to make himself beloved. His diplomatic talents were marred by his duplicity. His view of politics was that of the age in which he lived, an age that dealt but little in half-measures, not comprehending that the good men do lives after them, quite as eternal as the evil, and both go to form the minds of future generations.

Certainly he accomplished a great feat rather than a great work. He might, by refraining from so much unnecessary bloodshed, have gone down to history unstained by cruelty, as one who, with the slightest of resources, had preserved a rich and fertile province to the Crown of Spain. Instead, he laid, no doubt unwittingly, the seeds of hatred towards the mother country.

Still, taken from whatever angle he presents himself, he was a most commanding personality, not lovable, 'tis true, but perhaps the fittest instrument for the task awaiting him, that the Emperor could have found.

Without a moment's rest Valdivia set about enlisting men and fitting out a fleet.

He bought two ships for twenty-eight thousand dollars, upon the credit that La Gasca had extended to him.

A third he purchased from his own resources; then, as he says, within a month he put his fleet in order. As in those days navigation was " highly wearisome and slow," he named one Don Geronimo de Alderete, his deputy Captain General, giving him orders to bring the fleet to Atacama, and there wait for him.

He himself went to Arequipa to fetch the soldiers that his captains had recruited. On the last day of August, 1548, he set out with them towards the coast. Upon the way he was met by General Pedro de Hinojosa, with six stout musketmen.

It appeared that La Gasca, always suspicious, had been told Valdivia and his men were robbing everyone and levying contributions on the Indians.

Valdivia found himself in a most awkward situation. The journey back to Lima, a distance of a hundred and forty leagues, was long and arduous.

If he refused, he knew by the experience he had had of him, that he would be declared a rebel by the President. At the same time, he feared his fleet, left without his own authority, might mutiny and sail without him; and that his soldiers really might commit outrages.

Just at this juncture several of his captains appeared with forty mounted men. Pedro de Hinojosa and his six musketeers were thus outnumbered and reduced to impotency. He then produced what he knew, to such a man as Valdivia, was a trump card.

Calling him to a private conference, he handed him a

formal order from the Royal Audiencia of Charcas, the first authority in Peru.

Valdivia, who was loyal to the core, and above all things had a sort of veneration for the Emperor, did not hesitate. Ordering his horses to be saddled, and with but four followers, in a few hours he was ready for the road. After seven days' hard riding he reached Arequipa, and fortunately found his galley in the port.

In a few days he arrived at Lima, and was welcomed by the President. The wily priest embraced him, saying he was sure the rumours of his conduct were untrue, but that he rejoiced he had obeyed with so much patience and humility, for it would be a good example in the land. Whether Valdivia made the rabbit's laugh,[1] he does not say, but one would almost think that in his answer there was some irony, though carefully disguised. He says: "I told him I should do the like, at any time. Even though I should be at the world's end, I would come at full speed on the orders of His Majesty and those of the Lords of his Royal Council of the Indies, for I held obedience to be the chief piece of my armour, and had no will other than my King's and natural Lords', and to follow him always, without asking other reason."

He stayed a month in Lima with the President, and then set out again towards the coast. On Easter Eve he reached Arequipa, and then a sickness, from the anxiety and toil he had undergone, attacked him. He says it brought him to death's door, but that Our Lord was pleased to give him back his health after eight days. Then, though not thoroughly restored, he set off once again to the port in the valley of Arica, where he found Captain Alderete waiting for him with his ship.

On the 18th of January, 1549, he went on board the galleon *San Cristobal*, which, as he says, was making water in several places, and hardly seaworthy.

For all provision for two hundred men, he had fifty salted carcases of sheep and a considerable quantity of maize, but not a flask of wine.

[1] La risa del conejo.

As Valdivia explains, the voyage by sailing ship from Valparaiso to El Callao, the port of Lima, is a vastly different thing from the voyage back again. The strong south winds blow almost constantly up the coast, and in Valdivia's day the passage had to be made chiefly by rowing, or with boats going on ahead to tow the ship.

As the distance is somewhere about seven hundred and fifty miles,[1] it was an undertaking fit to appal all but the stoutest hearts. Before he set out on his voyage, one of those sudden movements arose that at that time seemed to afflict Peru, as to-day they shake the foundations of the state in Mexico.

La Gasca, who never trusted anybody, and certainly was not a generous man, yet found himself in a most difficult situation, from which it must have wanted all his tact and all Valdivia's loyalty to extricate himself. After the battle of Sacsahuana, the only means La Gasca had at his command of rewarding those who had assisted him was by dividing up the confiscated lands of his chief enemies. The land was cast into two hundred lots, but there were fifteen hundred claimants for them. Each one of these had fought under the royal standard, and probably had run deeply into debt.

La Gasca seems to have employed the usual Spanish method of putting off the evil hour. At last, the leaders lost all patience, and coming to Valdivia secretly, told him they had planned to kill the President and share the lands amongst themselves. All that they wanted for their project was a leader.

They played upon Valdivia's vanity, telling him that La Gasca owed the victory to his military skill. They hinted that for all that he had done he had not been rewarded, but used and then cast off, like an old alpargata[2] upon the road. They brought before him the lack of consideration with which La Gasca had forced him to return to Lima to justify himself, he to whom La Gasca owed almost everything.

[1] " 250 leguas ": Third letter to the Emperor.
[2] The " alpargata " is the same as the French " spadrille "—*i.e.*, a canvas shoe soled with hemp.

"Let us," they said, "at once kill Gasca, his officers, and all the priests and bishops in his train. Then we can share the land out between ourselves, and afterwards seize on the silver that is waiting at Las Charcas to be forwarded to Spain. You are the man to lead us, and when the feat is done, you shall be president, king, ruler, what you like, and the chief person in the realm. Choose now and quickly, for if not we will make you lead by force, or kill you if you refuse."

The stout old soldier never wavered for a moment in his loyalty. He must have borne a grudge against La Gasca, for he was human, and had been treated shamefully.

He answered, above all he was the servant and friend of everybody, but if His Majesty's authority was taken from him, as it would certainly have been had he joined such an abominable scheme, he was no more than a poor soldier, and as lonely as a wild asparagus.[1]

His answer did him honour, for he was in great danger of his life, and says himself: " And in all this I ran a risk, and might have run a greater, if I had not shown good temper and a fair bearing to them."

" Wisdom," he said, " lay in appeasing them and leaving the land quickly." This he did at once, " and God (who is at my side) gave me so good a voyage that in so ill-conditioned a vessel as I had, in two months and a half I came to Valparaiso, and was received with joy."

The first news that he received was that the Indians had risen and destroyed the town of La Serena, and had killed forty Christians[2] and as many horses.

---

[1] Tan solo que el esparrago. The wild asparagus, in Spain, grows amongst wheat in single plants, sometimes a yard or two from one another; hence the saying.

[2] Cuarenta Cristianos y otros tantos caballos. No doubt Valdivia felt the loss of his horses as much as the man in the old Spanish rhyme:

> " Mi caballo y mi muger
>   Se me murieron a un tiempo
> Que demonio y que muger
>   El caballo es lo que siento."

When he arrived in Santiago he enjoyed one of the few triumphs of his life.

With pride he tells that the town council, the magistrates, and all the people came out to greet him, and that he read out to them the Emperor's decree making him Governor and Captain General.

To such a man as was Valdivia, brave, honest, loyal, far-seeing, but not imaginative, this public recognition of his services must have been some recompense for the neglect with which La Gasca and the Emperor both had treated him.

After so many years of service, so many hardships undergone, and all the desperate enterprises he had engaged in, as much alone as the asparagus, to quote his own phrase, he was now the equal of any Spaniard in the New World.

His first act, in virtue of his new-made authority, was to refound La Serena, which he did in the year 1549, after punishing the revolted Indians.

All was going well with him, the town of La Serena refounded, a town council duly nominated, and the Indians (after due punishment) " very peaceful and ready for service," when one of those accidents occurred that go to prove the justice of the Arab proverb that " the grave of the horseman is ever open."

Valdivia had received supplies of men and horses from Peru, and had resolved to hold a great review or muster of them in September, upon " Our Lady's Day (may she be blessed)."

As he was riding with the cavalry, his horse fell with him suddenly. He came off on his right foot so heavily that he broke most of his toes and dislocated his thumb. Three months he lay in bed, suffering the barbarous surgery of the times. His cure, he says, was very wearisome, and well it might have been, for during it he had all the bones of his thumb extracted in little pieces. The pain was so acute that several times everyone thought he must have died.

At the beginning of December he was able to get up, but not to stand, only to sit in an armchair. In spite of everything, and against the wish of all the people, he determined to set out to found the town of Concepcion, as the crops had just been gathered in, and if he missed the present chance a whole year would be lost. As he could not walk, and still less get on horseback, he was carried in a chair by Indians, and set out with two hundred men upon his Calvary.

It took him twenty days to get beyond the bounds of the province of Santiago, and in that time, so great was the strength of his constitution and his determination to be well, that he had won back a little strength and could ride on horseback for an hour or two.

On the 24th of January, 1550, Valdivia reached the Biobio river, and in his attempt to cross it, for the first time encountered the Araucanians. At first he had thought to cross on rafts, as the " Biobio is a river very muddy, wide and deep."

A strong force of Indians immediately appeared to dispute his passage. They even crossed the river to attack him, trusting to their numbers; but by " God's will " Valdivia routed them and they fled, leaving ten or twelve of their number on the field.

Not to risk losing any of his horses, he went upstream to find a better crossing-place. After two leagues' march, and just as he had found a ford, he was again fiercely attacked by a strong force of Indians.

Captain Alderete charged them with twenty mounted men. The Indians threw themselves into the water, and Alderete and his men followed them closely, lancing many of them, for the water only came up to the stirrups and the horses were able to move quickly through it. Here, Valdivia says a very good soldier was drowned because he had a " treacherous horse."[1]

In the evening Alderete came into camp driving a flock of more than a thousand sheep. These sheep must have been llamas, for the Araucanians at that time had never seen a sheep. Moreover the Spaniards often referred to the llamas as Indian sheep.

The soldiers, who had been on short rations, were

[1] Un caballo atraidorado.

delighted to get fresh meat, for, as Valdivia says, " if the soldier does not die of hunger, he finds his merit in dying in the fight."

He marched on for several leagues and camped.

For the third time he was most furiously attacked.

By this time he must have been beginning to perceive that his future progress had to be won by fighting every step. However, he fell upon them, leading himself, with fifty horsemen, and gave them a good lesson,[1] leaving a number of them dead. He says with military precision and without comment, " we went on killing for a league and more. In the evening I returned to camp."

After a few days' rest he set out once more down the river, to find a good place for an encampment.

Half of his men were on guard till midnight, and the rest till daylight. On the second night, just as the guards were being changed, an enormous force of Indians fell upon them. Valdivia says they were fully twenty thousand, but the historians of every war, even the latest, have been inclined to magnify the number of the defeated foe. It is a practice that does no great harm to anyone, and merely causes historians to be classed with politicians and with fishermen.

The Indians only could attack upon one side, for Valdivia had camped upon the lake, and they had no canoes by means of which to cross and take him on the flank. The impact of the Indians was terrible, and though Valdivia had been a soldier from his youth upwards, he had never been in greater straits.

He says: "They began[2] to fight in such a way that I give my word that in the thirty years I have served Your Majesty, though I have fought against so many nationalities, I have never seen such stubborn fighters as these Indians."

[1] " . . . Pasé a ellos con 50 de a caballo, y di los una muy buena mano quedaron tendidos hartos por aquellos llanos, fuimos matando una legua y mas, y recogimos a la tarde."

[2] " . . . Comenzaron a pelear de tal manera que prometo fe que ha 30 años que servo a V. M. y he peleado contra muchas naciones y nunca vi tal teson de gente jamas en el pelear, como estos Indios."

For hours he could make no impression on their ranks, with a body of one hundred horsemen. When now and then they thought they had broken into the Indians' ranks, they made such stout resistance with their spears and clubs "that the Christians could not make their horses face the enemy."

When Valdivia saw his horsemen could make no way, he advanced his infantry, that well-drilled, steady and unemotional Spanish infantry, before whom in those days no other troops could stand. They lacked the dash of the French soldiers, who used to advance with the "furia francese" that was proverbial and has remained a heritage of France. Most certainly they had not the intellectual qualities and quick apprehension of the Italians, for quickness has never been a Spanish gift. But they excelled all European troops in stubbornness, and even in retreat were apt to rally and retrieve the victory. When all was lost, they always died to the last man.

These splendid soldiers—for Valdivia must have had many men who had served, as he himself had done, in the Italian wars—broke through the Indians' ranks and routed them, though none too easily. The Indians wounded "sixty horses and as many Christians" with their spears and arrows, but only one Spaniard was killed, and he by a chance shot from a brother soldier.

They lay upon their arms till daylight, and all next day cured the wounds of the horses and the men.

Valdivia took no rest, but at once started off to see a place at which, several years before, he had determined to found a settlement. It was upon the north bank of the Biobio and near the mouth, for there, he says, is a harbour "as good as any in the Indies, with a great river that falls into the sea, behind a headland, and the best fishing in the world, with many sardines, mullets, tunny fish, cod, lampreys, soles, and a thousand other kinds of fish."[1]

[1] " . . . La mejor pesqueria del mundo, de mucha sardina, cefalos, toninas, merluzas, lampreas, lenguados, y otros mil generos de pescados."

Valdivia's next act was to make a stockade of very thick trees set one against the other,[1] all made secure with wattles, and with a deep ditch on the outside. This he had finished by the third of March of the year 1550. Nine days later the largest army of Indians he had as yet encountered advanced to attack him in his stockade.

He puts the number at forty thousand, and says that in addition the Indians had strong reserves.

"At vespertide they came on with the utmost boldness, in four divisions of the most splendid and fine Indians that I have ever seen and with the best equipment of sheep and llama skins and undressed sealskins of many colours (which looked very handsome), and great plumes on headpieces of those skins like priests' hats, such that there is no battleaxe, however sharp, which can hurt those who wear them, and spears twenty and twenty-five palms[2] in length, clubs and bludgeons.[3] They do not use stones for fighting."

Valdivia gives an excellent description of the arms and equipment of the Araucanians, which is entirely in accord with that of Ercilla in his celebrated "Araucana."[4]

He instantly ordered a sally, and Captain Alderete charged with fifty horsemen on the Indians.

The Araucanians, who had never feared to face their invaders in spite of the disparity of arms, had not yet lost their natural fear of the strange animals on which their enemies thundered towards them at full speed.

They broke and fled, and the other squadrons seeing them waver also turned tail and tried to save themselves by flight. Fifteen hundred[5] to two thousand Indians were slain and many others lanced and some taken prisoners.

[1] Palo a pique.   [2] Palmos.   [3] Garrotes.
[4] "La Araucana," Alonso de Ercilla, Madrid, Año de MDCCLXXVI., con las licencias necesarias.
[5] "Matamos hasta mil y quinientos a dos mil Indios (Indio mas o menos) y alancearonse otros muchos, prendierase algunos, de los cuales mandé cortar a docientos las manos y narices por su rebeldia de que muchas veces les habia enviado mensageros y hecholes los requerimientos que V. M. manda.

"Despues de hecha justicia, estando todos juntos los torne a hablar porque habia entre ellos algunos caciques e indios principales

" From two hundred of the prisoners I had the hands and noses cut off for their rebellion, when I had many times sent them messengers and given them the commands as ordered by Your Majesty.[1]

" After this act of justice, when all had been gathered together, I spoke to them, for there were some caciques and leading Indians among them, and I told them why this was done, because I had sent often to summon them and bid them come in peace, telling them to what end Your Majesty had sent me to this land, and they had received the message, and not done as I bade them, and what seemed best to me for fulfilling Your Majesty's commands and for the satisfaction of your royal conscience."

This act of justice was to cost Valdivia his life in after years, but as he was unaware of it at the time, he went on just as gaily as a horse that has been nerved, until it treads upon a stone.

---

y les dije y declaré como aquello se hacia, porque los habia enviado muchas veces a llamar y requerir con la paz diciendoles que V. M. me enviaba a esa tierra y habian recibido el mensage y no cumplido lo que les mandaba, y lo que me pareció convenir en cumplimiento de los mandamientos de V. M. y satisfaction de su real conciencia. . . ."

[1] Valdivia does not say what the Cæsarian commands were; but, judging by those that Cortés and Pizarro acted on, they were probably to become Christians and acknowledge the Emperor's sovereignty.

CHAPTER VIII

THIS battle was the turning-point in Valdivia's career.

From that time forward, although he never ceased from exploring and founding towns, the Araucanians always were on his hands. His cruel barbarism, that has unfortunately not a few parallels in the conquest both of North and South America, seems to have been an isolated act. It failed, as it was bound to fail, to intimidate so brave and warlike a race as were the Araucanians, and cast a stain upon his name that nothing could wipe out.

It mattered little to the Indians to recognize or not recognize the Emperor Charles V. Not more than it does for the average Englishman to recognize the King as the head of his Church, or to the average Catholic to recognize the Pope.

Both Englishman and Catholic take the thing for granted, and perhaps not half a dozen times in all their lives does it come up before their minds as something definite.

As for Jehovah, possibly enough the Araucanians would have added him to their Pantheon, and only given him a thought when they were called upon for Peter's pence.

Their crime, though probably Valdivia had never put it into words, was that they thought themselves the equals of the Spaniards. If, as we read, hell holds no fury like a woman scorned,[1] your " poor white trash," as goes the phrase amongst the negroes in Georgia and in Carolina, cannot endure that a man who has never worn a shoddy suit, and may perhaps be a shade darker than themselves, should dare to equal them. Both have immortal souls, of course, equally precious, it is to be supposed, to the Creator of them;

---

[1] A man runs her a very good second on such occasions, especially if he is cow-houghed, blear-eyed, and altogether unpersonable.

but, then, a soul has little value, except its outward envelope has corns or consumes alcohol.

Perhaps of all the Indians of the New World, at that time, the Araucanians were the most interesting. Possessors of a small but thickly populated territory, they had developed a military system not unlike that of the Zulus under Cetewayo. They attacked in regular formation, and understood that it was not prudent to throw all their men into the battle at once. Regular officers from the chief class, known as ulmens and apo-ulmens, commanded their battalions.

When they declared war, they elected a supreme chief to lead them to the fight.

Besides Valdivia himself, the chief contemporary authorities about their customs are Gongora Marmolejo[1] and Alonso de Ercilla, who in his long epic poem " La Araucana "[2] describes many of the most interesting customs of the Indians. He also gives character sketches of the chief personages on either side, all of whom he either knew himself or had fought against.

Some see a great poem in his work, and certainly Cervantes makes the doctor and the priest save it from the auto de fe of the Knights' books on chivalry, with many words of praise.

Others can only see in it a newspaper in rhyme. Still it has several striking lines, especially the often-quoted one that may be paraphrased,[3] "The best of fortune's gifts is never to have had good luck at all."

He wrote it as Pedro de Cieza de Leon wrote his chronicle of the conquest of Peru, by the camp fire at night, after the battle of the day. He says himself: " Being thus retired one night, writing the events of the day."[4]

[1] " Historia de Chile."
[2] " La Araucana," Madrid, Año de MDCCLXXVI., por Antonio de Sancha, con las licencias necesarias.
[3] " El mas seguro don de la fortuna
   Es no la haber tenido vez alguna."
                              " La Araucana," Canto II.
[4] " Estando asi una noche retirado, escribiendo el suceso de aquel dia ": " La Araucana," Canto XXIII.

Such a chronicle written in the circumstances he describes is valuable as an actual record of the facts; but of necessity it must lack the atmosphere, that only comes when facts have had time to arrange themselves in the writer's brain.

Alonso de Ercilla y Çuniga was born in Madrid on the 7th August, 1533. He was the son of Dr. Fortun de Ercilla, a member of the Royal Council, and Doña Leonor de Çuniga. The family came from Bermeo, in Biscay.

From his early youth he was about the court.[1] Salazar says he was a studious youth, but also much inclined to arms.

Philip II. seems to have taken a fancy to the young student, for he took him with him all over Europe. With him, Alonso visited Spain, Italy, France, England, Flanders, Germany, Silesia, Austria, Hungary, Styria and Carinthia. In 1547 he went to Brussels with Philip, who had been called there to take possession of the Grand Duchy of Brabant. These travels did not satisfy the future historian, who from his childhood had been anxious to try his fortune in America, after the fashion of most high-spirited young men of that adventurous age.

He got his chance, curiously enough, in England, where he had accompanied Philip for his marriage with Queen Mary in 1554. They landed at Southampton, and Ercilla probably rode in Philip's company through that rainy day that so well ushered in the gloomy honeymoon at the old palace of Wolvesey just outside Winchester.

Geronimo de Alderete, a captain who had served some years in Chile under Valdivia, accompanied Philip to England. At Winchester, Philip named him " Capitan y Adelantado " of Chile,[2] and allowed the young Ercilla to accompany him.

He went out in the ship commanded by one Domingo Martin.[3]

Alderete went in the same ship with his wife and servants,

---

[1] Alonso se crió en Palacio: "Advertencias Historicas," Luis de Salazar, pp. 13-14.
[2] This was after Valdivia's death.
[3] En la nao de que es maestro Domingo Martin.

and arrived in America[1] in 1555. Alderete, whose health was broken by his long campaigns under Valdivia, died of a fever at Taboga, near Panama.

Ercilla, who was just twenty-one, had probably heard much of Alderete's old general Valdivia during the voyage, and as Valdivia had not long been dead, and died in tragic circumstances, his name must certainly have been in everybody's mouth.

Ercilla went on to Lima, and from there accompanied the new Captain General of Chile, Garcia Hurtado de Mendoza, to his government.

Having come out under the patronage of the late governor Alderete, it is probable that Ercilla arrived in Chile as an officer. No one for the next eight years had a better opportunity of observing the Araucanians at first hand, or of collecting from eye-witnesses the various stories about Valdivia from his contemporaries and friends. He himself was in seven pitched battles, and countless skirmishes. All of them he chronicled day by day, writing his poem on any paper he could find, sometimes on bits of hide.

He accompanied the governor, Hurtado de Mendoza, so far south as to be opposite the archipelago of Chiloe. Then, with ten soldiers, he crossed to the hitherto unvisited islands in a canoe, and cut his name upon a tree.[2]

In 1558 he returned to Santiago, where he nearly lost his life in most curious circumstances. A tournament was being held with running at the Quintain (Un estopero) to celebrate the coronation of Philip II. A dispute arose between Ercilla and one Don Juan Pineda. They drew their swords, and the other young men present took sides, and there was a scuffle. No one appears to have been injured,

[1] "Coleccion de Documentos Historicos," Juan Bautista de Monroy, Tomo 87.
[2] After his name he cut the following inscription:

"Aqui llegó donde otro no ha llegado
Don Alonso de Ercilla que el primero
Con solo diez, pasó el desaguadero."

"La Araucana," Canto XXXVI.

but the general was very angry, and the two young men were condemned to be beheaded on account of the disrespect which it was held they had shown to the King.

With great difficulty, and after repeated entreaties had been disregarded, they were reprieved, when actually standing on the scaffold. Ercilla himself says, "I was taken out into the public square unjustly, to be publicly beheaded."[1]

Though his life was spared, he was imprisoned for a long time; but as he was an able captain, having had several years of experience in the war with the Araucanians, he was sent out to fight whenever the Indians attacked the settlements, and saw much service. It was in these expeditions that he saw most of the Araucanians, and had the best opportunity of gathering the curious details about them, their military organization, and the constitution of their commonwealth, that makes "La Araucana" so valuable as a contemporary document, in spite of its somewhat pedestrian style.

His references to Valdivia are chiefly to be found in the first and second cantos of his poem, and are not of special interest, being all at second hand. Although a soldier and a conquistador, he was always revolted by unnecessary cruelty.

He was indignant at the barbarous execution of the celebrated Araucanian chief Caupolican[2] under Valdivia's successor, Villagra, and says, "If I had been there it would not have taken place."

It was a pity, indeed, that he was absent, for Caupolican, the Araucanian chief, about whose exploits Ercilla has much to say, was taken prisoner in fair warfare, and had often spared Spanish prisoners when he had them in his power. His death by impalement is one of the greatest stains upon the conquest of Chile, and, as is usual in such cases, drew reprisals of the same nature from the other side.

---

[1] "Fui sacado a la plaza injustamente a ser publicamente degollado": Canto XXXVII.

[2] "Que si yo a la sazon alli estuviera
La cruda execucion se suspendiera."

"La Araucana," Canto XXXIV.

Ercilla returned to Spain at the age of twenty-nine, and never subsequently revisited America. Philip II. again befriended him after his marriage with Doña Maria Bazan, a lady-in-waiting to the Queen.

In spite of all that he had undergone, Ercilla was so shy that, having had occasion to address Philip on some matter, he became dumb in the presence of the King. Philip, who knew him from his youth upwards, said, " Don Alonso, write to me."[1]

Ercilla, who wrote no other considerable work, is supposed to have died in Madrid in 1595.

His poem, though it deals copiously with the military equipment of the Araucanians, and contains long accounts of the many battles that took place after Valdivia's death, yet has not so many details of the domestic life and general conditions of the agriculture, houses, and character of the people as have Valdivia's letters to the Emperor. To Spaniards, quite naturally, all the achievements of their arms ministered to the national pride, in a way quite legitimate.

To the world at large, the intimate and favourable view that the wise governor Valdivia took of the Indians who fought so stoutly for their independence against him and his men constitutes a more perfect human document. Valdivia's view, so reasonable and just, seems strange in one who could perpetrate such a barbarity upon his two hundred defenceless prisoners. What " La Araucana " is chiefly interesting for is in the accounts he gives of what the writer himself endured, for they, more than whole pages of descriptions of battles, show of what stuff the conquistadores were made. The following shows how different was the soldier's lot in those days to our own:

" Rain water and a mere handful of blackened, mouldy biscuit was our fare, when we could get it, and at other times a handful of raw barley boiled with what herbs we could procure, and that without salt to season it.

[1] Don Alonso, hablad me por escrito.

"We slept and lived in armour, and I wrote, exchanging the lance for the pen[1] when I had time."

Ercilla's poem and Valdivia's letters supplement one another, and, to quite a remarkable extent, agree as to the main characteristics of the Araucanian Indians.

There were not wanting commentators, chiefly laymen, who held views far more radical as to the treatment of the Indians than either Valdivia or the author of "La Araucana." The licentiate Juan de Herrera was one of them.

In his most curious manuscript,[2] preserved in the National Library of Chile, he gives his views on how war in Chile should be carried on, and incidentally some interesting sidelights on the Indians' system of levying their troops.

Speaking of the Indians in the neighbourhood of the newly founded town of Concepcion, he says:

"The Indians in the outskirts of the said city of Concepcion in especial are extremely warlike, so much so that, in order to be more active on the day of battle,[3] they purge themselves and sometimes even have themselves bled. For their leader they elect the most courageous and strongest,[4] and

[1] "Armado siempre y siempre de ordenanza
La pluma ora en la mano ora la lanza."
"La Araucana," Canto XXXIV.

The sketch of Villagra's horse gives a fair example of his poetic powers:

"Estaba en un caballo derivado
De la española raza, poderoso
Ancho de quadra, espeso, bien trabado
Castaño de color, presto airoso
Veloz en la carrera y de especto furioso."

It might have been as well written in prose, and would probably have had more colour if it had been.

[2] "Relacion de las cosas de Chile," por el licenciado Juan de Herrera.

The manuscript may have been printed recently, for of late years throughout Spanish America there has been a great awakening of interest in the early history of the various republics.

[3] Guazábara. Nearly all the writers on the conquest make use of this word for a skirmish.

[4] "... Que para estar mas ligeros el dia de la patrulla ó Guazábara se purgan y aun se hacen sangrar": "Relacion de las cosas de Chile," por el licenciado Juan de Herrera.

he who can longest bear on his shoulders a massive beam of wood."

Ercilla also relates with circumstance the election of the unlucky chief Caupolican over all his fellows by the ordeal of the heavy beam.

Had Ercilla been an Andalucian instead of a Viscayan, he might have been accused of ponderation (ponderacion) in the account he gives of the proceedings[1] and the long hours the chiefs sustained the weight upon their backs. Herrera goes on to say, there is another kind of fighting Indians, who are like Italian soldiers, who serve for pay and bring their own arms with them.

In war-time they were accompanied by many "gay women,"[2] who gained a great deal at their lucrative trade.

"These Indians have many other particularities that I do not desire to treat of, as they do not fall into the scope of the memorial I have been charged with by Your Majesty." He draws a veil over these particularities, but his ideas of how war should be conducted against the Indians have a strangely modern ring.

"War in Chile should be a handsome war[3] as they call it, either cutting down the crops and by so doing reducing them by hunger, or by the strong hand, and by making victims[4] of the old Indians. . . . For otherwise the war will never end."

[1] Considered without national prejudice, the Araucanian method of electing chiefs is not a bit more foolish than the way we elect Prime Ministers. Our difficulty would be, that the average member of the House of Commons would hardly have brains enough for such a mental strain.

[2] Mugeres del partido. History repeats itself, for the same phenomenon was to be observed in the late War to end War.

[3] La guerra que en Chile se ha de hacer, ha de ser *guerra galana*, como dicen, talando las comidas, procurar tomarles por hambre y a manos, ó con mucha pujanza y hacer a los indios viejos "mitimas" (this is apparently a misprint for "victimas") . . . porque de otra manera no se acabara la guerra.

[4] Aeroplanes would have rejoiced the heart of the good licentiate. By their assistance he could not only have made "mitimas" of the old Indians, but of the women and children as well.

The licentiate goes on to say: " In Chile, whilst war is going on, the courts, the magistrates, and officials of the King are not wanted . . . and affairs ought to be carried on rather according as necessity requires than by the letter of the law, which rides as goes the saying, ' a lame, white horse that serves to frighten, not to kill.' "[1]

The licentiate's views were far in advance of the times in which he lived. No one could exactly call the Spanish conquerors, with few exceptions, merciful men; but they were warriors, and it was reserved for a wearer of the long gown to preach such disgraceful methods, methods, no doubt, the warriors practised by the light of nature, but measures which none of them advocated in their books. Even Cortés, it is said, had to restrain the evangelizing methods by fire and sword of several of his friars.[2]

The Araucanians who Ercilla and Herrera describe, were the people Valdivia now had to confront. His barbarity having failed to terrorize them, he was now faced with an interminable war. He had already founded several towns in their territory—Arauco, Concepcion, and other smaller settlements. Most probably the colonists who he established there were only masters of the immediate territory which he describes in all his letters as well populated.

" It is more thickly populated than New Spain (Mexico), very healthy, fruitful, and pleasant, with a most fair climate . . . abounding in men, cattle, and food . . . and in it the only things wanting are Spaniards and horses." Both men and horses were beginning to arrive in considerable numbers from Peru, but still the Araucanians were unbroken, and could put large armies in the field. " It has," Valdivia says, " so many dwellers in it that there are no wild beasts among the people—foxes, wolves, or other creatures of the kind . . . I have the hope (under God) to give food in it,

---

[1] " Un caballo blanco y manco que espanta y no mata ": "Relacion de las cosas de Chile," por el licenciado Juan de Herrera.

[2] It is only just to say that, the conquest once over, both the Jesuits and the Franciscans tried manfully to protect the Indians from the cupidity and the cruelty of the colonists.

in Your Majesty's name, to more conquistadores than are fed in New Spain and Madrid."

Now and again he speaks of indications of much gold, apparently because he knew it was expected of him, just as a missionary labouring amongst Arabs (a stony field in which to sow the Gospel seed) has to send home lists of his converts, although he knows that he will lose them all when Ramadan comes round.

Of all the conquistadores, Valdivia seems to have best comprehended the uses of a fleet, for he kept his ships continually cruising along the coast, always attempting to achieve a successful passage through the Straits, and conquering many of the islands of the archipelago of Chiloe. His pilot, the Genoese Juan Bautista de Pastene, made repeated voyages to the south, sailing by charts that he had brought from Spain. On one occasion, when he arrived in latitude 41 degrees, he was nearly lost, owing to a faulty chart.

Valdivia implores the Emperor to order new charts to be prepared, so that vessels coming from Spain could make their landfall with confidence. It appears that where the charts were wrong was in regard to the entrance to the Straits.[1] He says he will make no report on the matter till he has had the whole coast explored, so that the errors in the charts might be corrected. "The mistake did not lie in the number of degrees north and south (as I am informed), but in the east to the west."

Latitude 41 degrees (south) was the limit of Valdivia's government, as laid down by the Council of the Indies.

He writes the Emperor that south of 41 degrees the land was probably uninhabited, and begs him not to have another government marked out to the southward of that latitude, for it would only lead to trouble. Seven feet of ground would be enough for him, he says, but he asks to have his government prolonged down to the Straits, not from greed of territory, but to avoid confusion in His Majesty's affairs.

Upon the 5th of October, 1550, he founded the town of

[1] La demanda del estrecho.

Concepcion, and instituted a town council and a court of justice.

When these matters were satisfactorily arranged, in order that the colonists and the Indians should enjoy all the fruits of the civilization of the times, he set up a gallows tree.[1] Under its shadow he divided up all the Indians who had submitted to his rule amongst the colonists. " And they are living in content, praise be to God."

Neither the town council, tribunal, nor the tree of justice, attracted the bulk of the Araucanians, who manfully continued to defend their homes.

Their tenacity and patriotism evoked the admiration of the better educated Spaniards. Ercilla says of them in the preface to the second volume of his poems: " The Araucanians are worthy of all praise, for for more than thirty years they have persevered in their resistance, without ever laying down their arms, not striving to defend great cities or riches, for by their own action they have burned down their houses and destroyed what wealth they had, so that their enemies should not enjoy it, but only defending parched and stony fields that they have often watered with our blood."[2]

[1] Puse el arbol de justicia.
[2] They are supposed to number about sixty thousand to-day.

CHAPTER IX

VALDIVIA suffered, as did most of the conquistadores when once they had begun to settle down, from a want of labour.

The Spaniards of those days, who had but recently emerged from the long wars in their own country with the Moors, looked upon labour as derogatory to them. Those who had come to the Americas had come to make their fortunes, and nearly all of them were soldiers, or had served in the armies of the Emperor Charles V. in some capacity or other. Quite naturally enough, the last thing that they knew anything about was manual labour, or any kind of work. With few exceptions, none of the Indians were fitted for continuous toil, having never been obliged to work hard, owing to the conditions of their lives.

The Spaniards, as is well known, at first treated the natives with gross cruelty—witness the complete depopulation[1] of the West Indian islands in an incredibly short time.

Everyone saw the evil, and it was reserved for the great Las Casas, in his pity for the Indians' fate, to advocate a step that brought a heritage of trouble with it, by the introduction of the negro into America. Las Casas did not seem to see that he was only substituting one slavery for another just as bad. Undoubtedly the negro proved able to withstand hard work, and did not wilt and perish by his contact with the whites. Neither did he assimilate with them, as the Indians have done in certain of the republics, and formed a vigorous and athletic race. Had but the conquistadores known it, they were throwing away a source of real wealth, and of stability worth more than all the mines of Potosi, by their destruction of the Indians. Valdivia

[1] The last natives of Tasmania died, it is said, somewhere about 1852. So it appears that even our own withers are not entirely unwrung.

is not, therefore, to be blamed because he could not see further into the future than his contemporaries.

He writes to ask permission from the Emperor[1] to introduce two thousand negroes from the Cape Verde Islands.

It is not known whether these two thousand negroes, or any portion of them, ever arrived in Chile. One thing is certain, that Chile, at the time of her independence, had no negro problem to be solved.

Although Valdivia passed his life in action, always on horseback, exploring, founding towns, and putting down revolts, he yet had time to care for the spiritual welfare of the country that he conquered almost at his own expense, settled, and might have, if he had lived, placed on a far more stable basis than any other of the conquests of his day. He saw what practically no other of the conquistadores, except the great and really Christian Alvar Nuñez Cabeca de Vaca, ever comprehended, that agriculture and not mines was the true foundation of a state.

So as his ambition was to settle Spanish settlers on the land, he felt their spiritual welfare must not be neglected, if they were to make good citizens according to the ideas of the age.

Most of the conquistadores were men deeply imbued with what appeared to them religious principles, a fact that Protestant historians too often seem to miss.

Valdivia therefore sent the reverend Father Rodrigo Gonzalez back to Spain to render an account of all that he had done, and with a special request that he should be appointed the first bishop of the New Extreme.[2]

Valdivia's account of Father Gonzalez is most interesting and touching in a way, as it serves to show how strong a friendship existed between two men so different in character and in their mode of life.

"Father Gonzalez," Valdivia tells the Emperor, "was born in the town of Constantina, and is brother to Don Diego de Carmona, dean of the holy church of Seville. . . . The business of this reverend father here has been the service of God and the honour of His Church, and divine

---

[1] Third letter to Charles V.   [2] El Nuevo Extremo.

worship, and particularly Your Majesty's service. . . . I am sending him from this city of Concepcion, for owing to my business and his years, we cannot see one another to take farewell. . . . With the special love he has for this business,[1] I know he will obey and fulfil all unto death and do nought otherwise."

Valdivia was always in dread of some foolish or ill-considered appointment from Spain.

Therefore he begs the Emperor, in case someone should have been already appointed to be bishop of Chile, to appoint Father Gonzalez to be bishop of Arauco, a town that he promised to found as soon as he had time.

"Though St. Paul says: 'qui episcopatum desiderat, bonum opus desiderat,' I give Your Majesty my word that I know the appointment would be well conferred on this good knight of Jesus Christ."[2]

The Latin tag sounds as if Father Gonzalez had helped in the composition of the letter, but every now and then Valdivia intercalates a Latin phrase in almost all his letters, as did others of the conquistadores; but never those who really had been well educated.

Still pushing south below the Biobio, Valdivia founded another town that he called La Imperial, and in his report congratulates himself that the Indians were of a peaceful disposition and readily submitted to his rule, after he had explained to them the great truths of the Gospel and the advantages of being subjects of an unknown sovereign ten thousand miles away.

This he puts down to the exemplary punishment that he had meted out to the two hundred recalcitrants, whose hands and noses he had cut off to cure their lack of faith. The inhabitants in the south of Chile he describes in detail, and though he never alludes to them by name, they must have been the Araucanians, for many of their traits of character and their clothes are applicable to the Araucanian Indians even to-day.

[1] The conversion of the Indians.
[2] "Como buen caballero de Jesu Cristo."

"The country is all one town and one field and one gold mine, and if the houses are not put on the top of one another it will not hold more than it has; it is as rich in flocks as Peru, with wool that drags along the ground; abounds with all the foods that the Indians sow for their livelihood, such as maize, potatoes, quinua,[1] madi, pepper, and beans; the people are tall, fond of their houses, friendly, and white, and with handsome faces, both men and women, all clad in wool after their fashion, although they are very afraid of horses; they are very fond of their children, their wives, and houses, which are very well built and strong, with great planks, and many of them very large, with two, four, and eight doors. They have many and very fine vessels of clay and wood; they are very great husbandmen, and as great drinkers; their law lies in arms, and so they all have them in their houses to defend themselves against their neighbours and to attack the weaker."

This is the first and probably the most concise description of the Araucanians[2] ever penned, and tallies almost to the smallest detail with descriptions of all those who have observed the Araucanians in their homes.

Their coarse, blue woollen clothes have never varied, nor have their love of home and drinking habits. Naturally, in those days they were afraid of horses, as were all the Indians of America; but they have long ago become excellent and expert horsemen.

The one mistake Valdivia seems to make is when he says that they are "white." He may have said so by comparison with the darker Indians of Peru and Mexico, in both of which countries he had served. Their colour is a yellowish bronze, and Valdivia may have used the word "handsome" as the Elizabethans employed "tall," to signify that they were brave; though it is true he applies it both to women and to

---

[1] Quinua is usually spelt quinoa. It is the *Chenopodium quinoa* of botanists.

Madi seems to be a mistake for mani, a kind of oily ground nut.

[2] Valdivia never refers to them as Araucanians in his letters to Charles V. He always says Los Indios.

men. To most observers they appear as hard-featured a race as any upon earth. In February, 1552, the town of Valdivia was founded, and in April of the same year Villa Rica in latitude 40 degrees south.

This latter place he looked on as the most suitable in which to fit out an expedition to explore the Straits, and hoped to send his deputy captain, Francisco de Villagra, in command of it.

He had been planning also to bring out "his wife and transplant the house of Valdivia to these parts, so that Your Majesty, as the most Christian monarch, our natural King and lord, may be pleased to make it illustrious, for the sake of the services I have done to your imperial person."

Both Pizarro and Cortés had been ennobled. Quesada, the conqueror of New Granada, had been promised a marquisate that was never granted, owing to the intrigues of his enemies.

Most certainly Valdivia was as well deserving of such an honour as any of them, and without doubt it would have gratified him. Just as, in thinking of those times, it is to be remembered that most men really believed the faith that they professed, so titles that to-day we smile at, and certainly enrich neither the giver nor the recipient, were held in real esteem.

On the 26th of October, 1552, Valdivia wrote his last letter to the Emperor. It is dated Santiago, the city that he founded, fostered, and fought for, with a faith and a tenacity amazing even in those days of faith and steadfastness in toil.

It deals chiefly with business matters, and various sums he had laid out, which he expected to be relieved of by the Crown.

Once more he recommends Father Rodrigo Gonzalez to the Emperor for the new bishopric, and for the last time ends his letter, "Most sacred Cæsar, the most humble subject and vassal of Your Majesty that kisses your most sacred hands and feet."

Long ago the valiant soldier and the most sacred Cæsar

perhaps have met in the place appointed for them, where all distinctions have been levelled and they can talk their old campaigns over as men who, in their lives, were known one as " A Prince of Light Horsemen " and the other who, if fate so had ordered it, would have ridden by his side, their stirrups touching, into the gates of hell.

With the exception of the five letters that Cortés addressed to Charles V., no letters dealing with the conquest by actual actors of high rank are of more interest than the five letters of Valdivia. He had not the culture of Cortés, who had commenced life as a lawyer, nor his genius; but there is an air of truthfulness and of sincerity about his correspondence, that makes it interesting as a human document. To Chileans, his letters are one of the most precious records in the possession of their country. In them, preserved in the somewhat stiff Castilian of those days, are to be found the impression that the Araucanians, one of the most remarkable of all the Indian races of America, made on the mind of a straightforward soldier, shrewd and acute beyond the ordinary, and who, moreover, had served against all the best troops of Europe in the Emperor's wars.

He also saw and judged them from the standpoint of an Estremenian country gentleman of moderate means, who probably in his youth knew the small farmers round Villa Nueva de la Serena, intimately. Thus he was able to estimate them from the two standpoints of husbandmen and warriors. It is evident, in spite of his occasional cruelty, that he liked them, and had he lived long enough, most of the bitterness of the long warfare that ensued might have been avoided, for they seem to have both feared and respected him.

Those were the days in which men had to turn their hands to many occupations, for which their previous lives had not prepared them. Valdivia, though, as he says himself, he scarcely ever had his armour off his back, had to turn miner, agriculturist, explorer, navigator and statesman. The regulations that he drew up in the town council of Santiago, at whose sittings he frequently presided, fix prices for nearly all the trades then exercised in his newly founded town. Armourers, sword-makers, smiths, tailors, and shoe-makers, all had a scale of prices that they were forbidden to exceed. For every breach of the town council's ordinance a fine was to be imposed. Whether it was inflicted, taking into consideration the casual nature of the Spanish character, is another matter. Still, it showed that Valdivia, like many another governor, found it incumbent on him to endeavour to protect his people against the too strict application of the law of supply and demand, sacred to some minds and anathema to others.

A sword-maker, for sharpening a sword and making a new sheath, if he provided the material, was limited to five dollars.[1] If the leather was supplied to him, he had only right to two. A dagger cost two dollars to put in order and to sharpen. A lance head, half a dollar; the same price for a hoe, and so on throughout the scale of agricultural and warlike implements. Tailors and shoemakers were more strictly dealt with.

A plain cloak[2] was not to exceed two dollars and a half, the cloth to be supplied by the person who ordered it. A plain jacket,[3] two dollars and a half. Breeches,[4] three dollars. These prices may have been capable of being enforced; but in the next item even Valdivia could not have hoped to prevail against such odds.

For a woman's plain gown with sleeves, either of cloth or silk, the tailor never was to charge more than four dollars.[5] Only a conquistador could think that any woman, even in the Santiago of those days, would consent to be, so to speak, *adscripta glebæ*, to a panel tailor.

A velvet gown, with a sash and two rows of ornamental stitching, was rated at six dollars.

[1] Por aderezar una espada poniendo el oficial todo el aderezo y barnizandolo lleve cinco pesos, etc.: Actos del Cabildo de Santiago, 1541-1557.

Their record book was known as "El becerro," from being bound in calf skin.

[2] Una capa llana.   [3] Una chamarra llana.
[4] King Stephen's cost him but a crown.
[5] De un sayuelo de muger con mangas . . . de paño o de seda, 4 pesos.

Shoes were priced at one dollar, and riding boots at three. Buckles were a dollar the pair, and a buff jacket (for it appears that they were made by shoemakers in Santiago), five.

The penalty for the infraction of the scale of prices was fifty dollars'[1] worth of good gold. One part to be adjudged to the person who complained, and the other two to be given to the poor.

What is curious about both prices and the articles named in the list is that the prices could not have differed greatly from those charged in Spain. In spite of the great difficulty of communication, it would appear that Santiago was already well supplied with all the common goods and even luxuries of European life. That, too, though most of them must have come across the isthmus of Panama, and been reshipped to Chile from Peru, for, according to Valdivia's own letters, few vessels could have ventured through the Straits, with charts so faulty as those that he describes.

The regulations fixing a maximum in prices, though probably a counsel of perfection, at least as far as women's clothing was concerned, unless women in Santiago were strangely different from those of the two thousand years preceding them, were not unreasonable.

Probably they were enacted as so many Acts of Parliament are passed to-day, not in the hope of being acted on, but as a sop to a public outcry that has become a nuisance to the legislators. When the town council dealt with matters over which it had a real control, its ordinances were writ in blood.

At a meeting of the town council on the 8th of July, 1549, it was agreed that a guard should be appointed to look after all the mares " in this city," and take them to and from their grazing grounds.

If any Indian should wound them with arrows[2] or with stones, that his hand should be stricken off, and his master

---

[1] Cincuento pesos de buen oro, aplicados en tres partes; la una para la persona que lo denunció y las otros dos para los propios de esta dicha ciudad.

[2] Y el Indio que flechase o apedrease yeguas ú otra cualquiera bestia, que le sea cortada la mano por ello, y su amo pague el daño que hiciere.

should be liable to make good the damage to the owner of the animals.[1]

Trees were strictly protected, and a fine of two dollars of good gold was to be imposed for each tree cut or damaged, the money to be given to the poor.

This by-law was made public by the voice of Domingo Negrete, the town crier of "this city" of Santiago of the New Extreme, as all the people were coming out of church.

Some negroes must have arrived in Chile by the year 1551, probably brought from Peru, for Valdivia could have hardly had the time to receive an answer from the Emperor to his request to be allowed to bring them from the Cape de Verdes.

That they were there and were behaving badly is manifest from an enactment of the town council of Santiago on the 27th of March, 1551:

"We have learned that certain negroes have dared to run away and live at large, and that they do great injury to the natives of the country, forcing women against their will. We therefore order that in the future if any negro or negroes run away, and force any woman[2] or women against their will, the judge having received proof, may sentence him to have the offending member cut off,[3] and to the rest of the penalties that the judge shall think necessary for the service of the Lord our God, the King and the welfare of the realm." What other penalties were worth inflicting after the first had been duly carried out, is difficult to see.

Neither Indians nor negroes were allowed to play at any game of cards under pain of being publicly whipped. The council also rigidly enforced the curfew, and strictly pro-

[1] This ordinance is quite in the spirit of making a husband liable for his wife's debts, and, after all, is not more bloodthirsty than many an enactment in Manwood's "Laws of the Forest."
[2] ". . . Si forzase alguna india . . . contra su volundad."
[3] ". . . Puede el tal juez (recibiendo informacion bastante), ordenar por su sentencia en que le corten el miembro genital, y las demas peñas que el juez de la causa le pareciere conviene a la eficacia de la justicia y conforme a las leyes del reino."

hibited either Spaniards, Negroes, or Indians from carrying arms within the precincts of the town.

As Valdivia himself presided at almost all the council meetings, these curious ordinances, some so reasonable and others, as it seems to-day, so bloodthirsty and barbarous, are probably the reflection of his mind.

Most certainly he was a man who must have imposed his will on all the rest of the councillors, who probably also had been nominated by himself. His ordinances to regulate the price of commodities were bound to fail, as have all such attempts of legislators when they have sought to interfere with trade. Upon that field the noblest and the most ignoble minds have not infrequently met. The first from the desire to help mankind, the others from a wish to help themselves. Each has encountered the same difficulties, and both philanthropists and rogues have failed in their designs.

From the date of his fifth letter to the Emperor, nothing is known to have survived that Valdivia wrote, or if he wrote at all to Spain. The Indians, who he thought were cowed and bent beneath his rule, bore his yoke uneasily, and he himself, whether pushed by the greed of the home government, avid of gold from the New World, or because power had begun to sap his character, unwisely forced the Indians to work for him, both in plantations and in mines.

The result was certain when such a race as were the Araucanians became the victims of his greed.

CHAPTER X

ALTHOUGH none of the contemporary writers on the conquest of Chile are so authoritative as Valdivia, for he alone wrote as the events were still in progress, his last two years of life can be to some extent reconstructed from the works of Don Alonso de Ercilla and Captain Gongora Marmolejo who served under him.

Ercilla came to Chile a few years after Valdivia was killed. His rhyming chronicle contains but few details of Valdivia's life, and these, of course, he had gathered at second hand from retired soldiers and the older colonists. One actual contemporary historian and personal witness of the events that he describes, exists.

Captain Alonso Gongora Marmolejo served under Valdivia's orders and knew him and his successor, Villagra, personally.

Born in Spain, at Carmona, not far from Seville, Gongora Marmolejo appears to have come to the Indies as a young soldier.

His " Historia de Chile " long remained in manuscript; it was at last published by the well-known scholar Don Pascual de Gayangos in 1850, and is contained in the fourth volume of the " Memorial Historico Español."

Gongora[1] says there was no history of the conquest of Chile except that of Ercilla, in verse, so he determined to write one in prose. His style, though military, is modest and, on the whole, impartial. Sometimes he is rather obscure, and now and then spells a word in several different ways, on the same page.

[1] It is usual in Spanish to use the first of two names, not the second as in English.
This arises from the fact that the first name is generally that of the father, and the second that of the mother.

He had the same experience as most of the conquistadores, of lacking advancement in his youth, and of neglect in his old age. Especially does he complain of one of the governors, a Dr. Saravia, who he says gave the office of Protector of the Indians to a rich merchant, who had done no fighting, and had passed over an old soldier who had applied for it. Possibly the old soldier was Gongora himself, for he says "many old soldiers, of whom I myself was one, applied for the position." He says that he had served the King throughout the conquest, since Valdivia's day, and that up to that date had received no remuneration for his services.

After Valdivia had founded the town of Valdivia, he returned to pass the winter in Concepcion.

Next summer (1553) he went to Santiago, and from there sent Captain Alderete back to Spain with thirty thousand dollars as a present to the Emperor.

Alderete was charged to get the Emperor to confirm Valdivia in his governorship. Well did Valdivia know the constant want of money that the Spanish court always suffered from, and that nothing was to be expected without money.

In especial Valdivia was urgent with the Emperor to give him power to nominate his successor. He had no son of his own, and therefore this request was probably made from really patriotic motives, and a wish to advance the interests of the colony.

Probably he had Captain Villagra in his mind, who, though he was a little jealous of him, he knew to be a soldier of experience, well versed in Indian warfare, and an honourable and upright man.

This captain, Valdivia sent with eighty men from Concepcion to cross the Andes and explore the territory upon the Atlantic side. It must have been a terrible journey in those days. Nothing existed except trails known to the Indians alone.

The explorers had as little notion what was on the other side of the great chain of mountains as had the navigators of those days, of what lay beyond the seas that they set out to sail.

However, Villagra crossed the Andes with less difficulty than he had expected, and came upon a great and rapid river flowing eastward. This may have been either the Rio Negro or the Rio Colorado, for both of them flow eastward, and are deep and difficult to pass, and Villagra, after marching several days along the bank, could never find a ford. He came upon a fort held by Pehuelche Indians. In those days that tribe occupied territory both on the Rio Negro and the Rio Colorado. He attacked the fort, and took it, losing a man or two in the attack.

What were his motives in assaulting this isolated place so far from Chile only himself could tell, but all the conquistadores appear to have been animated by a love of fighting for its own sake. Without it, perhaps they would not have been conquistadores. He returned to Chile through the valley of Maguez, which he found well populated and very fertile. Valdivia, at this time, was at the height of his fame and position. All was going well with him. He had founded the towns of La Serena, Santiago, Concepcion, Confines, Imperial, Villa Rica, and Valdivia, and built three frontier forts, Tucapel, Arauco, and Puren, and a small military post in Quillota. Not a bad record for the life work of one man.

Most of these towns, now grown to be important cities, exist to-day on the same sites on which he founded them. Thus he has left more stable and greater material memorials of his work than any of the conquerors of the New World.

Besides his important explorations towards the Straits, he also conquered the provinces of Cuyo, that are now included in the Argentine Republic. The colonists all seem to have held Valdivia in great esteem, and looked on him as the father of the country, as indeed he was. His soldiers never troubled him after the first sharp lesson that he gave them. This was in marked contradiction with most of the conquistadores, who were often troubled with revolts. Valdivia had the advantage of being the one outstanding personality in the country, and it never would have occurred to any of his captains to dispute his will. Unluckily for him, the constant need of sending gold to Spain, or the increase of appetite on what it fed on, led him to draw the string so tightly that it snapped the bow.

Gongora, though he both admired and loved Valdivia, was not blind to his faults.

Few officers of an inferior rank, of any time or nationality, fail to perceive the spots upon the sun of their commanders. Gongora was no exception to the rule. He tells how gold mines were discovered somewhere between the cities of La Concepcion and La Imperial.

These mines must have been " placers," and not mines, for if they had been really mines, they would exist to-day. Moreover, Gongora gives a minute description of the trough[1] in which the gold was washed.

Valdivia had several hundred Indians employed at this work, and they produced about thirteen marks of gold a day. When he saw this gold, Valdivia, according to Gongora, exclaimed:

" I now begin, indeed, to be a lord."

Unluckily he omitted to give thanks to God for his good fortune, and this omission, some thought, was the cause of his death.

Gongora says: " It is hardly credible that a man of such good understanding should have omitted to give thanks to the Creator, who from a squire had raised him up to be a lord."

That, of course, may be so, but then the architects of their own fortunes frequently look on God but as a sleeping partner in the concern.

These placer diggings were worked almost exclusively, as it appears, by Araucanians who had submitted to the Spanish rule. Although a strong and sturdy folk, a little shorter than the average of the Spaniards,[2] deep-chested

---

[1] " Batea es, un palo redondo canado el fondo de el, de manera que viene a quedar como una fuente de plata, ansi grande mas honda con estas sacan el oro en las Indias."

[2] " Son los Indios de Chile de estatura algo menor que el comun de los Españoles muy robustos de pecho ": " Historia Militar, Civil y Sagrada de Chile," por Miguel de Olivares, Santiago, 1864.

Olivares, a native of Chillan, was a Jesuit, and wrote somewhere about 1740. His work long remained in manuscript.

and robust, few races of the world were less inclined to submit to servitude. Born in a temperate climate, in rather a poor country, to which, however, they were passionately attached, they were, moreover, quite unfitted for continuous labour, as were most of the races of the New World, for they had never been accustomed to any form of it. They were not hunters in the main, for game was not abundant in the country where they lived. Still less were they nomadic, for most of them, as do their descendants, cultivated sufficient ground for their immediate wants, but each one only worked for his own family.

Bascuñan, who was a captive[1] amongst the Araucanians, and grew to love them, has preserved many of their characteristics, which he had ample opportunities to study. He was born in Chile somewhere about 1607. His father was an old soldier, who, after forty years' service, from the age of fourteen, retired at sixty, having lost an eye and the use of his legs. He was a renowned warrior, who was known to the Indians as Martin Campo. His son, the captive, entered the army in 1625.

At that time the Chilians had two great frontier forts, one at Arauco, and the other at Yumbel. In 1622, Bascuñan, then a young captain, was at the disastrous battle of Las Cangrejeras, where the Spaniards suffered a severe defeat at the hands of the Araucanians.

Wounded in the wrist by an Indian's spear, he was knocked senseless off his horse by a blow from a club. So well delivered was the stroke that it drove his armour into his side. He recovered his senses to find himself a prisoner in the midst of a crowd of Indians clamouring for his death. Luckily for him, at that moment a chief rode up, called Lientur, who recognized him for the son of Martin Campo, who had once spared his life.

By this time the Araucanians had horses and Spanish

[1] "Cautiverio Feliz": Francisco Nuñez Pineda y Bascuñan, Santiago, 1863.
His most interesting work is contained in the third volume of "La Coleccion de Historiadores de Chile," Barros Arana.

arms, and the description of Lientur is most interesting. Bascuñan calls him a strong and generous Indian.[1]

"Then I saw Captain Lientur (the leader of that army) appear armed from the feet to the head.[2] A naked sword was in his hand, and on his head he wore a helmet. This warrior bestrode a fierce horse,[3] that breathed fire and pawed the ground."

A formidable pair Lientur and his horse must certainly have been; but what is most noteworthy about them is that both wore Spanish armour, and that in fifty years the horse had become as familiar to the Araucanians as to their foes.

This paladin rode into the middle of his followers, and, taking Bascuñan under his protection, declared no one should harm the son of his old enemy and friend, Martin Campo.

The young Spaniard—he was only twenty-four—became the captive of a chief called Maulican, who treated him as one of his own family.

Dressed in the Araucanian clothes, sleeping and eating with the chief's family, wrestling and running with the young men of the tribe, and playing with them at their national game, La Chueca, a kind of hockey, Bascuñan's captivity well merited the title that he gave his book, of "El Cautiverio Feliz."

He describes in detail their journeys, feastings, religious ceremonies, and drinking bouts, their marriage customs, and their love-making. At one of their great banquets, at which it appeared the ladies took an active part, a young Indian girl fell in love with him. Finding him obdurate to her advances, she with a companion, another girl, both of whom, it seemed, had partaken largely of the national beverage, chicha, appeared before the fire beside which Bascuñan was sleeping, together with an uncle of one of them. They explained the state of the girl's affections to him and then withdrew, leaving the lovesick maiden all alone with him.

---

[1] Indio esforzudo y generoso.
[2] "Armado desde los pies a la cabeza." In English, from head to foot.
[3] Feroz caballo.

Whether he spoke Araucanian or no, he does not tell us; but for such matters a knowledge of the grammar of a tongue is not of absolute necessity.

The girl at last, in desperation, lay down beside him, proceeding, as he says, to extremities no Christian could have tolerated. That may be so, of course, for who shall search the human heart?—still, on occasion Christians have tolerated a good deal.

Rising from his couch beside the fire, he told the temptress to begone, and at last the poor girl withdrew, as he tells us, " angry and ashamed."

Virtue so stern and so unbending is no doubt its own reward. Bascuñan's conduct was Christian in the highest sense of the term, so Christian as almost to transcend humanity. Still, some may think he might have stretched a point, after the kindness he had received. His Happy Captivity[1] might have been even happier still, if he had been more chivalrous in his behaviour. It lasted from the 15th of May (1629) to the 17th of November in the same year, when he was ransomed and returned home.

Bascuñan mentions Valdivia only cursorily in his book, for by that time his fame was getting dusted o'er a little, but he is interesting for the light he throws upon the Araucanians. Reading his book, it certainly appears that of all peoples upon earth, they were the last a prudent man would have forced to continuous toil.

A great secret conspiracy had been formed, embracing all the Indians who had submitted to Valdivia's rule in conjunction with those outside the pale.

The insurrection broke out in the province of Tucapel.[2] The Indians first made an attempt to take the little isolated fort of Tucapel.

It was commanded, as it happened, by a fierce old soldier, one Martin de Ariza, a Biscayan, who had grown grey in frontier warfare, and was well skilled in Indian stratagems

[1] " Cautiverio Feliz."
[2] " . . . La Provincia de Tucapel que es la gente mas belicosa de todos ellos ": Gongora Marmolejo.

and ambuscades. Having heard a plot was brewing, he sallied out and laid his hands on several Indian chiefs, and kept them prisoners in his fort.

Suddenly, some fifty Indians, apparently unarmed, and carrying bales of grass as fodder for the horses, appeared before the fortress. When they had passed the gate, they threw the bales upon the ground, and pulled out spears and clubs concealed within them.

Without their armour and unarmed, but for their swords, the Spanish garrison, after a brief, furious struggle, drove out the Indians, who left many dead upon the ground.

Although repulsed and unsuccessful in their first attempt, the Indians were not disheartened, and waited for the Spaniards to come out and fight. They sallied forth as soon as they had buckled on their armour, and drove the Indians back; but they returned in such overwhelming numbers that Captain Ariza was forced to evacuate the fort, under the cover of the night. He set out in the darkness to join Valdivia at Puren, some seven leagues away. Before the grim old Biscayan left the fort he killed all his prisoners with an iron bar. Gongora relates the fact, but does not comment on it, or try to excuse it in the modern way with sham regrets upon the fate of the poor Indians.

Valdivia, who seems to have looked on the revolt as unimportant, had not come to Puren, though he had promised Martin Ariza to relieve him on a certain day.

He still was at Concepcion. So much did he despise the Araucanians,[1] who at that time had not developed the fighting qualities they afterwards displayed, that when he marched to the relief of Tucapel, he only had with him some forty cavalry.[2]

[1] " No llevó mas numero de gente porque en aquel tiempo eran los indios tenidos en poco, como gente que no sabian pelear, ni aun tenian animo para ello; mas despues que conocian los caballos y tratavan a los Christianos supieron defender sus tierras ": Gongora Marmolejo, p. 35.

[2] Valdivia was much in debt at the time and could get no help from the Emperor, though he asked for it repeatedly. This, Ercilla says, prevented him from gathering a sufficient force.

No doubt Valdivia looked on the Indians as rebels, just as all Europeans so stigmatize those whose lands they have filched from them, when they rise to recover their own territories.

As soon as the Indians heard Valdivia was on the road, they burned the deserted fort of Tucapel.

Then they held a general council, and were debating on the best way of attacking the Christian settlements, when a young Indian called Alonso,[1] who had lived long amongst the Spaniards, as Valdivia's groom, rose up and harangued the assembled Indians.

His speech, or the essence of it, has been preserved, both by Ercilla in his "Araucana," and by Gongora Marmolejo in his history.

Possibly both have embroidered on it; but it is certainly just the kind of speech that would have occurred to any man in like circumstances. Moreover, both in North and South America, many of the Indians have been endowed with real eloquence.

"Brothers," Alonso is reported to have said, "the Christians are mortals like ourselves. The horses also are not immortal, and can be slain. More than that, when it is hot, they are tired easily, and cannot gallop[2] for any considerable time.

"Let us fight now, or else we shall be ever slaves.

"I will prepare a plan of battle, and show you what you must do to beat the enemy."

The assembled chiefs agreed to what he said, and he immediately relinquished the name Alonso, by which he had been known amongst the Spaniards, and assumed, or perhaps reassumed, that of Lautaro. Under that name he rose to be a chief, and the chief enemy of the Christians. Owing to him, the warfare that lasted down to the middle of the last century in Chile was initiated. Before his time the Araucanians had developed no special fighting powers, and might easily have been crushed. The young chief's advice was

[1] Gongora calls him Alonso. Some writers refer to him as Felipe.
[2] He knew what he was saying, for he had been a groom.

to draw up the Indian line of battle on a hill that had a river running at its foot. They were not to show themselves at first. Then they were to launch a squadron on the enemy, followed at short intervals by others, with the object of driving the Spaniards into broken, marshy ground, in which their horses could not gallop readily.

Upon the river bank he advised a squadron should be placed in ambush, hidden by the tall reeds. This squadron was to charge the Spaniards when they should see their horses struggling in the ford.

The plan was well considered, for the river was deep and strong, and the stream was very swift. Messengers were instantly dispatched to all the chiefs, and in a little space of time a strong force was collected, ready to attack. Gongora puts its number at fifty thousand, but it is hardly credible that such a small territory as Araucania could have furnished such a force, or that without any commissariat so great an army could have been kept together for more than a few days.

True it is that the Araucanians were extremely fruga in time of war, living most probably on the toasted flour[1] that is still used in Chile by the country people.

Valdivia, who seems to have been rendered careless by his success, lingered inactive in Concepcion for a considerable time, and then set off to relieve the garrison of Tucapel, accompanied by only forty men. He certainly sent out four mounted scouts to give him news of the movements of the Araucanians.

These men, raw soldiers, unused to Indian warfare, fell into an ambuscade, and all of them were slain. To challenge and defy Valdivia, the Indians cut off the arm of one of the dead scouts, and fastening his jacket sleeve to it, placed it upon the path by which they knew Valdivia must pass.

---

[1] Harina tostada. This is made either from wheat or maize and is often mixed with sugar and cinnamon. It is moistened at a river or a spring with water, and forms a kind of paste, that is said to have great sustaining qualities. It is, or was, usually carried either in a leather bag or in a horn.

One of his Indian servants, a young man called Agustinillo, when he saw the arm, pled with his master to return and wait the arrival of more men. He pointed out, from signs he had observed upon the road, that the Indians were in overwhelming force.

Gongora says Valdivia, being a man of great strength of character, would not listen to advice.[1]

His forty soldiers were chiefly gentlemen, accustomed to despise the Indians, young, rash, and inexperienced.[2] These youths seem to have urged him to advance against what might have been expected was his judgment, considering his long experience of Indian warfare. Whatever was the reason of his rashness, he and his forty men, the most of whom were officers,[3] pushed on till they arrived at Tucapel, upon the very day on which he had promised Captain Ariza to relieve him.

To his astonishment it was destroyed, and all he found was but a mass of smouldering ruins. Ariza evidently had not been able to get through to warn him. A man with Valdivia's experience, who had but such a slender following with him, ought to have retired at once. As he and his band of officers sat on their horses, hardly knowing what to do, from the woods near the ruined fortress the Indians suddenly emerged in force. To the sound of horns they set their squadrons in array, and came on steadily. Valdivia, seeing their numbers and their formidable appearance, formed his little band into three divisions, putting a guard over his baggage.

One of his little troops charged desperately upon the Indians, riding down and killing many of them; but without being able to penetrate their ranks. Then the second troop attacked, but with the same result.

Lastly Valdivia himself, with about twenty of his best

---

[1] "Valdivia como era hombre de grande animo lo despreció todo."

[2] "La poca edad y menos experiencia de los mozos livianos que alli habia": "La Araucana," p. 55.

[3] "Los mas de ellos capitanes": Gongora.

men, charged furiously, performing prodigies of valour, without being able to make the least impression on the main body of the Indians.

He sounded a retreat, and with the loss of many of his men fell back upon his baggage, that had remained upon a little hill.

He still had time to have retreated honourably after all that he had done, and still the way was open towards Concepcion, to which place Spaniards were hastening from all the settlements. Possibly he was what the Scotch call " fey," that is, foredoomed, or possibly he once again was overruled by his young officers.

Turning towards his yet surviving men, he said, " Gentlemen, what shall we do?" This from a man who from his youth had been accustomed to command, who had fought at Pavia, in the Peruvian wars, in Panama, and all the sixteen years that he had been in Chile had never had a sword out of his hand, shows that he either thought too much about the point of honour, or that his judgment was at fault.

One Captain Altamirano from Medellin answered him, " What does your lordship wish that we should do, except to fight and die?"

That answer sealed the fate of all that heroic little band. Without a word, Valdivia, who was mounted on the best horse of all the company, charged once again upon the Indians' ranks. Forced back to his position on the hill, where he had left his baggage, he then determined to retreat. He hoped, by abandoning his baggage, to secure time to take the road towards Arauco, where he would have been safe. Most likely this plan would have been successful, and the Indians, delayed by pillaging the baggage, would have given him time to pass the marshy ground that lay between him and the road, had it not been for Alonso, his ex-slave.

He instantly issued orders to leave the baggage, for what was most important was that Valdivia should not escape. Then he sent on light armed parties to guard the fords and marshes that lay between Valdivia and the Arauco road.

The desperate fighting under a hot sun all day had tired the horses, and as they struggled through the marshes towards the open road on which lay safety, the almost naked Indians, springing up out of beds of reeds, dragged the exhausted soldiers off their tired horses that could scarcely raise a trot, and dispatched them with their clubs.

At last only Valdivia, whose horse was relatively fresh, was left alive, accompanied by a priest,[1] called Pozo, whom he refused to leave.

Possibly Valdivia might have saved himself, for Gongora says his horse was still untired. That, though, was not the way of Spanish veterans of the Italian wars.

It seemed as if there yet was hope, but passing through a marsh, both of their horses bogged down to the girths. Instantly the Indians were upon them, and dragged them to the ground. Torn from his horse and badly wounded, both by clubs and spears, they stripped him of his clothes. His helmet they could not get off, in spite of all their efforts, for they did not know how it was fastened on. Tying his hands behind his back, and with blood pouring plentifully from numerous wounds, they forced him back more than a mile,[2] pricking him with their lances, for he could hardly walk.

A veritable Via Crucis, for the heat was tropical, and in the course of years Valdivia had become very corpulent.

When he could walk no more, they dragged him by his feet, until they came to a spot near a waterhole, where all the chiefs were waiting for him. With the chiefs was another of Valdivia's slaves called Agustinillo, who took his helmet off.

Through this man Valdivia is said both by Ercilla and by Gongora to have offered to withdraw from Araucania, if his life was spared. To show him that he could expect no mercy, they at once dispatched the slave and cut him into bits. Then Father Pozo, seeing that there was no escape, took up two straws from the ground, confessed his sins with a loud voice, and gave Valdivia absolution.

[1] Un clerigo de misa. [2] Media legua.

The Indians killed him almost before he had pronounced the sacramental words.

As to Valdivia's death, Ercilla and Gongora Marmolejo differ a little. Gongora says he was barbarously tortured before death. Ercilla, that his brains were dashed out with a club by an old warrior who was afraid that the Indians would accept his terms.[1]

Thus miserably perished Pedro de Valdivia,[2] one of the great figures of the great conquest of the New World. His death was due to his own imprudence, brought about by his contempt of a brave enemy, hardly to be believed in one of such experience in every kind of war.

Gongora says of him: "This was the end that Pedro de Valdivia had, a valiant man and fortunate, up to that time. He was fifty-six years of age, and had governed Chile sixteen years. . . . He was a man of good stature, and had a smiling countenance. His head was large, in just proportion with his body. He had become stout and bulky, and broad-chested. A man of a good understanding, although not

---

[1] Cordoba y Figueroa, who, though he did not write his "History of Chile" until 1740, yet was a descendant of a captain who had come to Chile with Valdivia and probably had the traditions, takes the most reasonable view.

He says (p. 77): "Even yet the circumstances of Valdivia's death are not known with certainty. They are related variously and confusedly. There was no Spaniard who saw it."

The story of Valdivia having been killed by molten gold poured down his throat, seems modern, for neither Ercilla nor Gongora Marmolejo mentions it.

All the historians concur in one respect, in that Valdivia was killed with a club. At any rate, he could not have lived long under torture, wounded and exhausted as he was.

[2] On the 1st of February, 1554, according to the letter of the treasurers of the city of Santiago to the Emperor Charles V.:

"Carta de los Tesoreros a S.M. sobre la muerte de Valdivia y el estado del pais.

"Desta ciudad de Santiago a 10 dias de Setiembre de 1555 anos."

This document is to be found in "Tomo I. de Documentos de Gay," in the Archives of the Indies at Seville. It is quoted in "La Coleccion de Documentos de Historiadores de Chile," Santiago, 1861.

cultured in his speech;[1] liberal and gracious when he did a favour. After he became a great lord, his greatest pleasure was to give anything he had. In all things he was generous, and it liked him well to wear fine clothes, and that all his friends should be well dressed; he loved to eat and drink all of the best. With everyone he was most affable and easy of approach.

"Two things he had that smirched his virtues. One that he hated men of noble birth. The other, that he was fond of women, and usually kept a common Spanish girl. . . . God has mysteries that a Christian should ponder on. Here was a man feared and obeyed by all, as a great lord, and yet he died a cruel death at the hands of savages."

These mysteries are, indeed, well worth a Christian's ponderation, and after pondering on them, all he can do is to point to the sky as do the Moors, and say " Allah," and if he chooses and has faith, add to Allah's name his attributes, the merciful, the compassionate.

Valdivia's followers loved and trusted him, and never once alleged against him, as it was alleged against greater men than himself, in the fraternity of the conquerors, that he kept back their pay, or took too large a share of booty for himself. His loyalty to his King and country was proverbial, even in an age of loyalty. The royal fifth, a condition that the shrewd Fleming, Charles V., always inserted in the capitulations into which he entered with the adventurers who set out to carve him empires with their swords, in almost every instance without a maravedi from the royal Treasury to aid them, Valdivia always scrupulously remitted to the Emperor. Never a letter came from Spain complaining that it was not punctually paid.

Moreover, Valdivia showed great gifts as an administrator. Even his well-meant attempt to regulate the prices of commodities showed that he had his people's welfare always in his mind.

A skilful soldier, having learned his trade under so great

[1] Hombre de buen entendimiento, aunque de palabras no bien " limadas."

a warrior as the Emperor Charles V., in the best school of those days, the Italian wars, he yet adapted himself readily to the guerilla warfare of the Indies. That he was a consummate horseman, no doubt in "both the saddles,"[1] and dexterous in the use of every weapon of the times, we know from his own letters and other testimony.

Valdivia was not, as it would seem, a man of the highest talent, such as were Quesada and Cortés. His qualities were largely those of his time and nationality, though sublimated, but not exactly to the point of genius. In common with all the other conquistadores, he possessed courage above proof, contempt of death, patience in hardships, great shrewdness, the power of rising to the height of unforeseen circumstances, and the gift of leadership.

These were the salient qualities of the stout cavalier who stepped into the breach, and with such slight resources conquered Chile, where such a skilled commander as Almagro failed to compass it.

His fall was brought about by avarice, one of the infirmities that have occasionally beset minds noble on all other sides.

Only the angels are untouched by it, and even they with wings of gold, radiant and free from care, in the bright empyrean where they were born—for surely heaven is peopled by themselves alone—may now and then accumulate more happiness than they can ever spend.

Valdivia's letters, remarkable in themselves both for their clarity, the wideness of their view, and for the knowledge they display both of the country and its inhabitants, form one of the most valuable contemporary accounts of the great adventure, the Conquest of the Indies, that have come down to us.

Inferior to the five letters of Hernando Cortés in literary style and in dramatic interest—for who in all the histories of the conquests of the world had such a subject as Cortés?—

---

[1] Ginete en ambas sillas.

even the conquest of Peru[1] is pale and tame compared to it, yet Valdivia's five letters reveal a personality of extreme interest and force of character. He and his fellow conquistadores are to be judged not by the standards of our times, but by those of the days in which they lived. Judged fairly by the proper standard, Valdivia was an upright, honest man, stern, though not cruel for the love of cruelty as were some others of his day, but never hesitating to commit actions, barbarous and brutal as they seem to us, if he thought them necessary for the welfare of the colony. What pierces through all his designs, whether in the sphere of politics, of economics, or of arms, is his determination that his colony should be successful.

His faith in Chile, its soil, its climate, and its capabilities, he has transmitted to the Chileans of to-day, who in some measure resemble him in their shrewd common sense, sternness of character, and unbounded patriotism.

[1] Perhaps the conquest of New Granada by Gonzalo Jimenez de Quesada, with the dramatic meeting of the three conquistadores, Quesada, Belalcazar and Federmann, on the Sabana of Bogotá, as it were in a *coup de théâtre*, comes next in interest to that of Mexico.

APPENDIX

CARTAS DE DON PEDRO DE VALDIVIA
AL
EMPERADOR CARLOS V

(From "Coleccion de Documentos de Historiadores de Chile," Tomo I., Santiago, 1861, pp. 1-62).

I

Letter from D. Pedro de Valdivia to H.M. Charles V., telling him of the conquest of Chile, of his labours, and of the state the colony was in.

To His Catholic Majesty:

It is five years since I came from the provinces of Peru as directed by the governor Marquis D. Francisco Pizarro, to conquer and settle these provinces of Nueva Extremadura, formerly called Chile, and to explore others beyond; and in all this time I have not been able to give Your Majesty an account of what I have done in them, for that I have spent it in your Imperial service. I know that the Marquis wrote to Your Majesty how he had sent me, and a year ago, when I reached this land, I sent for help to the Captain Alonso de Monroy in the town of Cuzco, my lieutenant; he came to the governor there, Vaca de Castro, who also wrote to Your Majesty with an account of me, as did the Captain Monroy, relating, though at short length, what he had done up to his leaving here; and it is my very great fortune that my labours have come to the knowledge of Your Majesty, though indirectly, before the importunities of my letters, which, on the grounds of these labours, ask favours which I am quite certain Your Majesty will grant me in your own good time, with that bounty you are wont to bestow on subjects and vassals for their services. And though mine are not of such account as I could wish (for I would make them as great as they could be), yet do I deem myself worthy of all the favours Your Majesty may deign to bestow on me, and of those I shall ask in this letter; so far as the labours of pacifying the dwellers leave me time to draw up and send a long account of this whole land, and what I have discovered in Your Majesty's name, and am going to conquer and settle,

I beg very humbly that they be granted me, since I ask them in the eager wish that my good intentions in your royal service may bear the fruit I wish for, which is the greatest wealth and happiness that can befall me.

Your Majesty shall know that when the Marquis D. Francisco Pizarro entrusted this enterprise to me, there was none that cared to come to this land, and those that most shunned it were they whom the frontier-governor, D. Diego de Almagro, brought with him, and when he left it, it got so evil a name, that it was shunned like the plague; and, moreover, many of those that were friendly to me and were deemed men of sense, did not hold me for such a one when they saw me spending the substance I had on an undertaking so far away from Peru, and where the frontier-governor had not held on, he and those that came in his company having spent over five hundred thousand gold *pesos*, and all he got by it was to give twice as much heart to these Indians. And when I saw the service that could be done to Your Majesty by entrusting oneself to it, settling and upholding it, so as by its means to make discoveries as far as the Strait of Maghellan and the North Sea, I set to sharpening my wits, and I raised money among the merchants; with what I had of mine, and with the help of friends, I raised up to one hundred and fifty men, mounted and on foot, with whom I came to these lands, all of us on the way going through great toil, fighting with the Indians, and such other evil haps as there have been in these parts in abundance down to this day.

In April, 1539, the Marquis gave me my orders, and I reached this valley of Mapocho towards the end of 1540. I at once set about coming to speech with the chiefs of the land, and owing to the diligence with which I moved about it, whereby they believed we were many Christians, most of them came in peacefully, and served us well for five or six months, which they did not to lose the provisions they got in the camp; and in this time they built us our wood and grass houses on the plan I gave them, on a spot where I founded this city of Santiago del Nuevo Extremo in Your

Majesty's name in this said valley, when I came there on the 24th February, 1541.[1]

The city having been founded, I began to bring some order into the land, fearing the Indians would do what they have always been wont to when they got food, which is to rise, and knowing well how they would behave towards us. And when they saw us settling in what seemed small numbers to them, after seeing the many with whom the frontier-governor withdrew (as they believed, through fear of themselves), they waited at this time to see whether we should do likewise; and seeing we did not, they resolved to make us do so by force, or to kill us. And that we might be able to defend and attack, the first thing I saw to was the keeping a very careful watch, and the storing of all the food possible, so that, should they start evil ways, we should not lack of it; and so I had as much collected as would last us two years and more, for there was plenty of it.

From Indians taken on the way as I came hither I knew that Mango Ynga, the native lord of Cuzco, a rebel against Your Majesty's sway, had sent to warn the chiefs of this land of our coming, and to tell them that if they wanted us to go back again like Almagro, they should hide all the gold, sheep (llamas?), clothing, stuffs, and food; for since we sought all this, if we did not find it, we should go away. And this they did so thoroughly that the sheep (llamas?) were eaten—as people do when they are leading a merry life— and the gold and all the rest burnt; and they did not even spare their very clothing, but left themselves bare; and so they have lived, are living, and will live till they come into obedience. And as they were thus well warned, they came to us peacefully, to see whether we were going back again, so that we should not destroy for them the provisions, since they had also burnt those of former years, only leaving enough for their needs till the harvest.

In this time, among the threats made against us by some

[1] Note says: Santiago was founded not on the 24th but on the 12th of this month and year, according to the account of its foundation standing at the head of the first book of its Council.

Indians who would not come to serve us, we were told that they were going to kill us all, just as Almagro's son, whom they called Armero, had killed Lapomocho (thus they called the governor Pizarro) at Pachacama, and that therefore all the Christians of Peru had gone away. And some of these Indians being taken and put to torture, they said that their chief (who was the chief lord of the Canconcagua valley, called Chile by the men of the frontier-governor) had news of it from the chiefs of Copoyapo, and these from the chiefs of Atacama; and therefore the *procurador* of the city resolved to request the *Cabildo* to choose me as governor in Your Majesty's name, owing to the news of the said Marquis's death, whose lieutenant I was, until Your Majesty, being informed, should send orders for what best befitted your royal service. And so they and the people, all with one opinion, met together and gave their approval, giving reasons why I should accept, and I giving mine why I should be excused; in the end they overcame me, though not by arguments, but through showing me the advantage to Your Majesty, and since it seemed to me that it were best for that state of things, I accepted. With this goes a report of the election as it was held, that Your Majesty may be pleased to see it.

This done, since I did not believe what the Indians said of the Marquis's death (for they lie), that I might send to give him an account of what was happening here, as was my duty, I had gone to the Canconcagua valley on the coast to set to work on building a brig, and with eight mounted men I was giving an escort to twelve men working on it. There I received a letter from the Captain Alonso de Monroy, wherein he gave me news of a certain plot on foot to kill me among some of the soldiers belonging to the frontier-governor's party that had come with me, and in whom I had trust. When I got this letter, which was at midnight, I came away, and came to this town, meaning to go back again in two days; I stayed longer, telling those left behind to go about with care, for thus the Indians would not dare to attack them. And they, not giving heed to this, went about with little care, and by day without arms; and so they killed them, and only two escaped that succeeded in hiding, and all the land rose in revolt. I made my enquiries here, and found many guilty, but with the straits in which I was I hanged five, being the leaders, and said nothing to the others; and with this I made sure of the men. They confessed in their statements that they had made arrangements in the provinces of Peru with the persons advising D. Diego to kill me here about this time, for so they were doing there to the Marquis Pizarro in April or May. And this was their resolve, and to go and lead an easy life in Peru with those of their party, and to leave the land if they could not administer it.

I then got news that they were making a levy of the whole land in two parts to come and make war on us, and I, with ninety men, went to attack the greater one, leaving my lieutenant to guard the town with fifty, thirty being horsed. And while I was dealing with the one part, the others came down on the town, and fought a whole day through with the Christians, and burning down the whole town, the food and clothing, and all that we had, so that we were left but with the tattered clothes we had for fighting, and with the arms at our sides, and two small pigs, a sucking-pig, a cock and a hen, and about two handfuls of wheat; and, in the end, when night came, the Christians got so much courage, together with that their leader put into them, that, although all wounded, with the favour of our Santiago they put the Indians to flight and killed very many of them. And next day the Captain Monroy gave me news of the bloody victory with the loss of what we had, and the burning of the town. And with this begins the war in earnest, as they waged it against us, not choosing to sow, feeding themselves with a few roots, and a small oatlike seed yielded by a plant, and other herbs this land grows of its own accord without sowing and in plenty; and with these and some maize (*maicejo*) they sowed among the mountains they contrived as they did.

Seeing the plight we were in, it seemed to me that, if we were to cling to the land and make it Your Majesty's for ever, we must eat of the fruits of our hands as in the beginning of the world, and I set about sowing. I divided my men into two sets, and we all dug, ploughed, and sowed in due order, being always armed and the horses saddled by day. One night the one half kept watch in its quarters, and so for the other half. When the seed had been sown, some kept guard over it and the town in the said way, while I, with the other half, moved all the time eight and ten leagues around it, breaking up the bands of Indians where I knew them to be, for they surrounded us on every side. And with the Christians and people we brought from Peru in our service, I built up the town again, and we made our houses and sowed to feed ourselves. It was no easy thing to find maize for seeds, and it was got with great risk. I also had the two handfuls of wheat sown, and from them that year twelve *fanegas* were harvested, whereof we provided ourselves with seeds.

When the Indians saw we were about sowing, since they would not, they tried to destroy our sowing by driving us to leave the land. And as I saw the need into which the ceaseless war would put us, to take measures for this war, if it could be done, while we could bear with the difficulties, I resolved to send the Captain Alonso de Monroy to the provinces of Peru with five men, and the best horses I had (I could not give him more), and he offered himself for so manifest a danger to serve Your Majesty and bring me help, which if it came not from God, I could hope for from none other; seeing I knew that no men would stir to come to these lands owing to its ill report, unless someone should go from here to bring them and take gold to buy men withal. And since the country they must go through was at war, and there were great wildernesses, they would have to go lightly equipped and unsheltered by night. I resolved for the encouragement of the soldiers who were to see the land to send no less than seven thousand *pesos*, which while I was in the Canconcagua valley on the business of the brig, the Anaconas and the Anaconcillas had got from the Christians, for the mines were there, and they gave them all to me for the common weal. And that the horses should not be distressed, I made six pairs of stirrups for them, and scabbards for the swords, and two vessels for them to drink out of; and from the iron stirrups and harness, and some other few things they found, I had horseshoes made by a smith whom I had brought with his forge, with which the horses were very well shod, and each carried for himself four more besides, and one hundred nails; and with my blessing I entrusted them to God, and sent them off, charging my lieutenant always to bethink himself of the lurking danger.

This done, I saw to the measures needed for ourselves, and seeing the great shamelessness and boldness shown by the Indians owing to the little they saw of it in us, and how they harried us, killing daily at our house-doors our Anaconcillas, who were our life-blood, and the children of the Christians, I resolved to make a fence one and a half *estados* high, and sixteen hundred feet square, which took two hundred thousand bricks a *vara* long and a *palmo* high, which Your Majesty's vassals, and I with them, made by their own toil; and with our arms at our sides we worked from start to finish without resting an hour; and when the warning of Indians was given, the people and baggage took refuge within it, and in it was the little food we had by us; and the men on foot stayed for the defence, while we horsemen rode out to move about, and fight the Indians, and defend our sown ground. This went on from when the land was planted—without taking off the arms at our sides for an hour—till the Captain Monroy came back to it with help, nearly three years' time.

The toils of war, ever-victorious Cæsar, men can bear, since it is the soldier's boast to die fighting; but if those of hunger are added to them, they must be more than men to bear them. Such men Your Majesty's vassals have shown themselves to be in both regards, under my care, and I under the care of God and Your Majesty, that I may hold this land for you. And up till the last of these three years, when we have sown very well and had food in plenty, we went through the two first in very great want, so great that I could not describe it; and many of the Christians had to go sometimes to dig up roots for food in the former and the other two years;

and when these came to an end, things were as before, and all the women, our servants, and children lived thus, and there was no meat, and the Christian who got fifty grains of maize a day thought himself well off; and he who had a fistful of wheat did not grind it to take away the husks. And in this wise have we lived, and the soldiers would have been very satisfied, had I left them to be in their houses with this subsistence; but I chose to have thirty or forty mounted men always about the plain in the winter; and when the food they took with them was finished, they came back, and others went out. And so we went about like ghosts, and the Indians called us *Cupais*, which is the name they give to their devils, for whenever they came in search of us (for they know how to attack at night) they found us awake, armed, and, if needful, on horseback. And so great was the care I took in this all this time, that though we were few, and they many, I had them in hand, and Your Majesty may know we did not do it with folded hands. So much for this short account.

From the provinces of Peru the Captain Alonso de Monroy wrote to Your Majesty, when he came there with only one of the soldiers he took from here, and destitute, the Indians in the Copoyapo valley having killed the other four and captured the two and taken the gold and dispatches they carried, so that he only saved a document pledging myself for moneys. And three months after they had been taken prisoners, the Captain Monroy with a knife he took from a Christian from among D. Diego de Almagro's men, and who had turned Indian there (he was the cause of the death of his fellows and the harm that fell on them), stabbed the head *cacique* to death, and taking the renegade Christian with him by main force, escaped, both of them, on two horses, and without weapons, and (he wrote) how he found these (in the said provinces) the governor Vaca de Castro, in Your Majesty's name after the victory he had won to your Imperial good fortune against the son of D. Diego de Almagro and his followers; and how he received him very well and showed him his favour.

And since the governor at this time had much to do—in

trying the guilty, bringing peace into the land and its dwellers, rewarding services, sending out captains who asked to be allowed to make discoveries, and in giving Your Majesty an account of everything by his own messengers and in duplicate dispatches—and Your Majesty's treasury being empty, and he himself having spent much and in debt, he sought persons among Your Majesty's vassals whom he knew to be zealous in your royal service, and to have money, that they might oblige me with it at such a time, and lend it me. He found one, and a Portuguese, telling them what was needed for Your Majesty's service, and the upkeep of this land, earnestly bringing all his authority to bear, and with so great energy and good will that my lieutenant told me that he knew him to be suffering in his soul, and if he had had money, or in the present state of things it had been lawful for him to borrow, he would have given money freely, so that the people should diligently serve God and Your Majesty.

Of those that obliged, one is called Cristobal de Escobar, who has all the time been employed in those parts in Your Majesty's service; he came forward with five thousand *castellanos*, which provided for seventy horsemen. And a reverend priest named Gonzalianez lent him another five thousand *castellanos* in gold, with which he further helped the men; and both came hither so as better to serve Your Majesty themselves. And, furthermore, the governor, seeing the need there was for the speedy accomplishment of this business among the more important ones, sent off my lieutenant first, asking many proper men of parts who were ready to seek their fortune with other captains to come away with mine for the sake of the service done to Your Majesty; and on his intervention, many of them came; and so he sent him off and bade him come with that help, and he himself would see about sending another ship laden with what these provinces need, so soon as he should have done something to clear away what business had to be done.

When the Captain Alonso de Monroy came to the town of Arequipa to buy arms and supplies for the men, and told certain persons of his need of a ship, and when the governor

Vaca de Castro had sent to call the master of one to arrange with him to come to these parts, and the master would not venture on it, a dweller in that town, called Lucas Martinez Vegazo, a subject of Your Majesty's, and full of zeal in your royal service (such is the report he has in those parts), learning what was being done for Your Majesty, and the will of the governor, being a well-wisher of his, loaded a vessel he had with arms, ironware, and other goods, depriving him of the profits of his moneys (so that he lost no little in them), and with wine (for four months divine service had not been held for want of it, nor had we heard Mass), and sent it me with a friend of his called Diego Garcia de Villalon; and when this was known to the governor, sent to thank him deeply, and assure him of Your Majesty's great regard.

The governor, Vaca de Castro, among many other things wrote me of the armies that the King of France had sent against Your Majesty in various places, and of the alliance with the Turks which was his last humiliation, and that Your Majesty had taken such measures that he had had not only to withdraw but to lose certain places in his kingdom.

He also sent me the royal proclamation of the war against France, of which I was glad to be warned, although we can live in these parts very safe from the French, for the more they come, the more they will ruin themselves.

He also wrote me to send the *quintos*[1] to Your Majesty. From this letter will be seen what has been able to be done in this matter, and I assure Your Majesty that I would look on it as salvation to find in this land two hundred thousand or three hundred thousand *castellanos* for Your Majesty's service, and to meet such heavy, so just and holy outlays; and I have trust in God and Your Majesty's good fortune to be able to do it one day.

In September, 1543, Lucas Martinez Vegazo's ship reached the harbour of Valparaiso of this town, and the Captain Alonso de Monroy came with his men by land from mid-December onwards; and from that time the Indians did not

[1] Royal fifth.

dare to come any more, nor did they come within four leagues round this town, and they all withdrew to the province of the Promaocaes, and would send me messengers daily, bidding me come to fight them and bring the Christians that had come, for they wanted to see whether they were as brave as we were, and if they were, they would submit to us, and if not, then they would do as they had before. I sent them answer that I would do so.

When the men and horses had recovered, for they had arrived all weak through not having seen one peaceful Indian from Peru to here, suffering much hunger through finding everywhere the food taken away, I went forth with all the men that had come very well equipped and on horseback, to keep my word to them, and went to seek the Indians. When I came to the strongholds, I found them all fled, they having gathered towards Mauli . . . leaving all their villages burned down, and deserting the best stretch of land in the world, so that it looks as if it had never had an Indian in it. And thus we were in the month of April, 1544, when there reached this coast a ship belonging to four or five men that bought it together, and loaded it with things wherewith to earn a livelihood, and found death. For when they reached this land, only three men came, and a negro, and no vessel; for the Indians of Copoyapo had tricked them, taken the ship, and killed the master and sailors, leaving by water; at thirty leagues from the harbour near Mauli, they met with a cross-storm, and the Indians killed the Christians that were left, and plundered and burned the vessel.

In June following, which is the height of winter, and filled it with rain and storms beyond all measure, so that as all this land is flat, we thought we must be drowned. The Indians say they have never seen the like, but have heard from their fathers that in their grandfathers' time one year was like it. In the same month another ship arrived, which was the one the governor Vaca de Castro promised to send; for a servant of his named Juan Calderon de la Barca, that he (the governor) might fulfil his word, seeing how his master wished to send me the necessaries I stood in want of, and that he had not the money to do this, used the ten or twelve thousand *pesos* he had, and loaded and came with them; the ship is called *San Pedro*.

The pilot and owner of the ship, who brought her (under God) and steered her hither, is called Juan Bautista de Pastene, from Genoa, a man highly skilled in bearings and things relating to navigation, one of those that best understand this craft of all that sail this southern sea, a man of much honour, faith, and truth, and that has been of great service to Your Majesty in the provinces of Peru, and to D. Francisco Pizarro, and after his death, in their recovery under the commission of the governor Vaca de Castro, who ordered him (for Your Majesty) to come to these provinces, as being a man of confidence, who would engage in your royal service, and whom he knew to be such. And he offered himself to come to do so great a service to Your Majesty besides those already done; with him the governor sent the news from France, and the proclamation against her I have spoken of.

The rage of the winter being over, in mid-August, when spring begins, I went to the harbour, and learning the wishes of the captain, which were to serve Your Majesty here as I should order him, and learning what a person he was, and what he had done in your royal service (which I already knew, and knew him from the time of the Marquis), I made him my lieutenant-general by sea, and sent him to explore this coast as far as the Maghellan Strait, giving him another ship, and a very good crew for both, and that he might take possession in Your Majesty's name of the land; and so it was. What he found and did, Your Majesty will see by the account herewith, and that of Juan de Cardenas as head clerk of the tribunal of these provinces, whom I appointed in Your Majesty's name, and whom I sent with him on Your Majesty's service.

I likewise sent my *maestre de campo*, Francisco de Villagra, owing to his warlike experience (who has been of great service to Your Majesty in these parts), that he might drive the Indians of these provinces hither, and should give me news of those beyond. And since then I have Francisco de

Aguirre, my captain, on this side of the river Mauli, in the province of Itata with men holding the frontier. And he does not allow the Indians there to cross to the other side, and if they are caught he punishes them; and he will be there till I go forward. And (the Indians) seeing themselves so followed, and that we stay in on the land, and that ships and men have come, have their wings clipped, and now, being wearied of going about through snow and mountains like animals, they are resolved to give in. And last summer they began to build their villages, and each *cacique* has given his Indians seed, both maize and wheat, and they have sown for seed and to feed themselves, and from now henceforward there will be a great abundance of food in this land, for there are two sowings in the year, the maize being gathered in April and May, and then wheat is sown; and in December it is harvested, and maize sown again.

Since this land had so evil a fame, as I have said, I had much toil to strain the men I brought to it, and I commanded them by dint of the strong arms of friendly soldiers who chose to come along with me (although I was going to destruction, as many thought), and through what I borrowed to help those who stood in need, which was up to fifteen thousand *pesos* in horses, arms, and clothing, pay being over seventy thousand in gold, and the ship and relief men that my lieutenant brought. I owe for all that was spent a hundred and ten thousand *pesos*, and on account of the last who came, I put myself another sixty thousand in debt; and at present there are in this land two hundred men, each of which stationed here costs me over a thousand *pesos*; for to other new lands men go owing to the good report of them, and all flee from this land for the ill report those have left of her who had no will to act in it like the former. And so up till to-day, for holding it I have had to buy the men I have for gold, and I assure Your Majesty that of all this sum I have mentioned, I have no document against anyone for a single *peso* to lessen it, and all of it I have spent for the good of the land and the soldiers who have defended it, since I cannot give them here what is just and what they deserve—full freedom.

And I shall go on doing this, for I have no other wish than to discover and settle lands for Your Majesty, and no other interest, together with the honour and favours you may be pleased to grant me therefor to leave a memory and good report of me, which I won in war as a poor soldier in the service of so enlightened a monarch, who, putting his most sacred person every hour into battles against the common enemy of Christianity and his allies, has upheld and upholds with his unconquered arm its honour and God's, breaking down even their pride against those that honour the name of Jesus.

Beside this, what I have aimed at since I came into the land, and the Indians rose against me, to carry out my intention to make it Your Majesty's for ever, is to have been governor in your royal name, with authority over your vassals and over it, and a captain to encourage them in war, and be the first in danger, for so it was best; a father to help them as I could, and grieve for their toils, aiding them like sons to bear up; and a friend to speak with them; a geometrician to trace out and people; an overseer to make channels and share out water; a tiller and worker at the sowings; a head-shepherd for the breeding of flocks; and, in short, peopler, breeder, defender, conqueror, and discoverer. And for all this I leave it to your imperial judgment to decide whether I deserve to have from Your Majesty the authority that your *Cabildo* and vassals have given me in your royal name, and to have it confirmed once more, that I may do you with it much greater services.

And why I am persuaded I most deserve it is that (with the help in the first place of God) I have been able to hold my own with two hundred Spaniards, so far from Christian peoples, when that happened in Peru which did happen, though there was so much there of all that soldiers wish to have, while I had to keep them here in restraint, hard-worked, dead from cold and hunger, with their arms at their side, ploughing and sowing with their own hands to feed themselves and their children; and withal they do not hate, but love me, for they begin to see all was needful that we might live and win for Your Majesty what we came to seek.

And therefore they are raging to go forward into your land, that I may in your royal name reward their services. And since I look at what is Your Majesty's advantage, I go forward little by little; for though I have had few men, if I had the same intention as other governors have had, which is, not to stop till I find gold to enrich myself, I could have gone searching with them, and they would have been enough. But, since thus it is best for Your Majesty's service and the holding of the land, I go with a leaden foot, as I settle it and make it sure. And if God wills I should do this service to Your Majesty, it will not be too late; and if not, then let him who comes after me at least find the land in good order, for my interest is not to buy a foot of it in Spain, even should I have a million ducats, but to serve Your Majesty with them, that you may grant me favours in this land, and that after me my heirs may enjoy these, and that memory may be left in the future of me and of them.

Nor should I have wished to have had greater possibilities, unless for (the choice of) leaving or taking, for if I did not go forward with me, though I should have more men, I should have more toil to feed them. With those that I have had, often risking their lives and mine, I have carried through what is needed to have security behind me when I shall go and really take up my station where I can settle men, and where the settlement can last.

Your Majesty shall know that from the Copoyapo valley hither there are a hundred leagues, and seven valleys between, and across there are twenty-five leagues and seven valleys between, at the most, and for others fifteen or less; and for those that come from the provinces of Peru to these, the hard part of their journey is from there to here; because as far as the valley of Atacama, as the Indians of Peru are at peace, owing to the good order brought in by the governor Vaca de Castro, they will find food everywhere, and in Atacama they will take fresh supplies of it to get through the great wilderness of a hundred and twenty leagues that lies as far as Copoyapo, the Indians of which and of all the others, being at once informed, take away the food to places whence it cannot be had; and not only do not give any to the stranger, but make war on him. And since in this land all that are here and that may come can be fed, bearing in mind that in three months from now, in December (which is midsummer), there will be harvested in this town ten or twelve thousand *fanegas* of wheat, and any amount of maize, and from the two small pigs and sucking-pig we saved when the Indians burned down the town there are now eight or ten thousand head, and of the cock and hen fowl as many as blades of grass, breeding in abundance in summer and winter. This last summer I tried, with the idea of making it easier to send to Peru, to found the town of Serena in the valley of Coquimbo, which is half-way; and so skilful has the lieutenant been whom I sent there with his men, that within two months he had peace in all those valleys; the captain's name is Juan Bohon; and thereby can come henceforward from Peru hither on horseback without danger or toil.

When the Captain Juan Bautista de Pastene, my lieutenant on sea, and my lieutenant by land had come back from where I sent them, and the Indians were beginning to settle and sow, that I may go forward and seek food for the two hundred men I have, for in the territory of this town, which goes up to Mauli, there are not more than twenty-five dwellers, and it is large—thirty leagues by fourteen or fifteen—and that horses and mares may be able to come to me for the men I have, for in fighting and its toils the most of those I brought have died; (to do all this) I have this last summer put the Anaconcillas, who were in our service, into the mines, and we ourselves, with our horses, brought them their food, so as not to tire the natives before they settle; these latter are at work, and we hold them for brothers, having found them such in our needs; and they are rejoiced at seeing they reap so much fruit; and in the rubbish left by the Indians of the land where they took out gold, they have got out twenty-three thousand *castellanos*, with which, and with fresh credits (for which I made myself responsible for a hundred thousand more), I have sent to the Captain Alonso de Monroy in the provinces of Peru, that he may undertake a second task; and to make answer to the governor Vaca de Castro in that land, whom I have found in all that was for the good of Your Majesty's service to be as I have here said; and that he may tell the merchants and people, if they wish to come and settle, to come. For this land is such that there is none better in the world for living in and settling down; this I say because it is very flat, very healthy, and very pleasant; it has four months of winter, not more, and in them it is only when the moon is at the quarter that it rains one day or two; on all the other days the sun is so fine that there is no need to draw near the fire. The summer is so temperate, with such delightful breezes, that a man can be out in the sun all day long without annoyance. It is the most abounding land in pastures and fields, and for yielding every kind of livestock and plant imaginable; much timber and very fine, for houses; endless wood for use in them; the mines most rich in gold, the whole land being full of it; and wherever men may wish to take it there they will find a place to sow, and the wherewithal to build, and water, wood, and grass for their beasts; so that it seems as though God made it purposely to be able to hold it all in His hand. And I must buy horses to give to those who lost them in the war as very good soldiers till they have the wherewithal to buy them, for it is not right they should go on foot, for they are good horsemen, and the land needs them; and some mares so that with the fifty I have here at present there may be no need in the future of sending to bring horses from elsewhere. (I have sent) that he may tell all the gentlemen and subjects of Your Majesty that there are without anything to eat to come with him if they wish to find food here. And through this journey I believe the roads will be opened out and the wills of these men, and many will come hither without money and will find it here; and if not, a man who has spent the cost of the journey hither, and expects to spend what he must now, will spend it and as much besides, and end by believing in the land, and keeping it in Your Majesty's possession for ever. And he that is, as I am, in the midst of the work, has spent and looks to spending what I say; and when the work is done Your

Majesty shall see what a man can do that comes through the Strait with fresh men.

I am also sending the Captain Juan Bautista de Pastene, my lieutenant on sea, with some money and credit, to bring me from there arms, ironware, powder, and men.

I also wish to let Your Majesty know this, that I sent to establish the town of Serena, for the said reason of the road being open, and I set up a *Cabildo*, and I have there all the other proper powers in Your Majesty's name; and this I chose to do and to say. And that those I sent thither might be in good disposition, I gave them the best Indians, that I might not have to tell them to go without them to fresh toils after having gone through the so heavy ones here. And I hold for myself that when my purpose in settling it has been effected, it will be best to move away if Indians are not found behind the snowy mountains to serve there: for there are not from Copoyapo as far as the Canconcagua valley, ten leagues away, three thousand Indians; and the settlers there are now about ten in number, here one hundred to two hundred Indians, no more. And therefore it is well for me, so long as people are safe in this land, to have a dozen of my servants looking after it as a check on those settlers; and the way those valleys can be of service to their owners in this town of Santiago will be through some tribute or other, and through each one having a rest-house where the Christians that come may be sheltered and fed. And this the Indians will do very willingly, and it will be no work to them, but rather a pastime.

So Your Majesty shall know that this town of Santiago de Nuevo Extremo is the first step on which to raise the others, and by them to settle all this land for Your Majesty as far as the Strait of Maghellans and the Northern Sea. And it is from here that the favour Your Majesty may show me shall begin, for the possession of this land for ever, and the toils I have gone through to maintain it, are not such that I cannot undertake what lies beyond; for had I not made this step, and if I went further into the land without colonizing here, if men and horses did not fall from the sky, it was not to be expected many would come by land, especially so through the want of supplies. And by sea horses cannot be brought, as the navigating conditions do not suit. And if a settlement is made here, and a shift made to hold Coquimbo, all may come and go at will that wish to. And as men, though not many, are coming to me now, for protecting this place, and some horses to give those I have on foot here, I will set forth with them to see where I can feed them, and settle the country, and go through it as far as the Strait, if need be. So that this is the account of what we have been able to do, and of what I think of doing; and the reasons of what has been done, although set forth briefly.

Also, I did share out this land, when I came here, without notice, for so it was best to soothe the soldiers' minds; and I broke up the power of the *caciques* to give each someone to serve him. And the account I was able to get was of the number of Indians from this valley of Mapocho to Mauli, and many names of *caciques*. And the truth is that these have never been able to serve since the Inca did not conquer beyond here, and all the chieftains were named on the people's choice, the number of Indians under each being twenty to thirty; and I appointed them thus after the war was over, and I have been to visit them. I am beginning to put things in order, taking their Indians away from the leading *caciques*, doing my best that what natives there are should not scatter, and that this land may be kept going. And I will take with me forward all those who here had something, and leave it behind, assuring Your Majesty that in particular and for no private interest of mine I shall not do injury to anyone; and if what is done shall seem to some to be an injury, it will be in the service of Your Majesty, and for the general weal of the land and its natives, whom I treat in accordance with Your Majesty's orders for the ease of your royal conscience and mine. And for this there are four priests, three of whom have come with me—whose names are Rodrigo Gonzalez, Diego Perez, and Juan Lobo; and they understand the conversion of the Indians, and give us the sacraments, and make good use of their priestly office.

Father Rodrigo Gonzalez, a *bachiller*, is very profitable in all things with his wisdom and preaching, since he knows the matter well; and all are of service to God and Your Majesty.

And so, victorious Cæsar, the great need of this land and its upholding and continuance, and discovery—and the same is true for that beyond—is that for the next five or six years there may not come to it from Spain through the Strait of Maghellan any captain sent by Your Majesty, nor from the provinces of Peru, to disturb me. To Peru I am so writing to the governor Vaca de Castro, who, indeed, does in all what is best for Your Majesty's service. To Your Majesty I here make this request and prayer, for should men come through the Strait, they cannot bring horses, which are needed, since the land is as flat as one's hand. And when men are not used to the food here, before they turn their bellies into skin-bags to profit of it, die, the half of them, and the Indians soon finish off the rest; and if they saw us disputing about the land, it is so brittle that it would break, and the game could not be started again in this life. I tell Your Majesty the exact truth, and may I find it and Your Majesty always on my side, that as to what I wish for, no one may come to turn me aside from Your Majesty's service, nor disturb me at this time, as this wish of mine is to use the life and means I have, and may have, to discover, settle, conquer, and pacify all this land down to the Strait of Maghellan and the northern sea, and find in it what subsistence I can for Your Majesty's vassals I have with me, and reward them for all they have done in it, and have your royal conscience and mine at ease as to them. And after this is done (which is my main aim), that Your Majesty may have an account of my services and of myself as is right, for I have done and am doing them towards your imperial person; and that I may be allowed to hear and see through Your Majesty's letters that they are acceptable to you, and that you deign to hold me among your loyal subjects and vassals, and servants of your royal house— and I can wish for no more. If Your Majesty shall choose to give the whole land to another or to others to govern without leaving any share to me (or with such as you may see fit to choose), I say that, if and when I am sure it is Your Majesty's will, I shall put in possession of it all, or of that part, that person whom Your Majesty shall send in command to me through the shortest letter signed by your imperial hand, or by the lords presiding over the Royal Council of these your Indies; and until Your Majesty can know this, and chooses to send me answer, I shall hold the land as up to now, and with the authority given me by your *Cabildo* and people. And if I see opposite orders to this given, I shall lay it away, and become a private soldier, and serve him who shall come with fresh instructions to these parts in your most sacred name, and with the zeal and the will with which I have done so in the past, and am now doing for Your Majesty. And these favours are those I said at the beginning of my letter I should ask for as a reward of the small services I have done up till now, and of the much greater ones that I wish to do all my life to add to the heritage and royal revenues of Your Majesty.

I mention one thing to Your Majesty, and beg for it very humbly, and that is if you choose to give this land to some person who asks earnestly for it, as having done services and making representations of them to your imperial consideration, let it be on condition that he make himself responsible to my creditors for the two hundred and thirty thousand *pesos* that I owe, and for the hundred thousand I am further asking them to lend me, and which will likewise be spent, and for the others which I shall have spent on behalf of the land and its maintenance; for up till now I have had no more from it than the seven thousand *pesos* which the Indians of Copoyapo took from the Captain Alonso de Monroy, the first time, and the twenty-three thousand that I send now also for its benefit to Peru; and this only so as not to lose credit, and as being reasonable, and according to my conscience. And I have no wish to leave with more substance than the knowledge that Your Majesty's service is being done in these matters, for I should in doublet and hose with sword and cape again undertake fresh service for Your Majesty with my friends, when I have not given what is just and what they deserve.

Once more and again and again, I beg Your Majesty (since I have begun the said work) that no dispatch be sent me till I send the account of the land, and write fully with my own messengers and duplicate dispatches, and till the *Cabildos* (write) likewise with an account of all that I and they have done in your royal service, and till I send to ask of you the favours, exemptions, and privileges which Your Majesty is wont to grant and which are the deserts of those that serve you well, and that you be pleased to give orders that no new steps be taken here; and if such has been done that an end be put to it, for so it is with Your Majesty's advantage, and for me it will be a favour such as I cannot properly prize or describe, for I would not that at the time my services will be accepted by Your Majesty some hindrance should come about without my wishing to be the cause of it, whereby everything will be turned to the contrary in your imperial sight.

I am so bounden to the Marquis Pizarro of blessed memory for having sent me whither Your Majesty can hear of my services and of me that I cannot repay him by setting his children so long as I live in his place; and since they have lost the care of such a father, who put such zeal into Your Majesty's service with such fruits for the growth of your royal heritage, that they may have advantage from such worthy toils.

I humbly beg Your Majesty to bear them in mind, granting them such favours whereby they may support themselves as the children of their father.

The bearer of this letter is called Antonio de Ulloa; he is esteemed by me and valued by those that know him for his deeds and bearing as a gentleman and nobleman, and such he has shown himself in these lands in your royal service, spending the means he has won, and found here to come and serve you in them; and therefore he is in debt and obliged to pay in his land to come in my company, and bring very good horses and arms to serve in the war, as he has served as a very good soldier, for he is skilled and practised in warlike things; and he has spent all for the good of this land, and therefore I handed over to him in Your Majesty's name two thousand Indians, and putting on one side the justice of his having them for his services, on their and many other accounts he deserves the favours Your Majesty may be pleased to grant him in these parts, both to him and to the person you may choose to send there to enjoy through him the fruits of the toils he has gone through in all this land. He is going away now when he should have had the satisfaction of gathering the fruit; and since the reason that moves him to go back to his own land is such a just one, I am letting him go, for were it not so strong in him, and he so pleased at going, if he waited until I had repaid him for his services in Your Majesty's name, or had given him as many gold *pesos* as should be rightly his that he might live there on the scale befitting him, I should not send him away from me. He has had letters from Spain from his kinsmen by the first ship that came here, wherein they told him that his elder brother, who had inherited, and had taken his father's place to support the house, had died childless, and so that the house should not die out by leaving the direct line, he is going to wed to leave someone to inherit it after him, so that its memory may not die. And so while I gave him of the little I had, and gladly, yet I should have wished to give him much. I gave him the leave he sought; and since I am on the road, and so busied about what I have said, and cannot send an account of the land until I have wherewith to give a good one, I am writing this letter for him to hand to Your Majesty, so that you may know the state I am in, and give orders that my prayers may be attended to. And since from him may be learned all that which I do not speak of here, I end by very humbly making prayer to Your Majesty in all he shall say and beg for in my name (being convinced he will say and act like the man he is), that you will have all the credit given him that you would graciously give to me myself.

Since the ship needed careening and hauling up dry, and there was no material for this in this town, while in La

Serena there is a certain pitch which God gives with his dew and which is yielded in plenty by certain plants (it is like wax, and said to be very fit for this purpose), therefore I am going thither to send off to Your Majesty, and to Cuzco while the caulking and putting to rights is being done, so as not to lose time. And I am leaving my second-in-command so that, meanwhile, he may see that the men are ready to leave when I come back, which will be the sign for the messengers to leave, and the ship be already; and she is so now, and I am sending her off, and she is leaving with the help of God and his blessed Mother, and to Your Majesty's happiness.

* * * * *

And may this letter come safely before your imperial consideration, and the election, and confirmation of possession, and the messenger, that Your Majesty may hear what my purpose is in your royal service. I have already spoken to the chiefs, and told them to serve the Christians very well, for if they do not do so, I shall send now to Your Majesty and Peru to bring me many men, and that when these have come I shall kill them (Indians) all. This is what I want them for, and beyond there are as many as blades of grass to serve Your Majesty and the Christians. And that if they behave like dogs and evil men towards those I brought, not one will be spared, and the snow will be of no help to them, nor to bury themselves alive in the earth whence they came, for I shall find them out there; therefore, let them see to it how they (the Christians) fare. And since they know me and up to now I have never told them anything that has not come true, and myself done as I have said, they feared, and do, indeed, fear; and they answered that they want to serve right well in all that I shall order them. And not even thus will they deceive me, for I shall leave measures of precaution here till forces come, and when all is safe, take away all the men here; and they (Indians) will serve the town of Santiago with a tribute to their lords, and by keeping up rest-houses on the road. And so I shall go away and come back to it with the blessing of God and of Your Majesty (for which I beg), whose most sacred person may Our Lord preserve for long years, with the headship and rule of Christendom and the monarchy of the world.

To His Catholic Majesty. The very humble subject of Your Majesty, who kisses your sacred feet and hands.

PEDRO DE VALDIVIA.

La Serena,
4th September, 1545.

II

Letter written to the King by Pedro de Valdivia from Lima on 15th June, 1548, giving an account of the fleet he had got together, and with which he was going forth from that harbour to the provinces of Nuevo Extremo.

MOST HIGH AND MIGHTY LORD,

Having come to this kingdom from Nueva Castilla, and the camp of the licentiate Gasca, President of that which in Your Highness's name was holding out against the tyranny of Gonzalo Pizarro and his fellow-rebels, I wrote to my lord, our monarch and emperor, holding it sure that the letter would go to his sacred hands or to Your Highness's, while I am not certain that any of those have gone which I have written up to now, and in which I gave an account to His Majesty and Your Highness of what I did in his royal service in that kingdom and government of Nuevo Extremo, and of the great expenses which came to me, and do come every day in maintaining, settling and exploring it, being steadfast in Your Highness's royal service—from a ship that by a great chance went to that country, I learned of the rebellion of these kingdoms and the tyranny of Gonzalo Pizarro; and I at once set about coming to Your Majesty's service, as I have always striven to do, and have been doing for twenty-eight years. When I had come to the headquarters of Your Highness, the President gave me charge of the camp, together with the General Alonso de Alvarado, and as I aimed at Your Highness's service, and to be ever more deserving in your royal eyes, I did as he ordered in Your Highness's name, and on my own side tried to do all that lay within me that the tyranny should not make any advance, and that there should be as little damage and as few deaths as possible of Your Highness's vassals. God was pleased to grant that to the imperial and royal happiness of our monarch, and Your Majesty, and through the mildness of the President, and the care of the captains in his camp, Your Highness won the victory with the death of only one man. The President executed Gonzalo Pizarro, and those he found most guilty, and he does the same daily to those deserving it; for Your Majesty may believe it that no one could have been sent to these kingdoms who should understand better than he how things are here, nor by whom Your Highness could be better served.

The vicissitudes of these kingdoms being at an end, when the President came to know what I have spent in Your Highness's service in the support and settling of that land, and the exploring of that beyond—over three hundred thousand *pesos*—and learning of my great wish to serve Your Majesty, he made me, in your royal name, governor and captain-general of that government of Nuevo Extremo, by virtue of the powers he had for that from our Cæsar, for the whole of my life, laying down to me as the boundaries of the government from 27 degrees to 41 degrees north-south meridian, and from east to west a distance of a hundred leagues, as is set forth at greater length in the provisions he gave me in virtue of his powers; and of them he sent an authorized copy together with the Instruction of Your Majesty's Tribunal of Audience established in these kingdoms. And he likewise gave me the orders (*capitulos*) which I asked of the President, and those he gave me in Your Highness's name. All of these he sent to Your Highness's royal council, so that they may be seen there, and Your Highness may command as you deem best.

From the statement sent to Your Highness you will see what I asked to be granted me; it was not all granted, as Your Majesty's commission only went so far. As a humble subject and vassal I beg of Your Majesty to give orders to send me your royal decree to confirm what the President gave me, and together with it to give orders for the favours to be granted me I ask for in the statement; for although Your Majesty has not the whole account of my services, they will be so acceptable to you that you will decide to grant me favours, for even if I had not spent three hundred thousand *pesos* in maintaining, settling, and exploring that land, only for that I have maintained it, when it had so evil a name as it had after the frontier-governor Almagro came back from it, and because of the will and strong desire wherewith I undertook the journey and offered to spend what I had on Your Majesty's service in any reasonable matter, (for this) Your Highness will order all favours to be shown me.

Besides the expenses that fell on me in maintaining the land, others have fallen on me, to come to Your Highness's service on this journey, and bring the fleet I am bringing; for, so as not to cause loss to the dwellers of this kingdom, very few men will go overland, and the most of them will go by sea, and for this purpose there will be, together with the galleon and galley that were in this harbour, belonging to Your Highness's royal navy and which I am bringing, likewise two other vessels, that cost me, apart from what I put into this land—which was more than eighty thousand *pesos* —over sixty thousand more.

The President sent hither, ordering Your Highness's officers to value the galleon and the galley, and the victuals there were, and give them to me, I undertaking to make payment to the officers at the time we arrange here; and the value was fixed at twenty-seven thousand odd *pesos*. This I am bound to pay to Your Highness, whom I humbly beseech, since all is spent in your royal service (I have no other wish but to spend it on this), to send them your bidding not to charge me for it; since I ask only for life to spend it in Your Highness's service.

I ask Your Highness to have the favours looked into which I ask for in the statement, and to order them to be granted to me, since Your Highness is wont to reward those who serve you, and grant them even more than the favours arising out of their services, and for that Your Highness will find it true that with what I have spent on this journey (whereon I have come to serve you), and the charges of the fleet I am bringing, the cost to me since I undertook the enterprise in your service has been over four hundred thousand *pesos*, which I hold for well laid out, it having been in Your Highness's service.

When I set to explore the coast, as I wrote to our monarch, and to take possession of the land in Your Highness's name, the ship I sent reached the neighbourhood of the Strait of Maghellan; and if it is Your Highness's wish that the Strait be sailed through, send me your orders to do so, for the navigation is nothing (under God's will) if Your Highness is served thereby; since even though I have to make efforts for this greater than those already made for the greater service of Your Highness, I will bring it about that from the day when Your Highness's orders shall come in a very short while there shall be a ship in Seville which has come through it; for in these kingdoms we all believe most surely that Your Highness's service will be thereby done, and the kingdoms enlarged.

May our Lord keep and exalt Your Highness's most lofty and powerful person, adding many kingdoms and dominions to it, and is the wish of us, Your Highness's vassals. Done in the city of the kings of Peru, 15th June, 1548. Most high and powerful lord, this humble subject and vassal who kisses the royal feet and hands of Your Highness.

PEDRO DE VALDIVIA.

III

Letter from Pedro de Valdivia to the Emperor, giving him an account of his doings in the government of Chile, and of his journey to Peru.

TO HIS CATHOLIC MAJESTY:

After having served your Majesty as was my duty, in Italy, in winning the State of Milan, and taking prisoner the King of France in the time of the famous Colonna, and of the Marquis de Pescara, I came to this part of the Indies in the year 1535. After labouring at the exploring and conquest of Venezuela following my wishes, I went on to Peru in 1536, where I served in the subduing of those provinces to Your Majesty with the post of *maestre de campo general* to the Marquis Pizarro, of good memory, until they were at peace both from the differences among the Christians, and from the rebellion of the Indians. The Marquis, being so zealous in Your Majesty's service, and knowing my disposition for it, opened me the door thereto, and with a letter and grant he held from Your Majesty (given at Monzon in the year 1537, countersigned by the Secretary Francisco de los Cobos, of Your Majesty's Secret Council), to send to conquer and settle the government of Nuevo Toledo and the province of Chile, as having been abandoned by D. Diego de Almagro who came thither—he appointing me for this purpose to fulfil it and hold the land as governor, and all the others that I might discover, conquer, and settle, until Your Majesty's pleasure should be known—I obeyed and gave up my mind to the task of winning for you such a land as this; and this though it was no ill-famed expedition, owing to Almagro having come away from the land and left it, though he took with him so many and so good men. And in Peru I also left food behind, as the Marquis had it, and that was the valley of Canela in Charcas, which was given to three *conquistadores* (being Diego Centeno, Lope de Mendoza, and Bobadilla), and a silver mine, which since has been worth over two hundred thousand *castellanos*, without having any profit of it, nor did the Marquis give me such towards the expedition.

Taking my leave from the Marquis, I left Cuzco in January, 1540; I journeyed to the valley of Copoyapo, which is where this land begins, passed the great wilderness of Atacama, and a hundred leagues farther to the valley known as Chile whither Almagro came, and turned back, wherefore this land got so bad a name. And for this reason, and that this name might be forgotten, I named that which he had discovered, and that which I was able to discover up to the Strait of Maghellan, Nueva Extremadura. I went on ten leagues, and founded, in a valley called Mapocho, twelve leagues from the sea, the city of Santiago del Nuevo Extremo, on 24th February, 1541, setting up a *Cabildo* and a tribunal of justice.

From that year down to this day I have sought to give and succeeded in giving Your Majesty the whole account of the people and the conquest of this city, and of the exploration of the land beyond, and its prosperity, and of the great toils I have gone through, and the so heavy expenditure I have made, and which falls on me daily when I go forward with so good purpose. I have written at times, by the messengers and when I shall say here, to show that what was possible for me I have done with that good faith, diligence, and duty which I owe Your Majesty. And that my letters and reports have not reached your imperial notice has not been my fault, but the fault of some of the bearers, as having been evil-minded and gone through a land so free, prosperous, and unquiet as Peru has been, while others have had their dispatches taken from them by the Indians on the long journey, and death has done this for the rest.

The settlement having been made, I brought the natives to a peaceful state by the war and conquest I waged on them; and while they had the purpose of serving us (for they at once seek treachery and rebellion, this being very natural among all these barbarians), I saw to it that the church and houses were built, and a good ward kept over all that needed it. To send for reinforcements and give a report to Your Majesty I ordered a brig to be built, and God knows what toil this gave. When it had been built, the Indians burned it for me, and killed eight out of the twelve Spaniards watching over it, owing to their disobeying the orders I gave them; and in one moment the land rose in rebellion against me (all this happened within six months); and they began waging a very hard war on me. Seeing the impossibility of doing otherwise, I sent by land, with much toil and risk for those that went and us that stayed, the Captain Alonso de Monroy, my lieutenant, with five mounted men, for I could not, nor would he allow me to, give him more. He left me in January, 1542; when he reached the Copoyapo valley the Indians killed four of his followers and took him and the other one[1] prisoners, taking from them eight to ten thousand *pesos* they had with them, and tearing up their dispatches. After three months the two killed the head chief, and fled to Peru on some of the horses the Indians had taken from them, and as they were on the edge of the wilderness they managed to escape, by the will of God, through their efforts. They came to the town of Cuzco during the government of Vaca de Castro, at the time he had routed the followers of Almagro's son, and taken him prisoner.

There he set about getting leave from Vaca de Castro to take men for this land; he got sixty mounted men, and with them came back to where I was; he was just two years on his journey. He got twelve thousand *pesos* of clothing and horses to bring these men to me, and equip them, and a ship on which he put four thousand of them. I paid here to the persons who let him have them eighty thousand odd *castellanos*.

In January, 1544, the Captain Alonso de Monroy was back in the town of Santiago with the sixty mounted men;

[1] Note in original: His name was Pedro de Miranda; see Gongora, Chapter IV.

and the ship he sent from Peru had cast anchor in the harbour of this town, which is called Valparaiso, four months earlier. My business in these two years was warlike operations and harassing the natives, and giving them no rest from them, and seeing after our victualling and guarding the crops; for we being few, and they many, we had much to do; and he found me so busied.

While the men were resting for a month, and rejoicing us all by their coming, I pressed the natives so hard, not allowing them to live or sleep quietly, that they had to come in and serve us, which they have done ever since.

While I was thus busied, in July of this year 1544, there arrived at the said harbour of Valparaiso the Captain Juan Bautista de Pastene, a Genoese, pilot-general in this South Sea for the lords of the Real Audiencia at Panama, with a ship of his own, which, to serve Your Majesty and through the action of the governor Vaca de Castro, he and a servant of his loaded with goods to come to the help of this land; and on them he laid out about fifteen thousand *pesos*. I bought of these goods for eighty thousand *castellanos* odd, which I shared out among my men for their use.

In the following September of this year, 1544, knowing the good will with which the captain-pilot Juan Bautista de Pastene had come, and offered himself to me to serve Your Majesty and me in your imperial name, and his fame as a pilot, and his skill and experience in navigating this sea, and exploring new lands, and all his other attainments needed for Your Majesty's service and the weal of all your vassals and of this land—I made him my lieutenant-general by sea, sending him at once to explore for me one hundred and fifty to two hundred leagues of coast as far as the Strait of Maghellan, and to bring me interpreters from it all, and so put him to work. And at the end of this month he had gone and come back on the commission I entrusted him with on Your Majesty's behalf.

Having heard the report given me by the captain and those who went with him of their voyage, and of what they took possession of, and of the wealth of the land, the abundance of men and cattle, and the reports given me by the interpreters he brought, I set about putting in the mines the Anaconcilla and Indian women in our service that we had brought from Peru, and to help us they went with good will. It was no small a task, for there were five hundred of them; and we carried them their food with our horses from the town, which is twelve leagues away, sharing equally with them what we had for the support of our children and ourselves, and which we had sown and gathered by our own hands and toil. All this was done so that I might again send messengers to Your Majesty, giving an account of myself and the land, and to Peru, that further help might be sent me for entering upon it and settling it. For without gold, it was impossible to bring a man, and even with it it would be no small work to bring one, owing to the privileges and amount the Spaniards have been given in those provinces, and the reputation this land has got for itself.

After nine months had been spent on the mines, and sixty thousand *castellanos* or a little more had been got out, I resolved to send off the captains Alonso de Monroy and Juan Bautista de Pastene with his ship, so that the one by land and the other by sea should try to bring me fresh supplies of men, horses and arms; and in this ship I sent one Antonio Ulloa, of Caceres, being with the reputation of a gentleman and nobleman, as messenger with the dispatches for Your Majesty. In them I gave an account of what there was to give you about myself and about the conquest, settling and exploring of the land. The gold that had been got was distributed among the three and two others, merchants, who also went to bring things needed, that Ulloa should have the wherewithal to go to Your Majesty, and the captains and merchants some possibility to bring what help they could.

I arranged with the men I had, while some of them looked after the getting of the gold, and the guarding of our goods, for the settling of the town of La Serena on the sea-coast at a very good harbour in the valley called Coquimbo, as being halfway on the road from the Copoyapo valley to where is the settlement of Santiago, which is the gateway for the men of Peru to come to serve Your Majesty in these provinces without risk. And I went there (Serena), and the *Cabildo* and Tribunal of Justice was established, and I appointed a lieutenant. And from there on 4th September, 1545, I sent away the messengers and said ship, confident that at the latest I should have an answer from Alonso de Monroy within seven or eight months; and for this end he took Indians from this land who offered themselves to come from Peru to where I should be with letters in four months or less.

When the ship had sailed from the town of Serena, leaving a strong guard there, I went back to Santiago. In the January of 1546, I gave orders that gold should again be got, as in the last time, for that year more wheat was harvested than in former years, and since it seemed to me the help could not be delayed I resolved to go and explore fifty leagues inland to see where I could plant another town; so soon as the captains had come back whom I had sent to engage men. I picked out sixty mounted men, well armed and lightly equipped, and set about my exploring, leaving instructions that the gold was to be worked while I was on my journey with the help of God, thinking the beginning of the inhabited land was farther off than when I found it.

On the 11th of February of the said year I left and went thirty leagues, which was land which obeyed us, and which we had ridden over. Ten leagues farther on we came upon a numerous population, and at sixteen leagues we met warriors who came out to defend the ways against us and to fight. We rode over the land, and those Indians that I took I sent as messengers to the *caciques* near, bidding them to peace. And on the morning of one day, three hundred Indians came out to fight with us, saying they had been already told what we wanted, and we were few, and they were going to kill us. We fell on them and killed fifty, and the rest fled.

That same night, a quarter after prime, there fell on us seven or eight thousand Indians, and we fought with them for over two hours; they defended themselves against us savagely, packed together in a squadron like Germans; in the end they turned, and we killed many of them, and their leader. They killed two of our horses and wounded five or six, and as many Christians. When the Indians had fled we spent what was left of the night in looking after our horses and ourselves; next day I went four leagues, and came to a very great river where it flows into the sea, called Biubiu, and half a league wide. Having seen a good spot for settlement, and the great quantity there was of Indians, and seeing I could not keep my ground among them with so few men (and I also knew that all the land on both sides of the river was coming upon me, and if misfortune befell me, I risked losing everything behind me), I came back to Santiago within forty days of leaving it, to the great joy of those that had come with me, and those that stayed to guard the town, seeing and knowing that we had so fair a land near, and with so many dwellers, where I could pay them for their toils and reward their services.

When I got back I was assured by the Indians who served the town of Santiago, and by those of the valleys who served in Serena, that they were somewhat anxious at my going onwards, and were certain that as the Indians were many and we few, they would kill us all; and therefore they had been waiting and watching so as when they heard of anything to attack the settlements and rise again; God chose to defeat their thoughts. I at once sent to Serena to tell them of my return and of the fair land I had found, whereat they were no little rejoiced. The following May I had a great quantity of wheat sown, believing for certain men would not be long coming, so that we should all have plenty to eat; and so with God's help we sowed widely.

It was seven months since my captain had gone to Peru, and I had no sure news or letter from them; and I had a vessel made ready which I had built for fishing with nets in the harbour so that seven or eight men might go to Peru if needed.

I shared up this land, as I founded the city of Santiago, without having real information about it, for so it was best so as to appease the minds of the *conquistadores*, and I separated the *caciques* to give each someone to serve him. And when afterwards I went about conquering the land and setting it at peace I got a true account and saw how few people there were, and that the few Indians there were were divided into sixty or so villages; and if this had not been remedied, the most of them would by now have been scattered and killed. I resolved, for the perpetuation of the Indians and the support of this city (for it is the gateway to the country beyond, and is where the men that have come and shall come to settle and conquer it do restore themselves)—I resolved to reduce the sixty odd *vecinos* to half, and divide up all the Indians among these, so that they should be somewhat better able to take into their houses those that come to help. I did this because of the good land I had found, which could very well feed the *vecinos*, when I took away the few Indians some had and distributed them amongst the others; and I assure Your Majesty that no better or more profitable thing could be done for the land to last long and be a support to Your Majesty, and that the natives should not scatter.

In August eleven months had gone by without my hearing anything from Peru. With the gold which some of my Indians had mined and that which the men had themselves, and all lent me (some of their own accord), I sent another messenger to Your Majesty, whose name was Juan Davalos, a native of Garrubillas, with copies of the dispatches taken by Antonio de Ulloa, and with what there was besides to tell of my journey, and the land I had found, and that he might bring help to anyone of my captains he might come upon on the way standing in need.

This vessel, as I say, left, taking nearly sixty thousand *pesos* belonging to me and others, which were it going elsewhere than Peru, was a great amount; but as that land has been, and is, so prosperous and rich in silver, they would hold that to be a small amount; while we here held it as much, since each *peso* cost us a hundred drops of blood and two hundred of sweat. They sailed from the harbour of Valparaiso in September of the said year, 1546.

As I awaited help any day, my care and concern was to see to the sowing of maize and wheat at their due times and to get the gold which can be got with the small means we had, so as to send always for men, horses, and arms, this being what we needed here; for as to the rest which we came to seek, so that there be no lack of men, there will be plenty of it, with God's help.

Thirteen months after the vessel had left the harbour of Valparaiso with the messenger Juan Davalos, the pilot and captain Juan Bautista de Pastene reached it again from Peru, standing in great need of food, and in a ship that was no more than a hull, without even a *peso* of goods, nor anything of the kind. Having lost all hope of seeing him again, for I held it sure (for they had been so long delayed that it was now twenty-seven months since they left these provinces, and I had had no news of them) that the ship and all had been lost and drowned—when I saw him, I was so overcome by joy that tears came up from my heart, when I bade him welcome; I clasped him as I asked him the reason for so long a delay and how and where the friends were he had taken with him. He answered telling me he would give me an account, and he had much indeed to tell me, and I should be filled with wonder in Peru, and that God had allowed the devil to have those provinces in his hand and those in them. And so they sat down, he and his fellows, to eat, whereof they had the utmost need.

He told me of how in twenty-four days' time they came to the Royal City, and learned of the arrival there of the Viceroy Blasco Nuñez Vela with the *ordenanzas* and *oidores* to establish an Audiencia, and of the deprival from the governorship and imprisonment of Vaca de Castro, and of the imprisonment of the Viceroy by the *oidores*, and of his being at liberty; and of how Gonzalo Pizarro went in pursuit with many soldiers against him to Quito, and how the Captain Alonso de Monroy died when landing, who had the most of my money; and that Antonio de Ulloa resolved to change his plans, and instead of going to Your Majesty and taking the dispatches, opened and read them before many foolish and presumptuous youths (as he showed himself there to be), and mocking at them, he tore them up; and through the favour he found in that town with one Lorenzo de Aldana, who was a cousin of his and who had been made his chief justice and lieutenant in the whole land by Gonzalo Pizarro, during his march against the Viceroy, he tried to have my gold which the dead man had left sequestrated until he should go to Gonzalo Pizarro and give an account of this land; and so it was done, and he at once went off to go into his service. He arrived there in time to be in the battle against the Viceroy, when the latter was killed, and for that service, with the favour, too, shown him by one Solis, who was his cousin and Pizarro's head steward, when he said he wished to come to me with help, and asked him for authority and leave to do this under a bond, he gave him the leave, and an order whereby he was to take all my gold wherever it might be found; and under this order he took what Alonso de Monroy had left, and laid it out in getting men to bring me, as he said.

When Antonio de Ulloa left for Quito, Lorenzo de Aldana gave orders under a penalty to the Captain Juan Bautista that he was not to leave that town. He was glad to have stayed until he had news of the Viceroy, and of how Pizarro's journey should end, although some signs he saw did not leave him without the suspicion that some business was afoot between the two cousins against my own interest. And meanwhile the news came of the Viceroy's defeat and death, and of the journey made by Ulloa, and of his representation of the greatness of his services in having been in the battle against the Viceroy. And I give my word that if those on the other side had been all of his kidney they (U.'s side) would not have won, he coming with greater presumption and prouder thoughts than he had brought from here, and always speaking ill of me. Aldana, seeing that these two who were bent on my harm might be useful for him, with the victory, too, they had won, gave fresh orders to the said Captain Juan Bautista, under pain of death and confiscation, not to leave the town without his express command; and he took the ship away from him.

At this time the *maestre de campo* Francisco de Carvajal seems to have arrived at that town, coming from Callao, where he had defeated one Lope de Mendoza and Diego Centeno, who were going about together with men stirring up those provinces of Callao, Charcas, and the towns of Cuzco and Arequipa against Pizarro; and he killed Mendoza, and took his followers prisoners, while Diego Centeno fled, and got into such hiding that he could not find him, although he sought him with the utmost diligence. And he got dispatches from Pizarro of his victory over the Viceroy; and news from others, who wrote him about how Ulloa was working against me with the help and favour of Aldana and the head steward Solis, his cousins. And when the said Captain Bautista went to call on Carvajal on my behalf, saying how we knew each other from Italy, and had been friends there, and that he held me for the best soldier that had come to these parts and would do for love of me whatever he could, having a great wish to forward my interests, he answered him, Why had he not gone to Quito to see about my interests? He made answer that it was because Aldana had forbidden him, under pain of death, to leave that town, and had taken his ship away from him; and since Carvajal was circumspect and experienced, and served Pizarro willingly, he hated Aldana, knowing him to be cautious, not at all brave, much too presumptuous; and not having the courage to undertake what they wished (declaring themselves to be my enemies), he showed that it was a great grief to him that under the law of friendship they were planning a Galalon-like[1] evil deed against one that trusted them. And so he said to him: "Know, then, captain, that Aldana and Ulloa are aiming at Pedro de Valdivia's death so as to govern, in the uttermost secret; and they want to make use of my lord the governor's friendship for Pedro de Valdivia to get the men, for they know that if it is not for Valdivia, he would not for anyone else at this time let one man out of the land, if it were for the sake of his own father

---

[1] Note in original: Adjective formed from Galalon, the traitor in the romances of the " Twelve Peers."

who should be where Valdivia is; and it is best for you to keep quiet, for they stand in great favour, and if you reveal everything that it may be remedied, you will not be believed, and they will kill you, and might thus carry out their aims. And when Valdivia hears, I know him to be such a man that he can make head against persons with teeth, and much more against these skinned rabbits; and if you do not save yourself for the business, I know not how it will go with him. Therefore take the advice I am going to give you for love for Valdivia and yourself, for I hold you for a man of truth and discretion: go at once to where my lord the governor Pizarro is, and I will give you leave to. And as the Captain Valdivia served the Marquis Pizarro, his brother, he bears him goodwill, and as you too were an old servant of his, he will do for you what you shall ask, so long as it is not to take away men from him, nor arms from the land, for he needs them; and those which Ulloa shall take away through the favour shown him by his cousins, not through love of Valdivia, but in his own interest. And as you are prudent, I do not say more to you. Set to work, having the favour of leave to go away alone with such sailors as you can get, and one ship, giving it to be understood that Aldana and Ulloa are friends of Pedro de Valdivia, saying to Ulloa that you will go as his captain, keeping him quiet with what money you can and with words till you get out to sea. And when there do what you see to be best for him who sent you, putting no trust in Ulloa not killing you like a coward, you being without heed owing to his protests of love towards you." And so he went off to Quito to see Gonzalo Pizarro; and while he went along the coast, Ulloa was coming to Los Reyes over the mountains. When he reached Quito, he asked for the permit, and an order was made to give it him, and he at once went back to Los Reyes. Pizarro told him that as he held me for a friend, he was sending me help by sea and land with Ulloa; that he was adding to all he was doing for me by consenting to men being raised at such a time, saying he had not relaxed for Hernando Pizarro, his brother, who had been here, while he had for me, owing to his love and esteem for me. And in truth he gave leave to those he held to be suspect, who belonged to the army that had been with the Viceroy, although Ulloa had for his officers and captains ten or twelve of the hottest and noisiest partisans of Pizarro, who had done very evil things in that land, and were coming here to sow that seed; and he urged the Captain Juan Bautista to be the friend and companion of Ulloa. He answered him he would do no more than what he should order him, with which he was very content; and with this he went back to Los Reyes. And as Ulloa held the Captain Bautista as very experienced, and did not trust him, he took the ship and put a captain of his own on her, and one on another ship that was loaded with merchant's goods, and had aboard ten or twelve married men with their wives, who had leave to come here to get away from the fire in that land; and he sent them both away to go up to the harbour of Tarapaca, which is two hundred leagues above Los Reyes, and await him there as he came with his men by land.

When the Captain Juan Bautista came to Los Reyes with Pizarro's permit, and saw he had no ship, and that they had indeed taken her from him, he showed it to Aldana and Ulloa, asking them to let him have her back; and when they saw it they did not dare to go against it, but told him he could go away when he should choose, since such was the order of their lord the governor, Pizarro; but that they could not give him the ship, since she was sailing with the things needed for the march, and they only took her from him as being in need of her; believing that once it was done he would not find the wherewithal to buy another, and while he was looking for it, Ulloa thought to come hither and carry through his evil.

When the Captain Juan Bautista saw how things were, he decided to keep them in check by making a partnership with Ulloa for merchandise, and spending with him the money he had, telling him it would be a very good thing that those two ships should go on beforehand, for when they had arrived here he would buy another, and he would come with merchandise so that they might help and do good to one another; and with this Ulloa took his leave, though not very pleased with the permit held by Juan Bautista, as got known later, and with some suspicion that following out his plans, he would contrive to get in front of him, although he should be left behind without money or ship, and with no one to lend him any, as he thought, for he was confident that Aldana in this case would put all the hindrances possible, as he did.

The Captain Juan Bautista managed the personal credit so well he had in that land from when he served the marquis that he found a man to sell him a ship for one thousand or so *pesos*, for which I should pay here seven thousand in gold; and with another two thousand he raised at the same rate he provided himself with provisions and supplies for the voyage, and with thirty men (soldiers and sailors with permits) he sailed away. He took six months to reach Arica and Tarapaca. During this time Ulloa and his two ships were between Tarapaca and Atacama; there the Captain Juan Bautista learned of how Ulloa had unfolded himself with his officers and advisers with great secrecy how he was coming to kill me, and was sending the two ships ahead that I might have been tricked by them when he should arrive; for when once I was dead he would share out all the Indians among those eight or ten, and the land he would give to Gonzalo Pizarro; and that for this reason if the Captain Juan Bautista should come with him, he would kill him as being certain that he could not bring him to his side; and with this reward he promised them, and through the land being given to Pizarro, all were satisfied, and very ready to carry out his will.

While Ulloa was making these decisions, the Captain Juan Bautista came in sight of his two ships with his one; he set about arranging with his friends to get him killed by some trick, and sent to greet and congratulate him, bidding him welcome, pretending to be greatly rejoiced, and asking him to come ashore and see him on such and such a day, for he wished him to take the other two ships with him. There was not found lacking a man who ventured himself on a raft and came and told him of Ulloa's intention and the trick he was going to play on him; although he was well informed.

When the Captain Juan Bautista answered the messenger he could not leave his ship, but must go on his way, and Ulloa learned of the answer, he started threatening him, and flung ashore there all his clothing and women, this coast being without water or sandy shores, wherefore nearly everything was lost; and he embarked with fifty musketmen to attack the captain's ship, and kill him if possible, or sink the ship. God willed that although they came in sight of him, they could not weather him, owing to Captain Bautista's seamanship being better than the one in command of Ulloa's ship; and so the former got ahead and left the other behind and out of sight.

The said captain told me further in his report how, after fighting the battle with the Viceroy and killing him, Gonzalo Pizarro seized the land, saying and swearing that, if Your Majesty would not give it him, he would hold and defend it, and that he had seized also Nombre de Dios and Panama, with a great fleet, and leaders, and men. This seemed to me so foul and hateful a deed that I stopped my ears, did not like to listen, and my body shook, that so low a man, so forgetful of his allegiance, should have not only spoken, and thought of it, but indeed have practised so abominable a treachery against the power of so great and so Catholic a monarch, his natural lord and King. I felt it so much that throwing aside all the losses, interests, and works that might come to me, with no thought beyond Your Majesty's service, I at once resolved to go to Peru, since I was confident in God and in Your Majesty's fair fortune, and that only with the trust given me by the faithfulness and duty I have towards your imperial and royal service, I should be an instrument to cast him down from that overweening madness, brought about by weakness and want of judgment and Lucifer-like pride.

I was grieved while the Captain Juan Bautista told me all this, that the ship in which he came had not reached the harbour of Valparaiso, but left it twelve leagues away, for not being able to come because of the strong south winds, he went ashore there with eight or ten men to come and give me the news, fearing that Ulloa, seeing him sail on, might have journeyed (by land) with a few lightly equipped men to carry out his evil aims; or at least might have put evil thoughts into those here, so that they should destroy us all and the land, and thinking he would reach the harbour with the ship if he (Ulloa) delayed any longer, so that his long labours would have been in vain.

Meanwhile, there arrived by land at the town of Santiago, eight Christians, and among them a servant of mine I had sent to Peru in the ship carrying Juan Davalos. They came in such a state as to seem from the other world, on some very weak mares. They gave me news of Ulloa, whom they had left at Atacama; and told me that as he could not overhaul the Captain Juan Bautista's ship, he turned the soldiers out of his and put aboard the women again he had turned out, and sent both ships off to Los Reyes. He would not let them come hither, although those in them wished it. He put on them captains from among his confederates, and he went back to Charcas, because the Captain Alonso de Mendoza (who was there for Pizarro, as has been said) sent to tell him to come to him with all his men, for Gonzalo Pizarro had written thus to him, and he was to write in turn to him (Ulloa), for he had need of his friends, and it was time for them to help him, for he had news that there had come to Panama a gentleman from Your Majesty, and that his captains had handed over to him (this gentleman) the fleet, although he did not believe it. And come what might, that he was resolved not to let him or any other that might come into the land, and he was confident he would succeed. And so he went off, and got no further satisfaction, for he already feared my coming from here, as he knew he could not escape me if I passed the wilderness.

When he went away, at the request of his friends there, he left in Atacama twenty men who wished to come hither, and among them were three or four who had sixty mares—the best and most needful and profitable goods that could come into this land. And as Ulloa could not do a good deed, when he gave them leave to stay, he took away the good horses they had with them, their armour, and lances; and this was the cause of their ruin.

Since there were so few people in Atacama, and the Indians being warlike, and they so hampered with mares, having few servants, they went into the wilderness, hoping to restore themselves in the Copoyapo valley; and as the Indians there had learned of the Atacama Indians that the captain had gone back, and that there were not more than twenty Christians, and unarmed, and Peru in revolt, they fell on the men as they came into the valley and killed twelve, while the others escaped badly wounded, on some unbroken mares. When night came they got out of the valley and reached the town of Serena, leaving behind all their clothes, mares, negroes, servants, and five or six small children. And the reason why they were not all killed was that the Indians of the valley got news from others that came with orders that Christians were coming out of Serena, and therefore did not follow them; and so they reached the town with the likeness of men lost through the toils and hunger they had gone through, and through their wounds. Of these and other things far worse Ulloa, I say it, was the cause, and Solis, his cousin, through favouring him, and Aldana, through his advice to him.

On the 1st of December, 1547, the ship arrived, and anchored in the harbour of Valparaiso, and on the 10th of the month I was embarked with ten noblemen, whom I took with me to go and serve in the provinces of Peru against Gonzalo Pizarro's rebellion, to serve him who should come on Your Majesty's behalf and with your authority to put them under your imperial and royal obedience.

I there appointed the Captain Francisco de Villagra my *maestre de campo*, since I held him a true servant and vassal of Your Majesty, and eager in your imperial service, as my lieutenant-general, charged with the defending, pacifying, and maintaining of the towns of Santiago and Serena, and

Your Majesty's vassal, and of all this land, and preserving the natives of it, as I had always done, while I should be away on the service I have said in Peru, and the return to this land with God's help; leaving him thereunto the instructions which seemed to me best for the good government and support of all. And I sent him at once to the town to present the ordinance in the *Cabildo*, and be received by it; and I waited that day in the ship until he had been received by them, and proclaimed in the town square. I got news on the morning of the third day that it (the *provision*) had been obeyed and fulfilled by the *Cabildo*, and they sent me their letters wherein they declared to Your Majesty how they were going to serve you, and see to the weal of all, and the maintenance of these provinces.

So soon as I saw the answer from the *Cabildo*, I asked Juan de Cardenas, the *escribano mayor* on the tribunal of these provinces of Nueva Extremadura, who was present and coming in my company, to bear witness for me, so that it should appear at any time before Your Majesty and the lords of your Royal Council, Chancellery, and Audiences of Spain and the Indies, or before any gentleman who should come with your royal commission to the provinces of Peru, (to bear witness) how I was leaving in these provinces of Nueva Extremadura the best directions I could for them to be maintained in Your Majesty's service, and was sailing in that ship, named *Santiago*, for the provinces of Peru to serve Your Majesty and any such gentleman (see above) against Gonzalo Pizarro and his followers in rebellion against your imperial service, and against all those who should presume to make an attempt, and to wage war against all and each with arms in hand, war by fire and sword, until they should lay down their arms and come of their own will or by force into the obedience, subjection, and sway of Your Majesty, and should all have been tried and punished (according to their guilt) with the rod of justice. And I asked the persons who were going with me and another ten or twelve gentlemen and nobles living in the said town of Santiago (who were there to take their leave of me and go back to their houses) to be my witnesses, and told them I made this declaration that it might always be known that I was the servant and loyal subject and vassal of Your Majesty, with no reserve, but as I should be. And therewith the persons left who were to go ashore in the boat, and going back aboard, I gave orders to make sail on the 13th of the said month, carrying forward Your Majesty's fortunes, and with the will to use my person, life, and honour, and a hundred thousand *castellanos* I took from here, and what else I could find in Peru by pledging myself (the sixty thousand belonging to me and to friends who had given with good will, and the forty thousand that I borrowed from other ten or twelve private persons—one thousand from one, one thousand five hundred from another—leaving orders that they could gradually be paid back out of what my gangs should get out of the mines, which would be twelve to fifteen thousand *pesos* yearly clear), and to spend it and lose it all with my life in your imperial service, or with both to destroy all your faithless and vile vassals.

I came in two days' sail to the town of Serena, which I had founded at the edge of the land, and went ashore, but stayed only a day. I gave orders to the lieutenant and the *Cabildo* for what they were to do, and how they were to guard themselves from the natives, and obey my lieutenant-general in everything, telling them how I was going to serve Your Majesty against Gonzalo Pizarro's rebellion, and of my eagerness; I went on board again on the 15th of the said month, and went on with my voyage. Hoisting sail, I ordered the sailors to throw overboard a great lot of plants they were bringing from these parts to Los Reyes, so that they should not use up water; telling them I should not stop until I found myself beside the person coming on Your Majesty's behalf; and so they threw them away.

On Christmas Eve I cast anchor in the harbour of Tarapaca, which is in the provinces of Peru, eighty leagues from the town of Arequipa and two hundred from Los Reyes. I had the boat lowered with half a dozen stout men who were to keep afloat to look after it, while one only was to land to find out from Indians what was happening ashore, or from a Christian. The man who landed (we were all to be seen) found two Spaniards, who told him that fifteen days before Gonzalo Pizarro, thirty leagues inland from there at Callao, had with five hundred men, who were no longer with him, defeated the Captain Diego Centeno, who led one thousand two hundred against him, and that he was more powerful than ever in Cuzco, and held the whole land. Being asked what news there was from Spain, they answered that there was said to be in Panama a president (the *licenciado* de la Gasca, he was said to be), and that Gonzalo Pizarro's captains had handed him over the fleet, but he had no men nor followers, and that I could be sure he would not come inland; and if he did, he and those with him would be killed, for Gonzalo Pizarro had sworn by Our Lady that at Candlemas he would be in the city of Los Reyes to meet him.

After having this report, I raised anchor and set sail the same night, and in eighteen days reached the neighbourhood of the city of Los Reyes, and learned how the President had landed there and was on his way to Cuzco with his men against Gonzalo Pizarro. I went into the harbour, and went off to the city with all the stout men I had with me; I left the ship with Your Majesty's navy, to be used like the others; I sent word to the President with all speed, letting him know of my arrival and of my purpose to serve him in Your Majesty's name, and I begged him to await me, as I should not stay in Los Reyes more than eight or ten days to buy equipment for the war. And so he did do, and I did not stay longer, and bought arms and horses and other things needed for myself and the good men of my following. And in this, and in helping other good men to go and serve Your Majesty, I spent in the ten days sixty thousand *castellanos* in gold; and so I set out with all to come to the President, making the journey in one day for which he had taken three, and thus I caught him up in Your Majesty's camp in the valley called Andaguailas, fifty leagues from Cuzco.

When the President saw me he showed great joy, and received me very well, setting great value in Your Majesty's name on the journey I had made and the toil I had taken in coming at such a time, and he said before all that he thought more of me in person than of the best eight hundred fighting men that might come to him in that hour; and I gave him my thanks, bearing him great gratitude therefor. He at once gave me all the authority that he held from Your Majesty for warlike matters, and handed me over the whole army, and put it in my hands, begging and praying for his and Your Majesty's sake all those gentlemen, captains and men, and ordering them to obey me in all my orders as to the war, and to carry out my commands as they would his own, for this was Your Majesty's pleasure; and so the whole army answered it would do; and he told me he entrusted me with Your Majesty's honour. I humbled myself and kissed his hand in your imperial name, and answered him that I took on myself your imperial and royal authority, and would use it in Your Majesty's service, and in defence of your victorious army with all the energy and wisdom and skill to be found in me in warlike matters, and with him and such gifts I trusted in God and in Your Majesty's good fortune to restore him the land, and set it under your obedience and lordship, and overcome Gonzalo Pizarro and his followers so that they might be punished according to their crimes or be left lifeless on the plain. And so the whole army rejoiced greatly with me, and I with it. Hereupon I showed the document I drew up in the harbour of Valparaiso before the *escribano mayor* of the tribunal, and the certificate he gave me showing how I was coming to seek him and serve him in Your Majesty's name; whereof he was mighty well pleased, it seeming to him to combine well the so great regard and confidence he had formed as to myself, with my faithful will and toils in the service and duty I owed Your Majesty; and he took it and said he wished to keep it to send to Your Majesty; and so he had it.

I at once inspected the companies, both the mounted ones and those on foot, and I made the musketeers into a separate one, and I set the squadrons in such order as was needed and was best for the march, having them supplied with powder and match, and with pikes and lances, and all the arms there were, so that each man should use them at the proper time, and putting the artillery where it was to march, and giving it the orders it must carry out daily; the General Pedro de Hinojosa and the Marshal Alonso de Alvarado being always with the army when on the march, and I used to ride ahead with such men as I chose over the ground, pitching the camp where it was best. From here I wrote to Your Majesty; my letter went with the dispatches which the President sent on 12th March, 1548.

In such wise and in such good order did Your Majesty's army march each day the distance which seemed to me fitting; sometimes great, owing to snow being gone through, whereby it might be harmed through the cold and want of food; other times the distances were small that the men and horses might be rested; and so we came to a great river, called Aporima, which is twelve leagues from Cuzco.

In a distance of twenty leagues there are five bridges over this river for those that come from the direction of Los Reyes to cross it, and from our direction; and all had been burned. This was done that the enemy might be gathered to stop our crossing, knowing where we should have to make it. Eight leagues before the army came to it, I had captains sent to all five with musketmen, and they were to make the material for the bridges, which are (of the kind) called rope-bridges; they are made of osier-like rods, woven together ten or twelve paces longer than the breadth of the river to be passed, and two *palmos* thick, six of these are enough for a bridge, being tied above afterwards to other lines; and in this wise the men and baggage were to cross that river, and the horses were to take their chance thrown into the river, which flows very deep down among the mountains, and is swift, and with no ford. And when the ropes had been woven, they were on no account to throw them to the other side of the river until I myself should come. And having given this order on Maunday Thursday, I went down to see how it stood with the bridge and the crossing, and having seen it, I gave orders to Lope

Martin, who was he that was making it, that he was not to throw the ropes or anything else to the other side till I came with all the forces, or should come again to where he was. And on Good Friday I went back to Your Majesty's camp, and the President and all the other commanders joined in begging me to give my opinion; and I told them that it would be best to strike camp at once, and that we should get across at that place as quickly as possible. On Saturday the preparations were made, and on Easter Day in the morning the Marshal Alonso de Alvarado and I went forth, and started marching with the vanguard.

At eight o'clock we came upon a Dominican, Brother Bartolome, who was riding at great speed up the mountain, and gave us the news that Lope Martin, as it seemed to him that it was worth taking the risk, and he knew not what risk he was taking, had thrown the bridge across on Saturday afternoon, and that the enemy had come that night and burned it; and all our men who had been making it had fled with Lope Martin, and he was lost; and there was no way of getting across there. When I saw how ill my charge had been kept, I told the captains of the musketeers who were with us to follow me; there was no time to tell the President who was with the rearguard; and so two hundred musketeers with the Captain Palomino came with me. I left the artillery up above a league from the bridge, and I sent down the Indians who were drawing it with four or five small pieces to defend the bridge should any men attack from the other side. In two hours under the sun I got there, and we saw the men who were on the other side, being twenty Christians and a few Indians, who managed that same night to throw down a worked pillar that was on the further side, of the kind used for fixing these bridges. And by doing this they gave us great trouble, for we had to go through twelve or thirteen leagues of snow to get to another bridge, and the army was very weary. And by going up to this other bridge we left the enemy behind us, and they could come to the city of Los Reyes, where Your Majesty's army could not support itself, for within a month all the food from the land would be used up, and when this was done Your Majesty's army could not feed the animals. On this I often spoke with the President, and some that could not see the difficulties nor understand them, through too little experience and too much presumption, complained a great deal of me for making them march as was needful (for on my word to Your Majesty, and with the truth I owe, if I had delayed one hour in telling the President of the destruction of the bridge, I do not know what would have befallen us; and to carry through my purpose I had to have God's help). And when I got, then, to the bridge, those who were on the farther side, seeing so many men coming down, went off upwards a league away. When I saw this, I made five musketeers swim over to the other side with a cord tied to a woven rope; and I set to work that night to make three or four rafts, and from midnight on I started all the noblemen with me on crossing over; and so two hundred men came across, whom I kept without eating a mouthful until they had dragged up all the woven ropes. I made the friendly Indians make ropes and other useful gear, for everything had been burned, and a great quantity of things for various purposes was needed, and for fastening the woven ropes (carrying the bridge).

Next day, the second Easter Day, at midday, the President and the whole army arrived. I made so much haste, without ever leaving the place, that on the last day of Easter the bridge was ready. On this same day I called the President thither, to near the bridge, and said to him: " Sir, it is my wish to cross and take the heights, for if the enemy take them from us, we shall see ourselves in difficulties to climb them." He told me to do so for the love of God, and that I should look to it that Your Majesty's honour lay in my hands. I answered him that I would lose my life, or carry everything through as it should be, and then at once, in his presence, I called the Marshal Alonso de Alvarado, and told him not to leave that bridge, and that the fighting men were to cross over it, without letting any baggage cross, until all were on the farther side, that the enemy should not come near it, and throw us into confusion; and that the horses were to be thrown into the river, as they had begun to do that same day; and so I crossed the bridge in God's name, and to Your Majesty's good fortune. And halfway up the mountain I came upon a soldier called Juan Nuñez de Prado, who was fleeing from the enemy's camp; and he told me that Juan de Acosta was on his way to defend the bridge against us with two hundred and ten musketmen and eighty on horseback. I said to him: "Go on to the President." I got up to the top, and took up what seemed to me a good position, where, should even Gonzalo Pizarro have come with all his army, I should have defeated him, although it was already night, and I had but two hundred men. Seeing which, and that the Captain Acosta was half a league away, I ordered the signal to be sounded at one in the morning for our men to come to my help; and so the signal was handed on to where the President was, and within two hours I had five hundred infantry with me, the four hundred musketmen, and fifty cavalry; and I kept them in readiness like a squadron all night.

Next day the whole army was gathered together; we stopped here two days. The enemy's forces were five leagues away, in the valley called Jaquijaguana. After two days, we went forward two leagues. There for another day, getting rid of all the sergeants, by myself I put the army into such order as seemed to me the right one. Meanwhile I sent out scouts, so that each day we might keep in one another's sight. When the order I have spoken of had been carried through, the marshal and I went out to where the scouts were (which was near the enemy's camp); we skirmished with them, and drove them all back into their camp. When I had very well seen the position they held, and the one it behoved us to take up, I said to the marshal: "Let us go back to our forces, although it is late, for we must bring them here, and to-morrow I promise you on my word, without using a lance, to scatter the enemy, and drive them from where they are." And so we went back and struck camp (it was already settled down for the night), and set it up in the said position, giving orders that all men were to keep in their squadrons as they had come, and that food was to be brought them there without their going to their tents; although all cursed Valdivia, and him who had betrayed him, for it was very cold, especially for the mounted men, for I had ordered them to keep their horses on the rein. And this whole night neither the marshal nor I got off our horses, and at midnight we made ready four companies of musketmen, which, after the President handed me over the army, I had ordered to be ready for when we should call them. And so at dawn we sent out the Captain Pardave with fifty musketmen under him to engage in a skirmish with the enemy towards our rearguard; and this he did. When it was day, the marshal and I heard Mass, and told the President what was going to be done; and we told him that the musketmen had no match, and were all shouting; and he went from man to man, so that if they had mattresses with cotton, it might be made into thread. And we told him the men must stay in their squadrons as they were, for we with the musketmen were going down to take a position we had seen the evening before, and when it was taken we should at once let the army know so that it should come down; and so we went down with the musketeers, and took the position. And I at once called Your Majesty's servant Geronimo de Alderete, and sent him to the President to tell him to bring down the artillery at once, and the army, as the position was taken, and what I had promised him many days before I would do; which was that not thirty of His Majesty's men should be killed. And as soon as Alderete came to where the President was, the artillery started to move and the army behind it; four pieces reached me where I was, which was a height commanding the enemy's camp, under which our camp was to be. And when these four pieces had come, I put them into position, and they had to be aimed by me, for the artillerymen were not as skilful as they should have been. I was so quick about firing, and with such good aim, that I drove all the enemy back within some works they had in their lines. The friends they had struck all their tents and camp, and began to flee from the other side of their camp to a very lofty height, and Christians behind them, some to Your Majesty's camp, and others seeking to escape. In this way Your Majesty's army was able to take the position which suited us, and which I wished, and when it was thus taken, I went on foot, for I could not on horseback, down to the level, where the position had been taken; and I ordered the artillery to come down after me, and I set it all together at a place where we could harass the enemy, but they could not do so to us. The fear brought on them by the artillery was so great, as Carvajal told me afterwards, that there was no one who could keep order among them; so that they were defeated, and Gonzalo Pizarro had to come and give himself up to a soldier, and beg that he should not be slain, while Your Majesty's army suffered no hurt. This matter being over, and the ringleaders taken prisoners, who were dealt with there, I went to the President in the presence of the above marshal and of the general Pedro de Hinojosa, and of three bishops and all the captains and gentlemen of the army, and spoke these words to them: " Sirs, I have carried out my word and bond, which I used to give you daily, and that which I gave the marshal yesterday, that I would break the enemy without losing thirty men." And the President answered this with: " Ah! Sir Governor! What a lot His Majesty owes you!" Now till then he had only called me captain, and the marshal said I had done far more than I had said. And therewith I handed back to the President the authority he had given me from Your Majesty for all the said purpose, and to all the captains and men I gave thanks for the good deed they had done in Your Majesty's service through having obeyed me with so much love and goodwill in the orders I had given them in your imperial name. And giving thanks to God for His mercies to us, we set to taking our pleasure, and the judges to trying the rebels. Of my services to Your Majesty on this day (the President is a man of conscience, from what I know of the integrity of his character, and a true servant of Your Majesty), of this case, I am sure, he had given, and would give, a true account.

The rebel Pizarro and some of his leaders having been tried and dealt with where they and their followers were routed—which was done in two days—the President went off to the city of Cuzco to take steps to bring the much-needed order into the land. I went with him, and was fifteen days in Cuzco, and during them I received the grant he made me of the governorship of these provinces in Your Majesty's name, in virtue of the powers he held to that end. And when I asked him for some favours as a reward for services he told me he had no powers to do more in my case than he had done, and that I must send and make request to the Real Consejo de Indias for them, for he could not but be a good friend to me with Your Majesty. I asked to be allowed to take men by sea and land from those provinces to come and serve Your Majesty in these, and this he granted me and every mark of favour. And seeing what I had spent in that journey and undertaking, and how I was in debt, having nothing wherewith to equip myself with ships, he gave orders to Your Majesty's officers to sell me a galleon and a galley from the fleet that was in the harbour of Los Reyes, and to give me credit for the cost, for I was going to put my fleet in order, and see about leaving, and that with all speed. And from Cuzco I sent a captain with eighty horsed men to go on ahead to the Atacama valley with all speed, and to gather together all the food possible, that they and the men I should bring might be able to get across the great wilderness of Atacama. For in three months from then all the food in that valley would have been gathered in, and if they had not taken it from the fields, the natives would not have time to hide it from us. And so we left together, the captain for Atacama, and I for Los Reyes. I sent other captains to the town of Arequipa to raise men and await me in those parts with them; and another to Las Charcas to do the same, and to go on to Atacama with such men as he could get.

I went to Los Reyes. Your Majesty's officers gave me two ships for two thousand eight hundred *pesos*, and I bought another, and I put the fleet in order and got all ready in a month. And since at the time I was sailing navigation there is highly wearisome and slow, to save time I left Geronimo de Alderete, Your Majesty's servant, as my deputy *capitan general* in it, to bring it up the coast, and I went ashore at Nasca, and came to Arequipa by land to take over the men my captains had, and go with them to Atacama.

When I got to Arequipa I did not stay there longer than ten days, that the men might do no damage, and I went on my journey with the men my captains had on the coast back to the valley of Arica, whither I had ordered my fleet to come; for if I got there first I would leave orders for it to go on with its voyage.

On the last day of August, 1548, I left by land, with the men I found in Arequipa, to continue on my way. While I was going on my journey, and came to the valley called Zama, I was met by the General Pedro de Hinojosa with eight or ten stout musketmen; I received him with the joy befitting a servant of Your Majesty's and friend of mine. I asked him why he had come. He answered me the President had been told that I was going along robbing the land, and harassing the natives, and that he had been ordered to come and look after me, and inspect the coast, and find out what was going on. I asked him what he had found out about all that. He said that it was to the contrary, and that he had also learned from the dwellers in Arequipa how well I had behaved towards everyone, and that he would like me to go back and see the President. I asked him whether he knew it to be necessary, and told him that if he was sending me the order, I would go at once back, but if it were not so, what was the good of my toiling to go back such a long and wearisome road as that to Los Reyes, a hundred and forty leagues of shifting sands; and what I most feared (I said) was the damage the soldiers might do while awaiting me in my absence; and I was already at the very farthest point of inhabited Peru; and perhaps the President would not be glad when he should know all the difficulties that might arise through my coming back. And herewith we left there for another valley called Tacana; and I also told him that if I did not go back I might succeed in founding a town the following Christmas, and if I went back I could not do so before another one and a half years; and they should see the disservice done to Your Majesty and the so evident damage to myself. The general said he would go thence to his house in Las Charcas, and I should go on my way; when I had come to Atacama two or three days later, one morning, having stationed the stout men who were with him with several loaded muskets in the courtyard of my lodging, he came into my room and handed me an order from the Royal Audiencia, wherein I was told to go back to the town of Los Reyes to give an explanation to Your Majesty of the charges that had been made against me, and were recited in it; and I do not know why the General Hinojosa should have denied having the order, for I had already willingly told him I would go back if ordered. My captains, who were there with forty mounted men and as many more musketmen, began to be disturbed. I at once gave orders that no one was to stir, for I must obey and carry out that order as a servant of Your Majesty's, and I told the general we would leave at once; and so I gave orders for saddling, and went back with only four stout men; and within four hours I arranged who should stay and guard my house in that valley till my return, and for a captain to take all those men to Atacama, for by the time they got there, I should, with God's help, have returned to them; and we left. We reached Arequipa in seven days; there I learned my galley was in the harbour of that town; we went on board so as to go quicker by her than on land; and the galleon had passed Arica, and the other vessel I bought had reached the city of Los Reyes in ten days. When we came to anchor in its harbour, and the President heard of our arrival, he came out to meet us on the sea. I told him that I was only grieved because of the trouble that had been taken in drawing up the order, for if I had been written an ordinary letter I should have come back at once. He was exceedingly obliged to me on Your Majesty's behalf, saying that he was well aware and satisfied, that all was untrue he had been told about me, and jealousy; but that he rejoiced that I had obeyed with such patience and humbleness, and given a very great example whereby others should know how to obey, a thing more needful at this time and in this land. I told him I should do the like always at any time, even should I be at the world's end, I should come at full speed on His Majesty's orders, and those of the lords of his Real Consejo de Indias; for I held obedience to be the first piece in my armour, and I had no will other than my King and natural Lord's, and to follow him always, without asking any other reason. I stayed a month with the President resting, and then he gave me leave to go, and I went on my return journey by land with but ten good men. I reached Arequipa on Easter Eve; a sickness came on me from the weariness and toil I had gone through which brought me nigh the end of my life. Our Lord chose to give me my health after eight days, and the feast days being over, though I was not properly convalescent, I set off for the valley of Tacana whence I had come. I went eight leagues farther to the harbour of Arica. There I found the Captain Alderete with the galleon which was awaiting me, and as the President had asked me to stay there the least possible time, that the men who were going wandering about the land on the pretext they were coming to go along with me should not do damage in those provinces, and because the silver which was to be taken to Your Majesty was in Las Charcas, and he could not bring it to Los Reyes until I should have left with all the men that were thereabouts. Having reached Arica on the 18th of January, 1549, on the 21st I was under sail to come back to this government. And so I went on board the galleon called *San Cristobal*, which was making water in three or four places, with two hundred men, and with no other food but maize and fifty salted sheep, and without a flask of wine or other refreshment, and on a very difficult voyage; for since the north winds do not come so far, and there are very stiff south winds, the voyage has to be made by strength of arm, and towing, going ahead three or four leagues a day, and other days losing twice as much and sometimes more, and before us were two hundred and fifty leagues, and as the voyage from here to Peru is pleasant, so is the return voyage full of toil.

When I left Los Reyes by land I left the galley there with a captain, that he should bring me her laden with men, and leave as soon as possible; for she needed caulking and careening, and I could not, and ought not, to wait to do it.

When I set out on my return the first time, the President had not finished dividing up the land; and as each one thought good fortune would fall to him, men had no wish to come and seek a living, although for two hundred shares that were unfilled there were one thousand five hundred seekers, and so only a few could draw a lot; and when I went back the strictest of the men were spent with waiting for the reward that could not be given them; and only a few could follow me, and these on foot, by sea; and I was not so rich I could help them, nor in a state to borrow. And so they stayed to await a better time, and I left with all possible speed, and I assure Your Majesty that the land was in so bad a state when I left to go back, and the people in so ill a mind owing to their many grievances, through there not being cloth in it to clothe any but those the President clothed, that many men of leading (though not of goodness) planned to kill the President and marshal, and the captains and bishops in his train, and when they had done so, to come to me and take me as their leader to rob Your Majesty's silver which lay in Las Charcas, and to seize on the land as was done before; and if I did not choose to do it of my free will, to make me do so by main force or kill me. And they told me of all this by hints, setting before me the injuries I had had to suffer and was suffering, it not being just that one should be so injured who had done such service as I had, and a thousand other grievances. When I answered that to go back again at Your Majesty's orders was no injury, but a favour shown me, and when I heard them, and saw whither their disposition was taking them, I dealt with the situation in the way of giving them to understand the contrary, believing they would be ever molesting me to trick and win me over for their own interests, and wishing to know what my opinion in this matter was. I used to answer those who made such discourse in general to me, telling me that this was what everyone in the land was saying, that I was the servant and friend of all, and if your Majesty's authority were stripped off me, no more than a poor soldier, and as much alone as the asparagus; while if I had any worth it was owing to my loyalty in your imperial service, and it was not to be thought of that such doings could be looked for from such loyal vassals, especially when they were being heaped with favours for the so great victory won only a few days before over the rebel Pizarro; and I told them that if, because I had been an instrument (under God's will) in destroying such an abomination, and bringing peace and rest under the allegiance of Your Majesty to the land, they thought I was of some worth—then they were to know they were under a mistake, for neither did they stand in need of me, nor would I follow them; and if for our sins God had not lifted his anger from that land, I should rather allow them to tear me limb from limb than through stress, through my own will, or through any interest to commit so abominable a treason, since the principle that brought me honour and profit was to serve Your Majesty by will and by deeds, showing it to you as I was declaring it by words. And in all this I ran a risk, and might have run a greater, if I had not used a good temper and bearing towards all; for at that conjuncture it was not wise—the minds of the men being so roused—to threaten or punish them, but wisdom lay in appeasing them as I did, and leaving the land quickly. God (who is at my side) gave me so good a voyage that after embarking under the necessity I have spoken of, and in a so ill-conditioned ship, in two and a half months I reached the harbour of Valparaiso. Great was the joy in the city of Santiago on hearing I had come.

Ten or twelve days after I reached the harbour, the galley came in that I had left in Los Reyes; I stayed one and a half months waiting for my lieutenant, Francisco de Villagra, who was in the Coquimbo valley punishing the natives; for while I was out of this land the Indians of Copoyapo and all those valleys had gathered, and slain over forty men and as many horses, and all the dwellers in the town of La Serena, burning it and destroying it, when the captain was already in the land whom I sent on ahead from Cuzco with the eighty men. And when he heard of my arrival he came at once and gave me an account of what he had done to administer the land in Your Majesty's service while I was away, and the work he had done to this end, which I am sure must have been very great.

I at once left for the city of Santiago, where I came on Corpus Christi. There came out to greet me the *Cabildo*, the tribunal, and the administration and all the people, with great good will and joy; I showed them Your Majesty's decree wherein you made me your governor and captain general in these provinces; and meeting in your *Cabildo* they gave it their obedience and fulfilment, and gave these to me by virtue of it as their governor and captain general in your imperial name; it was proclaimed publicly in the town square with all the fitting ceremony and rejoicing they could show.

Then I sent a captain to settle once again the town of La Serena, and I gave dwellers, and established a *Cabildo*, tribunal, and administration; and had those valleys punished for killing the Christians and burning the town; and so they are very peaceful and ready in service. It was founded again on 26th August, 1549.

This done, on 9th July I sent off the above lieutenant, Francisco de Villagra, in a frigate with thirty-six thousand *castellanos* I had been able to get among friends, to bring me some help in men and horses; for those who, in Peru, had nothing to do would now be more inclined to leave that there was a captain to bring them away; and (I sent him) to give an account to the President of how I had found this land, to serve Your Majesty although there was the loss of those Christians and that town; and of how I had been received, and with what pleasure, on my return, by Your Majesty's vassals. By him I wrote to Your Majesty, sending my letter to the President for him to forward it with him; the date was 9th July, 1549.

A month after my reception in the city of Santiago as governor, there also arrived the men I had sent by land with my three captains, although they were not many and had lost me over one hundred horses on the journey.

After the men had rested at Santiago over one and a half months, I resolved to hold a muster to see what there was for fighting, that they might get ready to go into the land in December. On Our Lady's Day in September (may she be blessed) I went forth for the purpose, and as I was riding about with the mounted men on the plain, my horse fell with me, and I came so heavily on to the right foot, that I broke all the toes to bits, dislocating (the base of ?) my thumb, and taking it all out in pieces during my cure. I was three months in bed, for this was a very wearisome one, and I had great troubles; so much so that I was often deemed dead by all.

Whether or no Your Majesty's vassals and *Cabildo* felt the want of me in your imperial service, and as to the good of all, that they know, and will bear their witness if it seem good so to them.

At the beginning of December I began to rise from my bed, but only to sit in a chair, for I could not stand. And so came the Christmas festival. Seeing that if I did not go to found this town of Concepcion, and the conquest of this land now that the food crops were on the land, and were beginning to be gathered, I should have to put off the foundation till next year, since it was best not to go into the country in the winter, which here begins in April, and that we might have shut houses to go into in the two or three months we might have of that season—although not yet well, and against the wishes of the whole people, for they saw that I could not possibly stand up on my foot, nor mount on horseback, I had myself carried in a chair by Indians, and so I left Santiago with two hundred men, on foot and mounted. I took twenty days till I got beyond the bounds assigned to Santiago, during which I had already won back something of my strength, and could ride on horseback. I set my men into order, and we went along keeping close together, with a force always in the rear, and our servants and baggage in the centre; sometimes I, other times my lieutenant, and other times the *maestre de campo* and other captains went out ahead every day with thirty or forty mounted men to explore and go over the ground, and to see its lay and where we should sleep, fighting with the Indians who came across our road; and we always found men trying to prevent our camping.

Sacred Majesty, I will proceed with my report of the conquest, first pointing out (though this makes me lengthy) how I carried through the orders I was given in Your Imperial name, and gave the summons Your Majesty orders should be given to the natives before war is started against them; and the lords of this land were informed of everything, and every day I did in this business what it is my duty and it is fitting should be done to carry out these orders.

Having crossed the Itata river, which is forty leagues from the city of Santiago, and where its bounds and jurisdiction end, I marched thirty leagues about fourteen or fifteen away from the sea, and I crossed a river two musket-shots wide, flowing very evenly and quietly, and coming up to the stirrups, which is called Nivequeten, and flows into the Biubiu five leagues from the sea; at its crossing my *maestre de campo* defeated two thousand Indians, going on ahead that day, and took two or three chiefs.

After crossing this river I came to the Biubiu river on the 24th January of this year, 1550; while I was getting rafts ready to cross it, for being very muddy, wide and deep, it could not be crossed on horseback, a great number of Indians arrived to hinder my crossing, and they even came over to my side, trusting in their numbers to attack me. By God's will I routed them on the bank; ten or twelve were slain, and they cast themselves into the river, and fled.

So as not to risk the horses, I went up the river to look for a better crossing; after we had gone two leagues, a great number of Indians showed themselves on our road; the Captain Alderete attacked them with twenty mounted men, and they threw themselves into the river, and he with his men after them. When I saw this I sent another thirty mounted men to support them, for over twenty thousand Indians had showed themselves on the other side; they crossed, and a very good soldier got drowned because he had a treacherous horse. They killed a great number of Indians, and came back in the evening with over one thousand sheep, whereat all the men were very glad, for after all, if the soldier does not die of hunger, he finds his merit in dying in the fight. I went on two or three leagues farther up the river, and camped there; for the third time a lot more Indians came up to stop my crossing; there, although the water came above the horses' saddles, it was gravelly; I fell on them with fifty horsemen, and gave them a right good lesson; very many were laid out on those plains, and we went on killing for a league and more; I came back in the evening.

Next day I again crossed the river with fifty mounted men, leaving the main body on this other side; and I rode two days towards the sea, above the neighbourhood of Arauco, where I came upon so thick a population as to frighten one, and I at once turned round, as I did not dare to stay longer away from my camp, in case it should suffer injury while I was away.

I rested eight days there, riding about hither and thither always, and taking cattle to feed us wherever we should camp; and so struck camp. I again crossed the Nivequeten river, and went towards the coast down the Biubiu. I camped half a league from it in a valley near some freshwater lakes, that I might look for the best district from there; I stayed there two days looking at places, giving all heed to keeping a good watch; half of us watched half the night, and half the other half of the night. On the second night as the first watch was going, a great number of Indians fell on us, more than twenty thousand. They attacked us on one side, for we were defended by the lake on the other, in three very big divisions, and with so heavy an onslaught and loud shouting that they seemed to overwhelm the land; and they began to fight in such a way that I give my word that in the thirty years I have been serving Your Majesty, and fighting against many nations, I have never seen such stubborn men for fighting, as were these Indians against us; and in the length of three hours I could not get into the one squadron with one hundred mounted men; and when we did get in a few times, there were so many men armed with spears and clubs that the Christians could not make their horses stand up against the Indians; and in this wise we fought for the length of time I have said; and seeing that the horses could not get in among the Indians, I threw my foot men against them; and when I got into their squadron, and we began to strike, feeling the swords on them, which were not idle, and how they were smiting, they were routed. They wounded sixty horses and as many Christians with arrows and spears, although both the ones and the others could not be better equipped; and only one horse died after eight days, and a soldier, who was killed by another firing off a musket. And the rest of the night and next day were given up altogether to looking after men and horses; while I went to look at where, in past years, I had resolved to make a settlement, which is one and a half leagues this side of the great river which I have called Biubiu, in a harbour and inlet than which there is none better in the Indies, and a big river falling into the sea round a headland, with the best fishing in the world, with many sardines, bream, tunny-fish, cod, lampreys, soles, and a thousand other kinds of fish; and on the other side another small stream that runs the whole year with very soft and clear water.

I moved camp hither on the 23rd of February to get supplies from the galley and a small vessel which the Captain Juan Bautista de Pastene (my lieutenant-general by sea) was bringing me; he was coming along the coast, and I had ordered him to look for me in the neighbourhood of this river. Next day I set to work in the morning to make a fence where we could come out to fight when we should choose, and not when the Indians should egg us on; (it was) of very thick trees set against one another, and fastened together like a wattle-fence, and a very wide and deep ditch around us; it was to give, too, some rest to the *conquistadores* in the matter of keeping the watches. For up till then the keeping watch had been a most wearisome thing owing to the men being always armed and every night, there being no one to look after sick and wounded. And we made it with our hands within eight days, so good a one and strong that it could be defended against the finest and most warlike nation in the world. When it had been made we all went inside of it, and I allotted quarters and lodging to each one; and we took up a convenient position for this on March 3 of this year 1550.

Nine days later, the 12th of this month, I having had news three days earlier that the whole land was gathered together, and that countless Indians were coming upon us, we had not been able to go and seek them out owing to our work on the stronghold, and we had been expecting those bulls every day—and so, at vespertide there appeared within sight of our fort, on some ridges, over forty thousand Indians, with as many more behind who could not show themselves. They came on with the utmost boldness in four divisions, of the most splendid and fine Indians that have ever been seen in these parts, and with the best equipment of sheep's and llamas' necks (skins) and undressed seal skins of many colours (which looked very handsome) and great plumes on headpieces of those skins like the great hats of priests, such that there is no battle-axe, however sharp, which can hurt those that wear them, with many arrows and spears twenty and twenty-five *palmos* long, clubs, and staves; they do not use stones for fighting.

Seeing how the Indians were coming to attack us from four sides, and that the squadrons could not give help to one another, as they meant to besiege us and fight with us for the fort, I ordered the Captain Geronimo Alderete to go out at one gate with fifty mounted men and break through a squadron that was coming against this same gate, and was a musket-shot away from it; and no sooner had the mounted men come up than the Indians gave way and turned; and the other three squadrons, seeing them broken, did the same; the pursuit went on till nightfall. Fifteen hundred to two thousand Indians were killed, and many others lanced, and some taken prisoners, from two hundred of whom I had the hands and noses cut off for their contumacy when I had many times sent them messengers and given them the commands as ordered by Your Majesty. After this act of justice, when all had been gathered together, I spoke to them, for among them were some *caciques* and leading Indians, and told them how this was done because I had sent often to summon them and bid them come in peace, telling them to what end Your Majesty had sent me to this land, and they had received the message, and not done as I bade them, and what seemed best to me for fulfilling Your Majesty's commands, and the satisfaction of your royal conscience; and so I sent them away.

Then I had what food there was in the district gathered and put in our fort, and I started going about the land and conquering it; and so successful have I been with the help of God, and Our Lady, and St. James the Apostle, who have shown me their favour, and through the very Indian natives themselves on this journey, as will be told below, that in four months I had the whole land at peace which is to be in the service of the city I have founded here.

I assure Your Majesty that since the first discovery of the Indians down to this day no such land has been discovered for Your Majesty. It is more thickly populated than New Spain, very healthy, fruitful, and pleasant, with most fair climate, very rich in gold mines, for nowhere has trial been made without gold being taken out, abounding in men, cattle, and food, great signs from very near of much gold on the land; and in it the only thing wanting is Spaniards and horses. It is very flat, and what is not flat shows gentle hills; it has much very fine wood. It has so many dwellers that there are no wild beasts among the people—foxes, wolves, or other creatures of this kind; and if there are any they must be domesticated, for they have nowhere else to bring up their young but in the houses and fields of the Indians. I have the hope (under God) to give food in it in Your Majesty's name to more *conquistadores* than were fed in New Spain and Peru; I say that I will give more allotments than there are in both places, and so that everyone will have one very great and befitting his services and standing. And it would seem the Lord wills it to be, that His worship be honoured in it, and the devil leave where he has been held in honour for so long. For, according to the words of the Indian natives, on the day they fell upon this fort of ours, when the mounted men rode on to them, an old man on a white horse fell into the midst of their squadrons, saying: " Flee, all of ye; for these Christians will kill you;" and the fear they felt was so great that they fled. They said furthermore that three days earlier, when they were crossing the Biubiu river to come against us, a comet fell among them one Saturday at midday (and from this fort where we were many Christians saw it go that way with a brightness far beyond that of other comets), and that when it had fallen a very beautiful lady came forth from it clad in white too, and that she said to them: " Obey the Christians, and do not strive against them, for they are very brave and will kill you all." And when she had gone from their midst, the devil their master came and put himself at their head, telling them " that a great multitude of men were to gather together, and that he would come with them, for when we (Christians) saw so many together, we should fall dead out of fear "; and so they went on with their march. They call us " Ingas " and our horses " hueques Ingas," which means " Ingas' llamas."

Eight days after we defeated the Indians in this fort, the captain and pilot Juan Bautista came in with the fleet; whereat we greatly rejoiced, and the Indians went about very gloomily. I at once sent it to Arauco to load maize and I sent the Captain Geronimo de Alderete with sixty horsed men by land to support him. They went and acted with wisdom, and loaded on an island ten leagues from here, and the islanders came peacefully, and they saw the greatest prosperity there is in the Indies, and wonderful conditions for founding a city greater than Seville; they brought me Indians from Arauco, who said they wished to come and serve.

In four months I again sent the same captain and pilot with the fleet to send messengers from among the Indians he should take in the island where he landed the first time when he left them at peace to the *caciques* of the district on the mainland where he should land, and of the islands he should meet with, bidding them to come peacefully to where I was, if I was not to send and have them killed, and that they might bring more food, for all was needed. He went on to another island twenty leagues farther, where he loaded with food; it was big and well populated. A month after he came back I sent the fleet again for the third time, ten days ago, for more food, and to go over the land along the coast they might pass, for the Indians sent to tell me they did not wish to come, since we did not go there.

Seeing how the *caciques* of this district had already come in peacefully and served with their Indians, I founded in this settlement and fort a town, which I named Concepcion del Nuevo Extremo. I founded a *Cabildo*, tribunal, and administration, and I set up the tree of Justice on the 5th day of October, 1550, and I appointed dwellers, and divided the *caciques* among them; and so they are living in content, God be praised.

I am dared to spend and get so far into debt, and I now begin again, since I have a great land with good fruits in my hands. And Your Majesty shall understand that so much of prosperity as the land of Peru at the beginning brought its explorers and conquerors, just as much toil does this one bring, and has brought up till now, and will bring till it is settled in order. . . . And what I above all wish for is to people so good a thing for the service done to God in the conversion of these people, and to Your Majesty in the increase of your royal crown, which is my main interest, and not in seeking at all costs to acquire estates. For of this metal and its help, once the land is settled at peace, there will be plenty, and all else that the over-fruitful land can produce for ease in living.

I assure Your Majesty that if the events in Peru had not happened after Vaca de Castro (of so evil a heart) came there, with all the zeal and skill I used in making war on the Indians and sending for help with the gold I have spent, I am convinced I should have explored, conquered, and settled down to the Strait of Maghellan and the North Sea, although the two hundred and a little more leagues have so many dwellers that they are more than the grass; and if I had had two thousand more men in the land so that I could have carried it out, leaving the others to guard them. The fruit that has come out of the toils which I here set forth myself as having gone through, and of the services I have done, and of what I have spent, is the bringing of peace and rest into the provinces of Peru and the founding in these provinces of Nueva Extremadura of the towns of Santiago, Serena, and this town of Concepcion; and that I have five hundred men in this government who, with the three hundred and the best mares and horses I have, can go on to settle another town in four months, with God's help and to Your Majesty's weal, thirty leagues from here in the land and situation in Arauco approved of.

I give my word to Your Majesty that from the 13th December, 1547, when I left the harbour of Valparaiso, until I came back there in May, 1549—seventeen months—I spent in gold and silver on Your Majesty's service one hundred and eighty-six thousand five hundred *castellanos* without any sorrow, and I would spend a million, if needful, for this purpose, if I had them or could borrow, and agree to be put in irons for their repayment. And this way of serving Your Majesty was shown me by my fathers, and I learnt it from them, who were generals of Your Majesty's and whom I have followed in my profession of arms.

And so, too, I give my word to Your Majesty, that I have spent for the good of this land from the day I undertook the journey down to this day on its upkeep and preservation, leaving on one side, as I do, the expenses of my person, house, and servants, two hundred and ninety-seven thousand *castellanos* in horses, arms, clothing, and ironware that I have given out among the *conquistadores* to help them live and serve, without asking anyone for a single gold *peso*, nay more, even a piece of writing for it; and when I get some leisure from the so great business I now have in conquering and settling—which is of greater importance—I shall send proofs showing clearly the truth of this.

Sacred Majesty, in the orders you gave me and the favour you showed me by virtue of your royal power which was wielded for this purpose by the licentiate De la Gasca, you marked down for me as the limits of government 41 degrees north-south down the coast, and a hundred leagues breadth west to east; and as from there to the Strait of Maghellan the land that can have a population is but little, and the person who might be given it would be rather a hindrance than of service, and I am settling it all, and sharing it among Your Majesty's vassals and its conquerors, I beg very humbly that you deign to have what has been given me confirmed, and grant me the fresh favour of extending its limits, and that the coast up to the said Strait be under me, and the land behind up to the North Sea. And why I ask it is that we have heard that the coast of the La Plata river from 40 degrees up to the mouth of the Strait is uninhabited, and I lear the land gets very narrow, for when I sent the pilot Juan Bautista de Pastene, my lieutenant-general on sea, to explore the coast towards the Strait, when he sailed by the charts he had from Spain, and was at 41 degrees, he was nigh being lost. Whereby it is to be seen that the charts made in Spain are mistaken so far as the Maghellan Strait is concerned, a mistake very great as to the entrance; and since the true state of things is not yet known, I do not send any report until I have had the whole coast explored, so that the mistake of the said maps in this respect may be corrected, so that the ships that come to these parts may not be in danger of being lost. And this mistake does not lie, as I am informed, in the number of degrees north and south, which is the way into the said Strait, but in the east to west direction. And I do not ask this favour like others do so as to grasp much land, since for me seven feet are enough, and what will fall to my successors that my memory may last among them will be that share Your Majesty shall deign to grant me for my slight services, the which, however small it may be, I shall value as I ought; but the only end whereunto I ask for this favour is the more to serve and to toil; and so soon as I see it or have a sure report, I will send this especially, and will give it to Your Majesty, that if you shall choose to divide it up and make two or more governments of it, this may be done.

So also, I beseech Your Majesty to deign to have the said government confirmed to me for life as I hold it, and to give me a fresh grant of it for the lifetime of two heirs in succession, or of the persons I shall name, so that after my days they may have and hold it like myself.

So also, I beg Your Majesty to deign to make me the grant of the public notaryships, and of the *Cabildo* of the cities, towns, and places I shall found in this government; and if Your Majesty has made any grant of them, I beg that mine may come next after it when the former ends.

So also, if my services shall be acceptable to Your Majesty, wholly or in part, since the good will with which I have done those up to now, and wish to do them in the future, is that of the most humble and loyal servant, subject, and vassal of your imperial person that can be found, I very humbly beg you as a reward for them to deign to make me a grant of the eighth part of the land I have conquered, settled, and explored, or shall explore, conquer, and settle in the course of time, in perpetuity for me and my descendants, and that I be allowed to take it where I choose with the title that Your Majesty may be pleased to grant me with it.

So also, I beseech Your Majesty for the confirmation of the grant allowing me to appoint three permanent *regidores* in each one of the settlements I shall found in Your Majesty's name in this government, and that you will also grant unto me that the said *regidores* by me appointed shall not be bound to go for confirmation to the Royal Council of the Indies, because of the expenses that might fall on them if sent, and of the hurt they might suffer on their long and toilsome journey.

So also, I beseech Your Majesty, seeing the heavy charges that must fall on me in the future, for up till to-day I have not ten thousand *pesos* profit, and what I shall spend each year is over a hundred thousand at the least, so that I may be somewhat armed against them, to deign to grant me the leave and favour to bring into this government up to two thousand negroes from Spain and the Cape Verde Islands, or from other places, free of all royal duties; and that no one shall be allowed to bring more than two slaves into the said government without my leave, until I shall have completed the above total.

So also, I pray Your Majesty that, seeing the so great expenses I have incurred since I undertook this expedition for the exploring, conquering, peopling, maintaining, and holding of these provinces, and those that fell to me when I went to serve against Gonzalo Pizarro's rebellion, as can be seen from the sections of this my letter—that you deign to give orders that I have acquittance and discharge from my notes lying in the royal chests of the cities of Los Reyes and Santiago, amounting to the following sum: one of fifty thousand *pesos* which I took in gold from Your Majesty's chest in the city of Santiago, when I went to serve in Peru as I have said, and another note I gave to the officers of the city of Los Reyes for the galleon and galley which they sold me on Your Majesty's behalf, and for the food they gave me in the harbour of Arica to feed the men I brought hither, amounting to thirty thousand *pesos*, and a further thirty-eight thousand *pesos* I owe on other notes to one Calderon de la Barca, who was a servant to Vaca de Castro, which I owe as the balance of sixty thousand *pesos* that I took from the money that was brought hither of the said Vaca de Castro in the ship of the pilot and captain Juan Bautista de Pastene, for the benefit of the men that were serving Your Majesty in this land, as already set forth, which money having been Vaca de Castro's, is now Your Majesty's; and these three amounts come to a hundred and eighteen thousand gold *pesos*. For them I pray Your Majesty, as I have already done, to give me acquittance and discharge.

So also, I pray Your Majesty to give orders for the further favour to be shown me that directions be given for me to be granted a further hundred thousand *pesos* from Your Majesty's chest to help me in part with the great expenses that fall on me daily, for my lieutenant, Francisco de Villagra, is not yet come back with the help for which I sent him, and I am now sending another captain, who leaves with the messengers bearing this letter, with a further sum of money to Peru, that he may get me more men; and when the lieutenant comes, another will go, and so it will be until my wishes in Your Majesty's service are carried out.

So also, I pray Your Majesty, since this land is powerful through its population, and warlike, and the people are by the coast, that, for the protection of your royal vassals, you be pleased to give me leave to establish three or four fortresses where it shall seem fitting to me between here and the Strait of Maghellan, and to assign to each one of them, for building and holding them, as many natives as shall seem good to me, and give them proper land, as to the *conquistadores*, for their support; which said fortresses may Your Majesty be pleased to give me to hold for myself and my heirs, with a yearly salary for each fortress of a million (*cuento*) of *maravedis*.

So also, I pray Your Majesty, seeing the land is so costly and far from our Spain, to be pleased to grant me ten thousand *pesos* salary and allowance in each year.

Sacred Majesty, I am sending as messengers with these dispatches and letter, the reverend Father Rodrigo Gonzalez, Bachelor in Theology, and priest, and Alonso de Aguilera, to give an account to Your Majesty and the lords of his Royal Council of the Indies of my small services in these lands, and of my so strong will to do far greater ones in the service of God, and Your Majesty, He in His infinite mercy allowing me to be the instrument for those coming after, as I have been for those living up to now, and with all powers to ask favours for myself, and to take the grants and bestowals of those which Your Majesty shall be pleased to make me, and is wont to bestow on your subjects and vassals who well and loyally serve, as I have always done and will do while I live, and to take the instructions that are to be sent me, that I may know what services I am to do, and not err in any wise; for my wish is to be clear about everything so as the better to know how to succeed.

The reverend Father Rodrigo Gonzalez is born in the town of Constantina and brother to Don Diego de Carmona, dean of the holy church of Seville; he came with me when I undertook this campaign, having only a few days before come back from that other very toilsome and dangerous one in Your Majesty's service made by the Captain Pedro de Candia among the Chunchos, wherein many Christians and a great number of the Peruvian natives who were taken as servants and carriers, died of hunger; and those that came back barely recovered and became themselves again for many a day. The business of this reverend father here has been the service of God and the honour of His churches, and divine worship, and particularly Your Majesty's service; in this, and with his religious life and habits in his priestly office administering the sacraments to Your Majesty's vassals, and putting forth all his powers, and holding it as his main interest and wealth. Some mares that he brought to the land with great toil, God multiplying them to him for the sake of his good works, and which are that kind of wealth which has been, and is, the most profitable for the exploration, conquest, settlement, and holding of these lands, he has given and sold to the *conquistadores* to this end, and the gold he has got from them, whenever I have needed it for Your Majesty's service, and to help me to send for the assistance already mentioned on behalf of these provinces, he has given and lent me with as good will as if he were giving me nothing; for his ends have always been, and are, on the spiritual side, to win souls for heaven from the natives, and to inspire the Christians not to lose theirs through their lusts, ever sowing the peace and love among them that the Son of God charged on His disciples when He went from this world; and on the temporal side, as a good vassal of Your Majesty, to help in augmenting your royal crown *viribus et posse*. The upshot in this case is that, having done these fruitful deeds, seeing himself to be so worn and old, he has resolved to go to Spain and die, and first to kiss Your Majesty's hands, if God is pleased to let him come in safety before your imperial notice, and give you an account of everything here, which as so good an eye-witness he can give as well as I. And to do further service, and see how the flock was that he had ministered to when he came for the founding and conquest of this town of Concepcion, having left it because of his age, and gone to the city of Santiago, he entrusted himself to fortune in a small vessel, and came here to hearten and rejoice us all in the love and service of God; and having made this journey he went back to that city to carry on his duties there. I am sending him from this city of Concepcion, for owing to my business and his years we cannot see one another to take farewell, and for the above reasons, and the fruits we have gathered from the good works and holy teachings that he has sown amongst us all this time, all we vassals of Your Majesty bewail his going, and have need in this land of such a prelate. On behalf of all us vassals of Your Majesty that have been here and know him, who have given me powers for this, and on my own behalf, as the most humble subject and vassal in your imperial service, we very humbly pray Your Majesty to be pleased when he shall have come into your royal presence, to order him to come back hither in your service, appointing him to the dignity of bishop of these provinces, granting him your royal patent, so that, this being presented in the public Consistory, our most Holy Father may invest him with the dignity; for I am so sure from his zeal that he will come and undertake this work only to serve God, at the bidding of Your Majesty or the lords of your Royal Council of the Indies, if you say it is for the good of your imperial service and the conversion of these natives that it should be so, for with the special love he has for this service, I know he will obey and fulfil all unto death, and do nought otherwise.

And should someone already be invested with the bishopric of Chile, Your Majesty can appoint him to the bishopric of Arauco and the town I shall found in that province; and though St. Paul says: *qui episcopatum desiderat bonum opus desiderat*, I give Your Majesty my word that I know he does not desire it. . . . The father has asked me to be sent, the *Cabildo* and people of that city of Santiago write me that they have thrown themselves at his feet, asking him for God's sake and Your Majesty's not to leave them, setting out before him the toils of the road, and his age. It may be that, touched by the prayers of so many children, he, like a good father, will do their bidding and give up his departure, but I cannot know this so soon. I pray Your Majesty once more and many times, whether or not he goes, to do us the favour of giving him to us as prelate, since the person that Your Majesty and the lords of your Royal Council will so earnestly bid seek in the cloisters and convents of your kingdoms and dominions for this purpose (even if he is of good life and conduct), him they have here already found, and such that he brings more fruit with his learning, preaching, and experience of these lands, than all the religious who might come from over there; and this I assure Your Majesty.

Alonso de Aguilera is from the town of Porcuna, held and esteemed for a nobleman, and gifted with every virtue and goodness; he came to this land to serve Your Majesty, and looking for me, being of my blood. He arrived at the time when I was in this fort where I founded this town of Concepcion, and was defending myself against the Indian natives, and carrying on war against them; he has helped in their conquest, and though his wish was to go with his service here, putting before him what is needed for Your Majesty's service— namely, that a person of his profession and quality should go and take an account of myself and what report I can give up to now of this land (for I know that if God grants him life he will not shut himself away (be lost ?) like the messengers up to now, since his personal character is of far higher parts in word and deed than theirs), I am sending him for the said purpose, and that I may put my house in order while I go to make settlements in Arauco; and I shall send the Captain Geronimo de Alderete from there, Your Majesty's servant and my deputy as captain general in this dominion, with the description of the land and an account of it all, and authentic proof from trustworthy witnesses of all the services I have done for Your Majesty, and my outlays, and my debts arising from doing them, and the small profit that has been got up to to-day from the land, and how much is needed to be spent by me until it is pacified and in order. And he will take the duplicate of what I am now sending with the above messengers that he may bring me my wife and transplant the house of Valdivia to these parts so that Your Majesty as the most Christian monarch, our natural King and lord, may be pleased to make it illustrious by your favours for the sake of the services I have done to your imperial person, and of the conversion of such populous provinces to our holy Catholic faith and the increase of your royal patrimony and crown being on the way.

And as to the rest I refer to the messengers, for whom I pray Your Majesty that they be given the same credit as I myself would have; for the confidence I have in them makes me sure that they will do everything befitting Your Majesty's service, and pleasing to me, . . . that I may have satisfaction, which for me will be no small one when I see a letter from Your Majesty whereby I learn that you hold yourself well served by what I have done in this land, and encouraging me to further service. Sacred Imperial and Catholic Majesty, may Our Lord preserve for long years the most sacred person of Your Majesty and increase it with greater kingdoms and dominions.

From this city of Concepcion del Nuevo Extremo, 15th October, 1550—S. C. C. M.—The most humble subject, servant, and vassal of Your Majesty, who kisses your most sacred feet and hands.

PEDRO DE VALDVIA.

IV

Letter from Pedro de Valdivia to the Emperor, under date 25th September, 1551, informing him of the affairs of his government.

To his most Catholic Majesty:

Having founded this city of Concepcion del Nuevo Extremo on 5th October of last year, 1550, and set up a *Cabildo*, and allotted Indians to the *conquistadores* who were to dwell in it, I sent off to Your Majesty ten days later, that is on the 15th, Alonso de Aguilera, and gave an account in my letters of what up to then I could give, and of what it seemed to me Your Majesty ought to know, as will have been seen by them, if God has been pleased to bring the messenger before your imperial presence; and in case he shall not have reached there (if through death, for no other mishap, I am certain, would prevent his going on with his journey and do on it what he owes to Your Majesty's service), I send with this a copy of what I sent by him, so that by one channel or another Your Majesty may have knowledge of what I have done in these lands to God's honour, and that of His most holy faith and belief, and to the increase of Your Majesty's royal patrimony and revenues.

After Alonso de Aguilera had left, I stayed on in this city for four months, during which I built a fort of *adobes* more than twice a man's height, and one and a half *varas* wide, wherein up to fifty inhabitants and *conquistadores* could find safety (of which latter twenty were horsemen), whom I left for the holding of this same town, while with one hundred and seventy (one hundred and twenty being horsemen) I went on to found another town where it should seem good to me. And when the fort had been built, in mid-February of this year 1551, I crossed the great river Biubiu with the aforesaid men, and I came to thirty leagues beyond this city of Concepcion, towards the Strait of Maghellan, to another mighty river, called in this country's tongue Cabtena, which is like the Guadalquivir, and far gentler-flowing, and with waters clear as crystal, and runs through highly fertile lands. As I went along looking at the land and coast, calling on the natives to come in peace that I might make them understand why we came, and what Your Majesty bids be done for their good (that they should come to the knowledge of our most holy faith, and to devotion towards Your Majesty) and looking for a site, I came upon a very likely one, four leagues from the coast up the river, and here I made a settlement. I built a fort in ten or twelve days, much better than the one I had built in this city at the beginning, but it was such as befitted the season, and was needed, for I decided to make it thus, seeing the great number there was of Indians, and therefore the need for us to keep a careful watch. Having founded it there, I called the town La Imperial; on this, and on going about the district and fighting the Indians so that they should come in to serve us, and in getting information for sharing the chiefs among the *conquistadores*, I spent one and a half months.

The whole land soon came in peacefully, and the main cause (after God and His Blessed Mother) was the punishment I gave the Indians when they attacked us in war when I founded this city of Concepcion, and their losses in the fight with me, both on that day and on earlier occasions.

I then shared out all the chiefs there are between here and the river, but did not give any of those on the other side; (the allotment was made) according to their *levos*, each with the name of one of them, which are names as it were (for the members), and by this the Indians acknowledge subjection to their superiors. I shared them out among one hundred and twenty-five *conquistadores*, that is the *levos* and their Indians for two leagues round for house service. And leaving them thus with a captain such time as, when the land had been well examined, the allotment should be made, and the grants given to such dwellers there as should and could be given their reward, on the 4th of April I came back to this city of Concepcion to winter there, and put it in order, since now I had the whole list of the chiefs that were to serve the dwellers, and to await and send off two ships coming from Peru with supplies for this land, as the harbour here being very good, I knew they would sail for it. And so I am leaving in this city forty dwellers, and have given them all their grants, and marked out their house sites, fields, and *peonias*, and all else it is customary to give them in Your Majesty's name. And all this I have done this winter—no small thing—and I have sent off the ships, and with them this letter for Your Majesty with the copy I have spoken of, and (I have sent) to Peru that all who choose may come to so fair a land; and having done this, I am leaving in eight days (with God's help) to inspect all the land that shall be allotted to those who are to dwell in the town of Imperial, and to punish certain chiefs that will not serve; and when I have the report I will give them their grants, as I have done here, and I will leave that town in proper order, it being now the time for it, that, when January of next year, 1552, comes, I may go on with what men I can (for almost one hundred men have now come to me in these ships, and we are better off for horses, of which there are some already in the land, and mares) another twenty leagues farther, to another river called the Valdivia (the name was given by those I sent to explore that coast by sea six years ago); and I shall found another town, and I will do for it and its maintenance what I have done for the others, if God grant me life.

What I can truly say of the goodness of this land is that all Your Majesty's vassals in it that have seen Nueva España say there are far more people in it than in this latter. It is all one town and one field and one gold mine, and if the houses are not put on top of one another, it will not hold more than it has; it is rich in flocks as Peru, with wool that drags along the ground; abounds with all the foods that the Indians sow for their livelihood, such as maize, potatoes, *quinua, madi,* pepper and beans; the people are tall, fond of their houses, friendly and white, and with handsome faces, both men and women, all clad in wool after their fashion, although their clothes are somewhat coarse. They are very much afraid of horses; they are very fond of their children, wives, and houses, which are very well built, and strong with great planks, and many of them very big and with two, four, and eight doors. They are full of every kind of food and wool; they have many and very fine vessels of clay and wood; they are very great husbandmen, and as great drinkers; their law lies in arms, and so they all have them in their houses, and very ready to hand to defend themselves against their neighbours, and to attack the weaker. The land has a very fine climate and every kind of Spanish plant will grow in it better than over there; this is what we have, so far, found out about this people.

Two months after I had come from the city of Imperial to bring order into Concepcion here, I received a cover from Your Majesty addressed to me, and in it, a letter signed by their Highnesses Prince Maxmilian and the Princess our Lady, in Your Majesty's name, in answer to one of mine which I wrote from the Andaguailas valley in the provinces of Peru, which they sent on to me from the Real Audiencia, which has its seat in those provinces. I have had a letter from a gentleman calling himself Don Miguel de Abendaño, brother to Doña Ana de Velasco, wife of the *comendador* Alonso de Alvarado, marshal of Peru, who is coming to serve Your Majesty in these parts, together with the lieutenant, Francisco de Villagra, and also brings me a dispatch from Your Majesty, and I am told it is the copy of this. In the cover I said I received there were four letters from Your Majesty for the cities of Santiago and Serena, and for Your Majesty's officers, and for the Captain Diego Maldonado. All were given to those they came for, and in like wise I shall give the others Your Majesty may please to send addressed to me. So, too, another was sent to me from Peru that Your Majesty had had written to my care to the President Pedro de la Gasca, who seems already to have gone to Spain, and other to the care of Leonardo Cortés, son of the licentiate Cortés, of Your Majesty's Council. I shall do in your royal name, to your honour and profit, what Your Majesty commands me in this case, for the so signal favour that was done to me and I received by seeing this letter, whereby Your Majesty assures me you hold yourself to have been served by me, as well in what I wrought in the provinces of Peru against the rebel Pizarro, as in the conquest, settling, and maintenance of these provinces of Nuevo Extremo, and that you will bid my person and small services to be kept in mind. I kiss Your Majesty's feet and hands one hundred thousand times, and I feel well assured that the more I distinguish myself in doing them, so much the greater will be the reward, and in accordance with the way Your Majesty is wont to treat your subjects and vassals in this case who serve your will, and have the same will to serve that I have.

Two days after these dispatches came from Your Majesty I received a letter of 18th May of this year 1551 from the Captain Francisco de Villagra, my deputy, whom, as I wrote to Your Majesty, directly I came back from the provinces of Peru, when I had been to serve against Pizarro's revolt, I sent with what money I could to bring me the men and horses he could; and in his company I sent the Captain Diego Maldonado, and he it was that dared with eight stout men to cross the mountains to give me the news of this, and God allowed him to find them bare of snow. He wrote me that he was bringing two hundred men and with them four hundred horses and mares, and was stopping in the neighbourhood of the city of Santiago on the other side of the snow, and that he was not going to cross through it until he had my answer, and saw what my orders were, and what he was to do in Your Majesty's service. I at once answered him and the said captain, who, that he might ever serve, as has always been his wont, decided to take on himself this twofold task.

Also the deputy wrote to me, and the captain likewise gave me an account, how, in the neighbourhood where I had founded the city of Serena, on the other side of the said mountains, he had found a captain settled called Juan

Nuñez de Prado, who is a soldier whom, as I tell in my letter and copy, I came upon on the mountain-side that day I crossed the bridge when we were going to give battle to Gonzalo Pizarro, and who was fleeing from his own side to ours; him the President, the licentiate Pedro de la Gasca, gave a commission, to go and settle a valley he had heard of, called Tucuma, and he founded a town, calling it the city of El Barco. It would seem that when the said deputy Villagra was going along thirty leagues away from El Barco, for he was thus ordered by the said President in Los Reyes, this Juan Nuñez de Prado, with mounted men, fell suddenly at night on Villagra's camp, firing muskets, harassing and killing soldiers and calling out: " Viva el rey y Juan Nuñez de Prado." His reason he must know himself; and from what could be gathered, it was to scatter those men, if he could, and take them for himself (for he could not hold his ground with those he had brought with him, and it was best for him to go back to Peru) and to play such pranks as they had been wont to in those provinces. After steps had been taken against this, Juan Nuñez de Prado, of his free will and without compulsion, gave up the authority he held, and which the President had given him, saying he could not maintain that town, and the *Cabildo* and townsfolk asked of Francisco de Villagra, since it fell within the bounds of this government of mine, to take it under his care, and in my name to administer it, that it might be maintained and kept in being. And he, seeing that it cannot be dependent on any other part of the South Sea but this, put it in Your Majesty's name under my protection and shelter, as, if you so please, you can see by the judicial decree that was drawn up in this regard, as also by the copy of the instruction I sent to the said deputy on what he was to do and have done in all things, both of which documents go with this letter, and with the copy of those taken by Alonso de Aguilera in a cover for Your Majesty directed to the Real Audiencia at Los Reyes, for forwarding to the care of the secretary, Juan de Samano.

In the dispatch taken by Alonso de Aguilera, I said in my letters that, when making settlements in the provinces of

Arauco, I should send the Captain Geronimo Alderete, Your Majesty's servant, with the description and account of all the land, and with the copy; and that as the eye-witness he is of the services done by me to Your Majesty both in these provinces and in those of Peru he could give a very complete account. His person is so necessary and important for Your Majesty's service in matters here, that both on this ground and because I am waiting to make a settlement on the Valdivia river, which I surely believe to be the core of the land, and where gold lies in it—until this is done, his going is put off for eight or ten months; and at the proper time he will be more opportune, and will bring clearer information as to what is best for Your Majesty's service and what I wish.

I likewise make known to Your Majesty that I am always keeping this Captain Geronimo Alderete very busied in warlike matters, and on matters the most important possible for Your Majesty's service in these lands; and for this reason he cannot give the heed he would and ought to give to the office of Treasurer of the Royal Revenues which Your Majesty granted him. And though I have sought to put another Treasurer until Your Majesty makes up your mind and takes measure in this matter, since I pity him seeing how hard his work is, he has not been willing to leave the post, saying he wishes to serve in it, although he has the other work, until Your Majesty be informed, and choose that it be given to another who has not so justifiable business for leaving it unserved as he has. I very humbly pray Your Majesty to deign to send to appoint a person to exercise and hold it as is needed and fitting. May Our Lord long preserve Your Majesty's most sacred person to the increase of Christianity and the monarchy of the universe.

From this city of La Concepcion del Nuevo Extremo, 25th September, 1551.

To his most Catholic Majesty: the most humble subject, vassal, and servant of Your Majesty, who kisses your most sacred feet and hands.

PEDRO DE VALDIVIA.

V

Letter from Pedro de Valdivia to the Emperor, giving him an account of matters in his government, 26th October, 1552.

MOST SACRED CÆSAR,

Your Majesty being so well taken up with the service of God, and the defence and upholding of Christianity against the common enemy, the Turks, and the Lutheran errors, it would be more fitting to help by deeds than to distract by words. Would to God I could find myself in Your Majesty's presence with much money that you might use me in your service, although I am not useless where I am, but in truth it would have been a great satisfaction to me; and so I shall strive not to be lengthy.

I have given Your Majesty an account in my letters how I went to Peru to serve against the rebellion of Gonzalo Pizarro; and I wrote from Andaguailas; and after long seventeen months, while I was engaged serving there, when I came back to this government, where I had founded this city of Santiago and La Serena, I found the whole land in arms, La Serena burned down, forty-three Christians killed by the natives; and of how I set about building and peopling it again, and of what else seemed to me proper, I gave a long account to Your Majesty by a messenger I sent from Concepcion, named Alonso de Aguilera, on 15th October, 1550.

The last letter I wrote to Your Majesty is of 25th September of last year, 1551; with it went the duplicate of that taken by Alonso de Aguilera; the whole dispatch was addressed to the Audiencia Real of Los Reyes, to be forwarded hence. I feel assured that it will have been duly cared for; if not, herewith is sent the duplicate of (that of) the 25th, whereby the reasons will be known why I did not at that time send the Captain Geronimo de Alderete, Your Majesty's servant.

As I said in those letters, on 5th October, 1550, I founded the city of Concepcion, and put forty settlers in it. In March next, in 1551, I founded the town of Imperial, where I put eighty other settlers; all have their grants. In February of this year, 1552, I founded the town of Valdivia, where one hundred settlers find their livelihood; I do not know whether, when I have to give them their grants, all can stay. Two months later, in April, I founded Villa Rica, which is the place whence the North Sea is to be explored; I put fifty settlers; all have Indians; and so I shall go along conquering and founding until I reach the mouth of the Strait; and if so Your Majesty wishes it, and there being found a site for founding a fort, steps will be taken that no enemy come in or go out without Your Majesty's leave.

That an account may be given to Your Majesty of all that has happened since I started on this journey down to to-day, the Captain Geronimo Alderete, servant and treasurer of Your Majesty, is going; he is one of the leading persons that came with me to this land, and have well succeeded in serving, both in the exploring, conquering and settling of it, and in Peru against Gonzalo Pizarro, for I took him with me on that expedition. He will very well be able to give the whole account of everything as an eye-witness, for I have given him honourable posts of great confidence in the war and in what relates to the custody of Your Majesty's royal revenues. And he has always acquitted himself as a nobleman, a true and loyal vassal of Your Majesty, and zealous in your imperial service, as indeed, he is; and therefore, and knowing him to be such, I am sending him.

I pray Your Majesty to make yourself acquainted from him with the services I have done Your Majesty to the augmentation of the royal crown of Spain, and in accordance with them to be pleased to hear me and grant me your favours with that bounty with which, as a so grateful lord and monarch, you are wont ever to grant them to all those gentlemen and noblemen that have served, and serve, you loyally and well, as I have done and will do until death. And of my aims and deeds and of what I did in Peru, I believe Your

Majesty will have knowledge through the report of the licentiate Pedro Gasca, and through other persons who likewise will have given an account of it all to Your Majesty, and now the Captain Geronimo Alderete will give it again at greater length, as one who was in it all, and to whom a good share of toil and expense has fallen through his good services; and thereby he is a heavy creditor of this land.

And such favours as in accordance with his report and my services Your Majesty may be pleased to grant me, I very humbly pray that the bearer may bring them confirmed by Your Majesty, for the expenses incurred by the messengers in going to such far lands and coming from them are very heavy indeed, and I am very much in debt and committed for a sum of over two hundred thousand *pesos*, not reckoning another five hundred thousand I have spent in the exploring, conquest, settlement, upkeep, and holding of these kingdoms, which are among the best which have been discovered for Your Majesty, and where you will be best served.

I am sending the Captain Francisco de Villagra, a true and loyal vassal of Your Majesty, who has done much service in these parts with the highest offices that I could give him in your imperial name, that from Villa Rica, which lies 40 degrees from this part of the equinoctial, he may go into the North Sea, for the natives that are serving this said town say that it is a hundred leagues from it. I will see to the exploring of that coast and settle it, for Your Majesty will benefit much thereby.

What I owe merchants for the help they gave the said Captain Francisco de Villagra in Peru in taking to this land the hundred and eighty men he brought with him, is more than sixty thousand gold *pesos*. So also I shall, with God's help, and if He so please, in the coming summer (for now I cannot do so, for the want of ships in this land)—I shall send and have the navigation of the Strait of Magellan explored and examined. I was this last summer within a hundred and fifty leagues of it, travelling among a chain of mountains coming from Peru and going through this whole kingdom, always fifteen and twenty leagues and less from the sea; and these mountains are crossed and cut by the Strait. And journeying between the coast and the mountains beyond the town of Valdivia, which lies at 40 degrees, and on the best sea and river harbour ever seen, the turn of the Strait being 42 degrees, I could not go farther because there came out of the great chain of mountains a very full river over a mile wide; and so I went up the river right to the mountains, and there I found a lake whence the river flowed, which in the opinion of all those with me stretched away for forty leagues. From there I came back to the town of Valdivia, for winter was coming on; and to send the Captain Alderete away to Your Majesty I came to this city of Santiago.

From here I have appointed two captains: one to go over the mountains behind this city of Santiago, and bring the natives on that side into service.

And in the neighbourhood of the town of Serena the Captain Francisco de Aguirre goes in, a very true and loyal vassal of Your Majesty, whom I have set there as deputy that he may likewise, by his energy and prudence, bring the other natives; for that land has been seen by the Captain Francisco de Villagra, and through it he brought me help when I sent him to Peru, as I wrote to Your Majesty, and write in this letter. It is a land partly inhabited, partly uninhabited. I shall do all I can to bring all those natives into subjection to Your Majesty, as I have done with the others; although one Juan Nuñez de Prado laid waste the town of El Barco which the said Villagra had fostered in Your Majesty's name, and left under my protection, in view of the fact it could be supplied from here, and not from elsewhere; and according to what has been written, went off to Peru, hanging an *alcalde* who defended its existence, for he knew the importance for such a journey that there should be a settlement there; for my intention is no other all the time God shall grant me life, than to spend it in Your Majesty's service, as I have done up till now.

From what I have learnt from the natives, and from what I hear astrologers and cosmographers say and tell, I am persuaded I am in a country where the service of the Lord can be very greatly advanced; and looking at one thing and another, I for my part deem that wherein Your Majesty can be to-day best served is in the navigation of the Strait of Maghellan, and for three reasons, leaving others aside that might be given: first, because Your Majesty in Spain will have all this land and sea of the south, and none will dare to do what he should not; second, you will have well in your hands all the spice trade; and third, the other side of the Strait can be explored and settled, which, as I am informed, is a very well inhabited land. And for the rest, as it is not for me to give an opinion, but to let Your Majesty know what I find here, and hear, as a man who has matters in his hands, I do not give it; and that I may serve Your Majesty too, in this, as I have done in other things, the Captain Alderete is going with the determination to do this service, and set up the first flag of Your Majesty in the Strait, wherefrom these kingdoms will have very great content, and Your Majesty very decided service. Unto all which, and for what concerns my own business, I very humbly pray Your Majesty once again and many times to be pleased to order that all favour and help may be given him, so that such a high service as this may be done for Your Majesty, he being granted the rewards proportionate to his services in the past, and for those he again wishes to set out upon. And since, as I have said, he will know how to give an account of all he is asked for, and is taking the report on the land, although the detailed description cannot go now, seeing that I am taking both inland and along the coast geographers to make it perfect to send to Your Majesty, and it is not finished; I will send it by the first ships that sail.

So also the Captain Alderete is taking the gold that has been got from the royal fifth, since what was in Your Majesty's royal chest was sent here with a captain named Esteban de Sosa, directed to the President Gasca, whom he did not find in Los Reyes, as he had gone to Spain, and he left it there with Your Majesty's officers. And since at the present time gold is not mined except in this city of Santiago and Serena, since I do not allow it to be mined so soon in the others I have founded, that the natives may be well brought into order and quiet, and that the settlers may keep on building their houses, and giving themselves to sowing and breeding so as to improve the land for their support, what he brings is little. When mining is begun in all the towns I have founded till now, Your Majesty will be given much fruit and help for your needs and outlay, since this is so holy a one, and so good and profitable for the service of the Lord, and the maintenance of Christianity, His Roman Church, and universal Shepherd, who fills and holds St. Peter's chair, as Christ's vicar.

That wherein I have had special care, toiled, and gone to the limits of my strength since I came to this land, is the treatment of the natives to the end that they may be preserved and taught; and I assure Your Majesty that in this regard this land has had the advantage over all which have been discovered, conquered, and settled up to this day in the Indies, as Your Majesty may learn not only from the messenger, but from the other persons that from here have gone down to-day, and shall go hereafter to our Spain.

In the conversion of the natives to our holy faith and belief, the Bachelor in Theology, Rodrigo Gonzalez, a priest, brother to Don Diego de Carmona, dean of the holy church of Seville, has been of great help through his teaching and preaching, as I wrote lately to Your Majesty by Alonso de Aguilera. In my letter I begged on behalf of all Your Majesty's vassals, and on my own, of us who know him and have had experience of his good and seemly life, that Your Majesty be pleased to appoint him as our prelate in this government; this same prayer we make now, since the grounds and reasons there are that he should be raised to this dignity, if Your Majesty be pleased to grant us this favour, are full well known to all here.

The orders Your Majesty has had sent me about the married men in these provinces, that they are to go, or to send for their wives; and the order as to the procedure to be followed in lawsuits of the Indians; and all others that shall come within my province, will be obeyed and fulfilled by me, in accordance with the instructions in them, and with what shall seem best to me for Your Majesty's service, the peace and tranquillity of your vassals and this land, and of the natives, and their preservation; for all this is my main interest; and the wish I have to do right in all and to serve well is that one which I have declared, and do declare always in my letters to Your Majesty; whose most sacred person may the Lord keep for endless years, with the addition of greater kingdoms and the monarchy of Christendom.

From this city of Santiago, 26th October, 1552. Most sacred Cæsar, the most humble subject and vassal of Your Majesty, that kisses your most sacred feet and hands.

PEDRO DE VALDIVIA.

INDEX

ABENDAÑO, MIGUEL DE, 210
Acosta, Juan de, 66, 180
Agraz, 14 and *n*.
Aguilera, Alonso de, Valdivia's dispatches sent with, 202, 205, 207, 212 *et seq.*, 219
Aguirre, Francisco de, 40, 139, 217
Agustinillo, 117, 119
Alcantara, Fulano de, 3
Alcantara, Martin de, 3 *n*.
Aldana, Lorenzo de, plot against Valdivia and Pastene by, 61, 62, 165 *et seq.*, 172
Alderete, Geronimo de, Captain General to Valdivia, 76, 77; appointed Captain and Adelantado of Chile by Philip II., 88 and *n*.; death, 89; sent to Spain, 108, 215 *et seq.*; Valdivia's tribute to services of, 214 *et seq.*, 218; other references, 22, 81, 84, 181, 184, 186, 194, 196, 206
Almagro, Diego de, conference of Mara between Pizarro and, 2, 17; birth and early career of, 6; compact between Pizarro and, 6, 11 *et seq.*; expedition of, to Peru, 7 *et seq.*; quarrels and ill-feeling between Pizarro and, 15-16, 23; made Marshal of Peru, 16, 20; execution of, 16 *n*., 23, 49; expedition of, to Chile, 17 *et seq.*, 24, 25, 128, 129; and its failure, 21 *et seq.*, 122, 154, 156, 157; character of, 19
Almagro, Diego de (son), murder of Pizarro by, 23 and *n*., 29, 130, 131; defeat and execution of, 36 and *n*., 134, 158; other reference, 11
Alonso. *See* Lautoro, 115
Altamarino, Captain, 118
Alvarado, Alonso de, 152, 177 *et seq.*, 210
Alvarado, Pedro de, vii
Anaconas, the, 132
Anaconcillas, the, 132, 133, 142
Andes, the, difficulties of crossing, 18 *et seq.*, 41, 108-109; bridge-building in, 65, 177 *et seq.*

Aporima, River, bridge-building across, 65, 177 *et seq.*
"Araucana, La" (Ercilla), literary value of, and as an authority on Araucanians, 87 *et seq.*; references to Valdivia in, 89, 90; Lautoro's speech in, 115; quoted and cited, 28 and *n*., 84 and *n*., 89 *n*., 90 *n*., 92 *n*., 107, 117 *n*.
Araucanian Indians, military skill, patriotism, and character of, viii, 20, 27, 28 *et seq.*, 46-47, 82 *et seq.*, 87, 96, 161-162, 192 *et seq.*; Valdivia's actions against, 28 *et seq.*, 44, 129, 131 *et seq.*, 137, 139, 157 *et seq.*, 163; their fear of horses, 84, 115; authorities on customs of, 87, 92; Herrera on, 92 *et seq.*; Valdivia's description of, 99-100, 102, 194, 209-210; treatment of, by Valdivia, 106, 114-115, 160, 194-195; and their unfitness for servitude, 110-111, 113; Bascuñan's description of, 111 *et seq.*; organised revolt of, against Valdivia and the Spanish, 113 *et seq.*
Arauco, 94, 99, 109, 111, 118, 196, 205, 206
Arequipa, Monroy at, 39, 135
Ariza, Martin de, 113-114, 117
Armero, Indian name for Almagro, 23, 130
Atacama desert, difficulties of crossing, 21-22, 33, 35, 36, 42; other references, 141, 157, 172
Atahualpa, Inca, 18
Avila, 4

Balboa, Vasco Nuñez de, 5 and *n*.
Bartolome, Brother, 178
Bascuñan, Francisco Nuñez Pineda y, captivity of, among the Araucanians, viii, 111 *et seq.*
Bazan, Maria, 91
Beam, the ordeal of the, 93
Belalcazar, Sebastian de, v, 2, 60, 123
Biobio, river, settlement on, 81, 83 *et seq.*, 99, 162, 191, 207

221

Bobadilla, 157
Bogotá, 7, 11, 123 n.
Bohon, Juan, 142
Bolivar the Liberator, 22 n.
Boscanillo, the horse, 70
Briceño, Alonzo, 10 n.
Bridges, osier, in the Andes, 65-66, 177 et seq.

Cabtena, river, 208
Campo, Martin, 111, 112
Canconcagua valley, 130, 144
Candia, Pedro de, 10 and n., 12-13, 203
Canela, valley of, 157
" Canes, The," game of, 58 and n., 64 and n.
Capac, Huayna, 16 n., 17 n.
Capac, Manco, 18, 28-29
Cardenas, Juan de, 138, 173
Carmona, Diego de, 98, 203, 219
Carrion, Anton de, 10 n.
Carvajal, Francisco de, friendship of, with Gonzalo Pizarro, 52 et seq.; and with Valdivia, 61; assistance of, to Pastene, 62, 166; at the battle of Sacsahuana, 66, 69-70, 182; execution of, 67, 71; career of, 71 et seq.; character of, 73
Castellano, the coin, 38 and n.
Castillo de la Mota, El, 5 n., 16 n.
Castro, Vaca de, defeat of Almagro (son) by, 36, 158; help and news sent to Valdivia by, 38 et seq.; 134 et seq., 159, 201; as Viceroy of Peru, 42, 49, 127, 134-135, 141, 198; imprisonment of, by Vela, 50, 51, 164; trial and acquittal of, 51, 52
Castuera, 1 and n.
Caupolican, chief, execution of, 90; method of election of, 93
" Cautivero Feliz " (Bascuñan), 111 n.
Centeno, Diego de, 57, 58, 64, 65, 70-71, 157, 166, 175
Cepeda, licentiate, 68-69
Cervantes, vi, 87
Chapas, battle of, 10-11
Charcas, 18, 20, 21, 186, 187
Charles V., Emperor, military expedition of, in Italy, 1; Pizarro's capitulations with, 10; and visit to, regarding Peru, 11 et seq.; honours Pizarro, 16; character of, 43, 53 et seq.; attitude of, to Gonzalo Pizarro, 54 et seq.; treatment of Valdivia by, 80; agreements of, with conquistadores, 121; military qualities of, 122; letters from Pedro de Valdivia to: I., September 4th, 1545, 127-151; II., June 15th, 1548, 152-155; III., October 15th, 1550, 156-206; IV., September 25th, 1551, 207-213; V., October 26, 1552, 214-220; references to, vii, viii, 25, 26 and n., 28, 29 and n., 31 and n., 32 and n., 33, 34, 37, 39 et seq., 43 et seq., 48, 61, 62 and n., 64 n., 65-66, 82 n., 84, 85, 95, 98 et seq., 106, 177; value of, 43-44, 91, 92, 102, 122, 123; letters to Valdivia from, 210-211; letter to Gonzalo Pizarro from, 56
Charts of South America, need for correct, 95, 199
Chaves, Nuflo, de, ix
Chibcha Empire, 7
Chile, Indians of, viii-ix, see also under Araucanian Indians; Valdivia's impression on, ix, 123; Almagro's expedition into, 17 et seq., 24, 25; Valdivia undertakes subjugation of, 24 et seq.; ill-repute of, 39, 128, 139, 154, 157; climate of, and prospects for colonists in, 42, 94-95, 143, 195-196, 209-210; results of Valdivia's policy in, 42-43; Southern, explored by Pastene, 45, 138; history of, see under " Colecciones de Documentos de Historiadores de Chile," " General Biographical Dictionary of Chile," " Historia de Chile " (Marmolejo), " Historia Militar " (Olivares), " Relacions de la Cosas de Chile," and under Molina and Figueroa
Chiloe, 89, 95
Christianity, introduction of, into America, vi-vii
" Chueca, La," game of, 112
" Civil Wars of Peru " (Cieza de Leon), translated by Sir Clements R. Markham, 50 n., 67 n.
" Coleccion de Documentos de Historiadores de Chile, La," 111 n., 120 n., 125
Colorado, Rio, 109
" Comentarios Reales " (Garcilaso), see under Garcilaso
Concepcion, founding of, 81, 92, 94, 96, 108, 109, 190, 193 et seq., 198, 204, 207 et seq., 215; situation of, 193, 195
Confines, founding of, 109
Conquistadores, the, English opinion of, vi; aims of, vi-vii; fate of, ix; treatment of, by the Crown, 14; and by the Council of the Indies, 43; courage of, 22; as chroniclers,

INDEX

38, 48; character of, 48, 91, 109; religious principles of, 98
Copoyapo valley, 20, 134, 141, 144, 157, 172, 188
Coquimbo, valley of, 25, 45, 160, 188
Cordoba, Gonzalo de, 55
Cortés, Hernando de, v, vii, ix, 7, 9, 11, 14, 16 and *n*., 38, 43, 45, 55, 60, 85 *n*., 94, 101, 122
Cortés, Leonardo, 210
Council of the Indies, Pizarro before, 14, 16; other references, 43, 50, 147
Cuellar, Francisco de, 10 *n*.
Cuyo, 109
Cuzco, 5, 16, 17, 20-21, 157

Davalos, Juan, 48, 163, 164, 171
Davila, Pedrarias, 5 and *n*.
"Description of Patagonia, A" (Falkner), 28 and *n*.
Diaz, Bernal, 10, 38, 47 *n*., 60
Diaz, Ruy, 20
Don Benito, Pedro Martin de, 69
"Don Quixote," vi, 87
Drake, Sir Francis, vi, vii
Du Chaillu, 15 *n*.

El Barco, 212
Elizabeth, Queen, vi
"Encomiendas," 51
Ercilla, Alonso de, "La Araucana," by (*q.v.*), cited and quoted, viii, 28 and *n*., 93, 96, 114 *n*.; on Valdivia, 107, 119-120; career of, 88 *et seq.*; marriage and death of, 91
Escobar, Cristobal, 38, 135
Estremadura, v, vi, 1, 2

Falkner, Thomas, cited, 28
Faravia, 8 and *n*.
Federmann, 123 *n*.
Ferdinand V., 55
Figueroa, "History of Chile," and "Biographical Dictionary of Chile," by, cited and quoted, viii, 17 *n*., 27 *n*., 120 *n*
"Florida" (Garcilaso), 34
France, war with Spain and alliance with the Turks, 39, 136
Francis I., vi
Friars, treatment of the Indians by, 94
Frobisher, Martin, vi

Gacte, Maria Ortez de, 1
"Game of Canes, The," 58 and *n*., 64 and *n*.
Garcilaso de la Vega (father), 59, 68

Garcilaso, the Inca, "Comentarios Reales," by, cited and quoted, 4 *n*., 6 and *n*., 7 and *n*., 8 *n*., 9, 10, 12, 14, 15, 17 and *n*., 18 and *n*., 19, 22 and *n*., 23, 52 and *n*., 54 *et seq.*, 67 *et seq.*, 70 *n*., 71 *et seq.*; "Florida," by, 34; charm and value of writings by, 67 *et seq.*
Gayangos, Pascual de, 107
"General Biographical Dictionary of Chile" (Figueroa), quoted, 26 and *n*.
Gómara, Francisco Lopez de, cited and quoted, 2 and *n*., 3 *n*., 6, 9, 10, 19 and *n*., 22, 23, 49, 55-56, 62 *n*.
Gomez, Pedro, 24
Gongora, Alonso de. *See* Marmolejo
Gonzalez, Father Rodrigo, recommended by Valdivia as prelate of Chile, 98-99, 101, 202, 219; other references, 145, 146
Gonzalianez, Father, 38, 135
Guadalupe, 14

Harina tostada, 116 *n*.
Hawkins, Sir John, vi
Heredia, 60
Herrera, Juan de, with Almagro, 20; on the Araucanians, 92 *et seq.*
Hinojosa, Pedro de, 76, 177, 184-185
"Historia de Chile" (Marmolejo), 107
"Historia del Peru" (Zárate), cited, 6
"Historia General de las Indias" (Gómara), cited, 2 *n*., 9 and *n*. *See also under* Gómara
"Historia Militar, Civil y Sagrada de Chile" (Olivares), 110 *n*.
Horses, value of, in South America, 38-39, 42, 47, 68, 73, 143, 145, 171-172; Indian fear of, 35, 84, 100, 115; regulation regarding mares, 104; use of, by Araucanians, 112
Hoz, Pedro de la, 24
Huarinas, battle of, 58-59, 68
Huayna Capac, the Inca, 16 *n*., 17 *n*.

Indians, protection of, by the Laws of the Indies, 49; conversion of, 94, 99; treatment of, by Spaniards, 97; laws regarding, at Santiago, 104 *et seq.*; forced labour of, by Valdivia, 110. *See also under* Araucanian Indians
Indies, Council of the. *See under* Council of the Indies
Indies, Laws of the. *See under* Laws of the Indies

Irala, Domingo de, vii
Itata, river, 191

James, Saint (Santiago), 26, 28, 31
Jérez, Garcia de, 10 and *n*., 23

La Barca, Juan Calderon de, 137, 201
Labour, problem of, in Spanish America, 97
La Gasca, Pedro de, appointment of, as President in Peru by Charles V., 55, 171; description and character of, 55-56, 67 *n*., 73 *et seq.*; policy of, toward Gonzalo Pizarro, 56-57; routed by Pizarro, 58-59; Valdivia joins forces of, 64-65, 152-153, 175-176; battle of Sacsahuana won by, 66 *et seq.*, 177 *et seq.*; execution and vindictive treatment of Pizarro and Carvajal by, 67, 72; attitude to and treatment of Valdivia by, 73-74, 76-77, 80, 182 *et seq.*, 199; plot against, 78-79, 187-188; return of, to Spain, 210, 218; other references, 212, 216
La Imperial, founded, 99, 109, 208 *et seq.*
La Plata, 199
Lapomocho, Indian name for F. Pizarro, 23, 130
Las Cangrejeras, battle of, 111
Las Casas, Bartolome de, 49, 50, 97
La Serena (Chile), founding of, 1 *n*., 25, 42, 46, 64, 109, 142, 160, 161, 198, 214; Indian rising at, 79; destruction of, 80, 189, 214; and rebuilding of, 80, 189, 214; other references, 150, 162, 172, 174, 210, 211
La Serena (Estremadura), vi, 1 and *n*.
Las Salinas, battle of, 24
La Torre, Juan de la, 10 and *n*., 11
Lautoro, Chief, organisation of Araucanians against Spanish by, 115 *et seq.*
"Laws of the Forest" (Manwood), 105 *n*.
Laws of the Indies, 49, 50, 51, 56
Legaspi, v
Leon, Pedro Cieza de, quoted and cited, 10, 13, 50 and *n*.; value of writings of, 13, 67; other references, 38, 87
Leyton, Catalina, 71
Lientur, chief, 111-112
Lima, 5 *n*., 152, 164 *et seq.*, 175, 183 *et seq.*
Llamas, 81
Lobo, Father, 31, 145

Los Cobos, Francisco de, 156
Los Reyes. *See* Lima
Los Rios, Pedro de, 9
Luce, Domingo de Soria, 10 *n*.
Luque, Hernando de, compact of, with Pizarro and Almagro, 6 and *n*., 7, 11 *et seq.*
Luther, Martin, 55

Magellan, Straits of, 40, 45, 95, 128, 146, 155, 159, 198, 199-200, 216 *et seq.*
Maguez, valley of, 109
Malagon, 6 and *n*.
Maldonado, Diego, 210, 211
Manco Capac, Inca, 18, 28-29
Mango Ynga, 129
Mapocho, valley of, 128, 157
Mara, conference of, 2, 17
Markham, Sir Clements R., translator of " War of Chupas," 50 *n*., 51 *n*.; on executions after Sacsahuana, 67 *n*.
Marmolejo, Alonso de Gongora, " History of Chile " by, cited and quoted, viii and ix *n*., 25 *n*., 31 and *n*., 87 and *n*., 107, 110, 113 *n*., 114, 115, 117, 119 *et seq.*, 158; career of, 26 and *n*., 107, 108
Marquis, value of the title of, 16
Martin, Domingo, 88 and *n*.
Martin, Lope, 178
Mary I., Queen, marriage of, to Philip II., 88
Maulé, river, 40, 137, 139
Maulican, chief, 112
Maxmilian, Prince and Princess, 210
Melo, Pedro Oncas de, 1
" Memorial Historico Español," 107
Mendoza, Alonso de, 171
Mendoza, Garcia Hurtado de, Captain General of Chile, 89
Mendoza, Lope de, 157, 166
Mendoza, Pedro de, v, 14
Milan, siege of, 1
Miranda, Pedro de, 158
Molina, Alonzo de, 10 *n*.
Molina, Ignatius, cited, 17 and *n*.
Moncada, Pedro de, 24
Monroy, Alonso de, accompanies Valdivia, 24, 127; warns Valdivia of plot, 29, 130; defence of Santiago by, 30-31; journey to Peru and adventures in Atacama desert, 33 *et seq.*, 132 *et seq.*, 134, 136, 147, 158; return of, to Chile, 38, 39, 158-159; sent by Valdivia to Lima, 46, 142-143, 160-161; character of, 60; death of, 60, 61, 164, 165

INDEX

Monroy, Juan Bautista de, cited, 89 n.
Montaña, the, 49 and n., 72
Montezuma, 7

Negrete Domingo, town crier of Santiago, 103
Negro, Rio, 109
Negroes, introduction of, into America, 97, 98; into Chile, 105, 106, 201; laws regarding, at Santiago, 105, 106
New Castile, 16
New Extreme, the name for Chile (q.v.), 25
New Granada, 43, 123 n.
New Toledo, 16
"Noche Triste, La," 11
Nuñez, Alvar, vii, 52, 98

Ojeda, Alonso de, 5, 14, 60
Olivares, Miguel de, 110

Palomino, Captain, 178
Panama, Spanish settlement at, 2, 8, 9
Pardave, Captain, 181
Pastene, Juan Bautista, sent by Castro to Chile, 40, 138, 159, 201; sent to explore Magellan Straits and Southern Chile, 40, 45, 95, 138, 142, 159-160, 199; his errand to and return from Peru (Lima), 48, 49, 60, 62-63, 144, 164 et seq., 169 et seq.; plot against, in Lima, 61, 165-166; at Concepcion, 196, 197
Paullu, Inca, 18 et seq.
Pavia, vi, 1, 118
Paz, Martin de, 10 n.
Pehuelche Indians, 109
Peralta, Cristoval de, 10 n.
Perez, Diego, 145
Peru, wealth of, 7-8 and n., 14-15, 48; conquest of, 11, 13, 16, 123
Pescara, Marquis de, 156
Philip II., friendship of, for Ercilla, 88, 89
Pineda, Juan, 89
Pizarro, Francisco de, birth and early career of, 2 et seq.; Conference of Mara between Almagro and, 2, 17; assassination of, by Almagro (son), 5, 23, 26, 29 and n., 49, 130, 131, 138; compact of, with Almagro, 6, 11 et seq.; expedition of, to Peru, 7 et seq.; visit of, to Charles V., 11 et seq.; made Adelantado Mayor of Peru, 15; and a Marquis, 16, 101; ill-feeling between Almagro and, 15, 16, 21; and civil war, 23; character of, 16, 19; battle of Las Salinas fought by, 24; grant of Encomiendas by, 51; sends Valdivia to Chile, 127, 128, 156-157; Valdivia's tribute to, 148; and service with, 167; other reference, 85 n.; Life of, by Tena. See under Tena
Pizarro, Gonzalo (father of Francisco), 2 et seq.
Pizarro, Gonzalo (brother of Francisco, 3 n.); character of, vii, 52 et seq., 61; desire of, for Governorship of Peru, 49; defeat of Vela by, 52, 164 et seq.; Charles V.'s letter to, 54-55; struggle with La Gasca, 56 et seq., 63, 152, 170 et seq., 201, 211, 212, 214; fleet of, joins La Gasca, 57, 171; Valdivia's friendship with, 62, 167, 168, but takes action against, 63 et seq., 173; defeats Centeno, 64, 175; defeat of, at battle of Sacsahuana, 65 et seq., 180, 18e, 183; execution of, 67, 72, 153, 182, 183; other references, 17
Pizarro, Hernando, confinement of, in El Castillo de la Mota, 5 n., 16 n., 23; enmity of Almagro and, 15, 23; news of conquest of Peru taken to Spain by, 16; marriage of, 16 n.; other references, 3 n., 167
Pizarro, Juan Francisco, 3, n., 17
Pizarros, the, v, 60
Pozo, Father, 119-120
Prado, Juan Nuñez, 66, 180, 212, 217
Prescott, William, vi, 67 n.
Prices, regulations regarding, at Santiago, 102 et seq.
Puren, 114

Quesada, Gonzalo Jimenez de, v, vii, ix, 7, 11, 38, 43, 60, 101, 122, 123 n.
Quillota, 109

"Relacion de la Cosas de Chile" (Herrera), 92 n., 93 n., 94 and n.
Ribera, Nicolas de, 10 n.
Rojas, Gabriel de, 17
Ruiz, Bartolomé, 10 n.

Saavedra, Juan de, 18
Sacsahuana, battle of, 65 et seq., 73, 78, 181-182
Saint Domingo, 5
Salazar, Luis de, 88

Salinillas, the horse, 59, 68
Samano, Juan de, 212
San Cristobal, galleon, 77, 186
San Pedro, ship, 138
Santiago, founding of, by Valdivia, 25 *et seq.*, 101, 109, 128-129 and *n.*, 144, 157, 198, 214; burnt by Indians, 31, 41, 131; and rebuilt, 36, 132 *et seq.*; Valdivia's reception at, 80, 189; regulations of town council of, 102 *et seq.*; letter from treasurer of, to Charles V. on Valdivia's death, 120 *n.*; importance of situation of, 162-163; other references, 108, 210
Santiago, ship, 173
Saravia, Dr., 108
Silvestre, Gonzalo de, 58, 60
Solis, 165, 172
Sosa, Esteban de, 218
Soto, de, 60
Spanish proverbs and sayings, 6 and *n.*, 9 and *n.*, 53, 54, 78, 79 and *n.*, 87, 94
Sylvestre, Gonzalo de, 34

Taboga, 6 *n.*, 7 *n.*, 89
Tafur, Fulano, 9
Tasmania, extinction of natives in, 97 *n.*
Tenochtitlán, 11
Tena, Presbyter Juan, "Life of Pizarro" by, quoted and cited, 2 *n.*, 4 *n.*, 5 *n.*
Torre, Juan de la, 10 and *n.*, 11
Torres, Hernando de, 52
Trujillo (Estremadura), 2 *et seq.*
Trujillo (Peru), 17
Tucapel, fort of, 109, 113 *et seq.*
Tumbez, vale of, 12

Ulloa, Antonio de, takes Valdivia's dispatches to Peru, 61, 160, 163; treachery of and plot against Valdivia and Pastene, 61-63, 164 *et seq.*, 169 *et seq.*; Valdivia's esteem for, 148-149
"Unknown Conqueror," an, 22 and *n.*
"Unknown Warrior," the, 22 *n.*
Uraáb, 5 and *n.*

Vaca, Alvar Nuñez Cabeca de, vii, 52, 98
Valdivia, Isabel Gutierrez de, 1
Valdivia, Pedro de, birth and parentage of, v, 1; character and description of, v, vii *et seq.*, 48, 102, 103, 120-121; early military service of, v, vi, 1-2, 156; at conference of Mara, 17; service of, for Pizarros, 24, 156; sent to Chile, 21, 24, 127 *et seq.*, 156-157; founding of Santiago by, and difficulties with Indians at, 25, 28 *et seq.*, 37, 44, 128, 129, 157-158, 161-162; plot against, 29-30, 130-131; sends to Peru, 33, 134; financial difficulties of, and statements by, 39, 136, 139, 197 *et seq.*, 201, 202, 206, 216; Indian challenge to, 39-40, 137; aims, ambitions and policy of, 40 *et seq.*, 98, 140; desire of, for non-interference in Chile, 43, 146 *et seq.*; helps La Gasca against Gonzalo Pizarro, 44, 59, 63, 65 *et seq.*, 73-74, 152 *et seq.*, 172 *et seq.*, 214, 215; exploring zeal of, 45 *et seq.*, 95, 99-101, 109, 128, 138 *et seq.*, 155, 159-160, 161, 191, 198, 216 *et seq.*; sends Monroy, Pastene and Ulloa to Lima, 46, 142-143, 160-161; Ulloa's plot against, 61, 62, 164 *et seq.*, 166, 169 *et seq.*; loyalty of, to Charles V., 63; confirmed Governor of Chile by La Gasca, 74-75, 153, 183; leaves for Chile, 75-76, 183-184; and is recalled by La Gasca, 76, 77, 184 *et seq.*; invited to plot against La Gasca, 78-79, 187-188; reception of, at Santiago, 80, 188 *et seq.*; accident to, 80, 81, 190; military action against Araucanians on the Biobio, 81 *et seq.*, 94; death of, 89, 119-120; Ercilla's accounts of, in "La Araucana," 89, 90, 107; labour troubles of, 97, 98, 110; recommends Gonzalez as prelate, 98, 101, 202; ordinances of, at Santiago, 102 *et seq.*; versatility of, 102-103; treatment of, and policy to Indians by, 106, 114-115, 145, 160, 163, 194-195; Marmolejo on, 107; desire of, for power to nominate succession, 108, 201; colonists' esteem for, 109; settlement and establishment of towns by, 109, 144-145, 190, 207 *et seq.*, 214, 215; Indian conspiracy against, 113 *et seq.*; and last battle of, 116 *et seq.*; estimate of his work, 121 *et seq.*; letters of, to Charles V. *See under* Charles V.
Valdivia, town and river, 101, 108, 109, 209, 213, 217
Valparaiso, 39, 78, 79, 136, 159
Vargas, Isabel de, 4
Vega, Garcilaso de la. *See under* Garcilaso
Vegazo, Lucas Martinez, 39, 136

INDEX

Vela, Blasco Nuñez, appointed Governor General of Peru, 49, 164; appearance and character of, 50; action of, against Castro, 50, 51; defeated by Gonzalo Pizarro, and death of, 52, 54, 56, 164 *et seq.*

Velasco, Ana de, 210

Venezuela, conquest of, 1, 156

Villagra, Francisco de, as Valdivia's Maestre de Campo, 40, 63, 138, 172, 188, 210; execution of Caupolican by, 90; his horse described in " La Araucana," 92 *n.*; suggested exploration of Magellan Straits by, 101, 216; succeeds Valdivia, 107; character of, 108, 216; expedition of, across the Andes, 108-109; sent to Peru, 189, 202; letter to Valdivia from, 211-212; at El Barco, 212

Villalon, Diego Garcia de, 136

Villa Rica, town of, founded, 101, 109, 215

" War of Chupas " (Cieza de Leon), translated by Sir Clements R. Markham, quoted, 50 and *n*.

West Indies, depopulation of, 97

Wolvesey, palace of, 88

Xeres, 49

Yumbel, 111

Yuste, friars of, 43

Zárate, Augustine de, quoted and cited, 6, 10, 23, 49, 57 *n.*, 71